ABOUT THE AUTHOR

Debra was born in Halifax and has always enjoyed cycling and walking in the countryside. In her teens, she visited and fell in love with the beautiful Lake District, dreaming that she might one day live there.

Living opposite the famous chocolate factory, Rowntree Mackintosh, she soon developed a sweet tooth. Unsurprisingly, Debra's cycle rides and walks always involved chocolate, such as a Yorkie Bar, Toffee Crisp, or Quality Street. But Debra is also quite partial to Cadbury Dairy Milk.

Debra now lives in Scotland with her Scottish husband and their Border Collie, eating chocolate, walking, cycling, and writing, continuing to dream that one day, she might live in the Lake District.

Find out more at https//mothermurphys.co.uk/ or follow Debra on Facebook, Instagram and LinkedIn.

Also by Debra Murphy

The Magical Tearoom on the Hill
Beatrix the Time Travelling Collie

The Magical Adventures of Florence the Border Collie Series

The Tale of Florence and the King
The Tale of Florence and the Dragon
The Tale of Florence and the Lost Sea Kelpies

Published in 2025 by Lawers Publishing
Copyright @ Debra Murphy 2025

Debra Murphy has asserted her right to be identified as the author of the Work, in accordance with the Copyright, Designs and Patents Act 1988

All rights reserved. No part of this publication may be reproduced, stored in a retrieval system, or transmitted in any form or by any means, electronic, mechanical, photocopying, recording or otherwise, without the copyright owner's prior permission.

A CIP catalogue copy of this book can be found in the British Library.

ISBN Paperback: 978-1-917875-02-8
ISBN Ebook: 978-1-917875-03-5
ISBN Audio Book: 978-1-917875-04-2

Illustrations - Jessica Leech @ The Ricketty Desk

For further information about this book contact the author at
https//mothermurphys.co.uk/

CAMPERVAN CAPERS

Have you turned
the water on?

Debra Murphy

For Jim

May you forever be the chalk to my cheese

Introduction

"I wish I'd known that!"

Over the years (which sometimes seems so many), I've had a varied life with different jobs–medical secretary, photographic researcher, vocational assessor, teacher, motorbike instructor, tearoom owner and author. So why on earth would I want to write a book about campervans?

Well, I am a writer. I love putting words on paper. But my earlier books were about recipes, tales, and adventures–often including my beloved Border Collie, Beatrix.

I've always been an outdoor girl–cycling, walking, hiking and baking goodies to take with me on my exploits. In my late teens, I discovered the love of camping. I soon began dreaming of owning a campervan and living in the Lake District, but thought these were just pipe dreams.

Then, in 2021, I suddenly had the finances to follow my campervan dream. That's when it dawned on me that I knew absolutely nothing about campervans. What makes a good campervan, and how would I know which ones to avoid like the plague?

"I know," I said in a discussion with my long-suffering husband, Jim (those of you who have read my earlier books will know him as Mr M), "I'll go to Waterstones. They'll have loads of books about campervan life."

I strolled into the Waterstones store at Falkirk in Central Scotland and asked where to find books on campervan life. The lovely manager, Laura, already familiar with my writing and my books, replied,

"I'm just saying, Debra. There are not that many."

Even with this subtle hint, the idea of writing a campervan book still didn't reach my already full mind.

"Oh well, the internet will have to do," I sighed.

Forging my path to becoming a campervan owner, there were so many times I uttered the words,

"I wish I'd known that."

Mr M would sigh and tell me to write it all down.

As my journey into campervan life began, another book naturally developed, and various notebooks filled up quickly. Yes, I usually handwrite first, then type. One of my fears for today's younger generation is that they will not experience the unadulterated joy of simply scribbling thoughts down on scraps of paper using an actual pen or pencil. I've even written in crayons when I couldn't get my hands on a pen! I can touch type, so words appear quickly on my laptop, but I prefer old-fashioned writing.

Mind you, this is no thanks to some of my schoolteachers who repeatedly scolded me for writing with my left hand. In my primary school, we began our writing journey using a pencil. One teacher (I can remember her name, but will refrain from naming and shaming) told me I could have a pen once I'd learned to write with my right hand. If that had been the case throughout life, I would still be writing in pencil! Thankfully, the world now recognises that we lefties are unique and not thought to be spawn of the devil or that we are witches.

When I was researching which campervan would suit me, I wanted to read and learn how people chose their dream van. Were they enjoying campervan life? What did they have to get the hang of? What mistakes did they make? What could I find out from them?

CAMPERVAN CAPERS

And so, ideas for a book began to grow. It wouldn't be a technical guide by any stretch of the imagination. Buying and owning one campervan certainly didn't give me the credibility, knowledge or desire to write that kind of book. My book would take my readers along my journey, from deciding which campervan to buy, to my experiences in the van, including the many lessons learned and even more mistakes made.

With my uneducated mind, I assumed I'd be able to buy a campervan, drive off into the sunset, be self-sufficient, and soon be camping all over the country wherever the notion took me.

I wasn't at a stage in my life when I could live full-time in a campervan, and I was certainly not ready for a life of wild campervanning. My staying in tents in my pre-Mr M life never involved wild camping. I like the security offered by campsites where you can still relax in peace and tranquillity, but the fear of getting murdered as you sleep is much reduced. Extreme fear, I know!

So, dear reader, as you journey with me through my book, you'll discover whether my dream has become a reality. Does campervan life meet my expectations? Has Mr M, the camping-hater, learned to love campervan life? What does Beatrix, our Border Collie, think?

There have been many laughs, moans, and tears along my campervan journey, and I'm happy to share them all with you.

As you would imagine, the start of my journey focused on determining what type of van I needed and then finding it, before including stories about our adventures, mistakes, discussions, and thoughts. I've tried to include helpful information for would-be campervanners, but I also wanted to share personal experiences, places I've visited, and my feelings along my journey to become a seasoned campervan woman.

Would I become another Lady in the Van?

Chapter 1

Was I Being Selfish?- July 2021

Born in Yorkshire, surrounded by sublime scenery, including nearby Haworth and remote moors made famous by Emily Bronte's Wuthering Heights, it's hardly surprising that I love being outdoors. My home has always been a clue to this. Maps on the table, muddy walking boots, waterproofs dripping on the clothes horse, cycling shoes drying next to the fire, and umpteen rucksacks, walking poles, and crampons are always on show. Since my mid-teens, I've loved camping and listening to the wind howling around the canvas and the rain bouncing on the tent, often praying the guy ropes would hold out.

As you read this book, you'll soon discover that I love learning, and I'm always looking to research different things, especially how something got its name or why we say certain words. Whilst writing this chapter, I realised that even after all my years of camping, I still didn't know why the ropes that hold up a tent are called guy ropes. Now, with the ever-accessible internet, I was slightly disappointed to learn it was a simple translation from the French word 'guie', meaning to guide. Then there is also the suggestion that it might be from the Dutch word, 'gei', which was something used to attach sails to a mast on ships. From my experience, they could just as well be called hazard ropes, as I have tripped over many a guy rope in my camping life. Nowadays, there are bright, luminous guy ropes, sometimes with lights, to prevent injuries or collapsed tents from people tripping over the hidden ropes.

I've camped across our wonderful nation, from Land's End in Cornwall, through Wales, Cumbria, Yorkshire, and up to John O'Groats in the far north of Scotland. Good weather or bad, it doesn't matter; being close to nature and having a feeling of freedom are the attractions for me.

Despite loving camping in all weathers, the hankering for a campervan was loitering in the back of my mind. Not a huge motorhome that looks like a house on wheels, just a small one with the essentials. An old-style VW campervan would be perfect. We didn't even have a car when I was a small child, but I'd see these amazing vans driving around. Many looked like they'd been painted in the 1960s with bright colours and daisies. If I ever managed to peek inside one parked at the side of the road, I imagined how cosy it would feel to sleep in the tiny bed, curled up in a favourite blanket. I dreamed about sitting in such a van, looking out onto the sea or hills, drinking a cup of hot chocolate, and munching on crisp sandwiches. Yes, crisp sandwiches. White bread, butter, and Walker's Tomato Ketchup crisps. Don't mock it until you've tried it. More importantly, these vans oozed peace and comfort to me.

Have you seen the price of those things? You could easily buy a house for the same money as a fancy motorhome. Maybe even one in the Lake District!

Still, I continued to dream. As the years passed, two wonderful children came along, Benjamin and Chloe. Real life sometimes took its toll. Other priorities never allowed my dream of a campervan to reach anywhere near the top of the list.

I felt time was drifting by, and I should accept that I'd never be able to afford the luxury of a campervan, but I still dared to dream.

Then, in 2021, at the age of 56, I discovered I'd been left an inheritance that was 'to buy your dream campervan'.

Words can't describe how this made me feel, and my mind was in overdrive. Of course, there was the overwhelming sadness that the money from this inheritance meant that a special person was no longer here.

Then, I began a long battle with my thoughts. The sensible part of my mind told me how ridiculous it would be to spend that amount of money on a campervan, whilst my adventurous head kept shouting at me,

"Think of all the things you could do with the money."

I felt I was the custodian of my inheritance and appreciated the massive gift of love and money, so I wanted to do the right thing. I pondered long and hard about the dilemma and had lots of fighting going on in my head. Should I follow my heart and get the campervan, or follow my sensible conscience and spend it wisely?

Mr M gently and tactfully told me that it was a once-in-a-lifetime opportunity for me and that I should choose what I wanted to do with the money and not think about anyone else. Whatever I decided, he would support me. And so, my mental debate began.

I wondered about investing the money, but the inheritance was not so large that it would generate a tremendous amount of interest, so what would be the point? The money had been left for me to enjoy.

Everyone I know always seems to be spending money on their houses. Maybe I should do that and use the kitty to improve our house. Although we didn't, and still don't, have a vast disposable income, we were in a reasonably sound financial position. With no debts, no mortgage, and a house in pretty good nick, spending the money on home improvements was not my priority. Neither Mr M nor I are very materialistic people and never feel the need to keep up with the Joneses. Heck, we're the odd couple who gave away all our televisions as we decided we wanted to live a TV-less life. That was about eight years ago, and we have never regretted that decision. So, no, I didn't feel I needed to spend the money on our house.

CAMPERVAN CAPERS

My next thought was that I could give the money to my children. That would be something a good mother would do, isn't it? The selfish voice inside me suddenly popped up and cried out,

"The money was left to me!"

That made me take a long, hard look at myself.

Was I really such a selfish person?

Why wouldn't I give everything I could to my children?

Well, quite honestly, I felt I still had a long time to live and deserved to have a dream come true. Would I have thought that twenty years ago? Most probably not. I also knew my children had seen my many struggles over the years and would be 100% behind me following my dream. When I told my daughter, she cried, telling me she couldn't believe somebody had been so wonderful in making my dream possible and that I should definitely buy a campervan.

So, should I go with my heart and buy the campervan? If I kept the inheritance to spend on future holidays, how many trips would I be able to pay for with the money? Four or five good ones? How many holidays, trips and adventures would I be able to have in a campervan? Oh, my mind boggled thinking of that: day trips and holidays without looking for dog-friendly accommodation. The children could borrow the campervan to have holidays themselves. I could take my grandchildren away on trips in a campervan. I'd be the coolest grandma ever!

Then I started to think of the times I've taken my children, grandchildren, and dogs to the beach, carrying bags full of the necessary food, drinks, clothes, toys, and blankets to keep everyone happy. If I could park my campervan close to the beach, we could eat, drink, wash off the sand, change clothes in the van, and enjoy more time playing on the beach and in the sea.

I will never forget taking my granddaughter Minnie, who was then four, to Barassie Beach, just outside Ardrossan on the West Coast of Scotland. We travelled to Barassie on the train, and both Mr M and I each hauled a large rucksack filled with food, drinks, towels, spare clothes, and extra food, water, and towels for the dog. After having a fabulous day, we packed up, leaving nothing but footprints in the sand, of course. When we were leaving the beach, Minnie announced that she needed the toilet. I told her it was OK and she could do a little wee on the sand, and nobody would mind.

"Oh no, Grandma, I need to do a big poo," she said, smiling.

With no toilets in sight and a little girl who may not be able to last until we were back on the train (and would the train toilets even be working or clean?), I needed to help Minnie manoeuvre herself to do what was indeed a massive poo on the beach. She was unconcerned about this, but I was none too happy at having to pick up human poo with a dog-poo bag and dispose of it in a dog-waste bin. If we'd had a campervan parked nearby, Minnie could have used the toilet.

Now, although I love camping, Mr M hates it. We discussed whether he could see himself in a campervan rather than a tent. Much to my relief, he agreed that a campervan could be a good idea and that he would probably enjoy staying in one.

Decision made. I would buy my dream campervan.

My imagination was going wild, thinking of the adventures we could have: Mr M, Beatrix, our Border Collie dog, and myself—The Travelling Murphys.

"Just wait one minute," said the sensible Mr M, or 'Mr Doom and Gloom,' some might say.

"Who will drive this campervan, and where will you keep it?"

Chapter 2

Choosing My Ideal Campervan

So began my search on the internet. Do you know how many different places you can buy a campervan from? Private sales, small companies, and large dealers. It seems campervans and motorhomes are crying out to be bought all over the length and breadth of the country. And just as many companies are desperate to buy your campervan or motorhome from you.

Mr M was very upbeat about this.

"You know, Debra. If you buy one and don't like it, you could probably resell it, no problem."

Once I'd decided that I was brave and selfish enough to fritter my new pot of money on a dream, I spent the next few weeks admiring some amazing campervans and motorhomes. I was bamboozled by the different types you can choose from.

When did a campervan become a motorhome? I wondered. The internet quickly answered that, and I discovered five main differences between a campervan and a motorhome.

Firstly, campervans are based around an existing van body, whereas motorhomes have a purpose-built body.

Next, the cabs on campervans are not usually part of the living space, but in motorhomes, they often are.

Not surprisingly, campervans are generally smaller than motorhomes, with fewer features.

Then, naturally, because of their size, campervans are usually more economical to run than motorhomes.

Last, but not least, campervans are easier to drive and park than motorhomes.

The last two points grabbed my attention, so I was already finding myself veering towards a campervan rather than a motorhome. A massive motorhome would be OK on America's long, straight highways, but on the twisty, winding, narrow roads of Scotland, Yorkshire, or the Lake District?

I think not!

The choices were still vast. You can get motorhomes that sleep between two and six people, or more if you go for a ginormous one. Some have two seats with seatbelts, while others have additional ones. You can choose whether to have an end, central, or corner washroom. Do you want a front lounge, an end lounge, or a dining area? What about your sleeping arrangements: twin singles, a corner double, an island double, or a dropdown double bed? There are even some incredible ones that have side slide-outs. With these, once parked, you can increase the width of the living room, kitchen, or bedroom – or all three, depending on how many slide-outs you have.

When we still had our tearoom, I would chat to customers about my dream of owning a campervan. One of our regular customers, Ian, told me if he won the lottery, he would buy me a large American-style motorhome that would be so big that the sides would expand when parked and the boot (which I now know should be referred to as the garage, and will do so throughout the book) would hold a small car for me to drive around in once I'd arrived at my campsite.

"That's a lovely thought," I told him. "Could you also pay for a chauffeur, as I could never drive something so big?"

I just wanted a simple campervan. This internet search gave me more questions than answers. Online searching was not enough. I had to see the campervans 'in person'. I needed a plan.

CAMPERVAN CAPERS

Remember, this was when the world was a strange and scary place to live, with COVID-19 hanging around and social distancing still a necessary evil. I phoned a few campervan dealers in Scotland to see if we could arrange a visit. Some of them were booked up, and some didn't have any campervans available. Some dealers were still not letting people visit because they feared COVID-19 might get left in their vans. Eventually, I found a local place forty minutes or so from home.

Driving to the dealer, both Mr M and I were looking at the roads in a different light. Despite there still being a pandemic, it seemed that the roads were full of people enjoying their campervans and motorhomes.

"Don't forget, Debra. We're just looking today. Let's not make any rash decisions," said Mr M, but I could tell he was just as excited as I was.

We were given a set time to arrive at the dealers and told how long we could look at the campervans before their next potential customer was booked in. At least I was going to see actual campervans and not just pictures.

Wow! What an eye-opener that visit was. The prices and selection were an awe-inspiring experience: large ones, small, old, and new. Tidy ones, untidy, smelly, and pristine ones. Oh, so many!

We arrived back home no wiser than before we set off. We needed to narrow our choices down.

Chapter 3

Identifying Our Essential Features

Mr M and I sat around the kitchen table after tea one evening and began to make our list of essential features for a campervan.

I decided the first thing I had to be clear on was how much I was prepared to spend. So, I set my budget, an amount I wouldn't go over, even if I saw something and loved it. A budget is probably the most important thing to take into consideration. It's easy to get carried away when you see these fantastic vehicles. Of course, the budget for your van is entirely personal for you to decide on, and I can't advise you on that.

I couldn't quite believe I was in the amazing position of having the money for a cash purchase. I also knew I needed to leave myself enough to cover the insurance, breakdown cover, and any repairs over the next few years. Mr M kept reminding me of that!

So, we had choices to make. We could buy a new one (for the cost of a chateau in the south of France!) or opt for a second-hand one.

Buying a new one would mean we could be almost 100% sure that the van would not fail in the next few years, or at least the warranty should cover us if it does have any faults. Buying second-hand, as with anything, is risky, like buying a second-hand car.

CAMPERVAN CAPERS

This decision is down to you, as only you know your budget. For me, there was no way on this earth I could afford a new campervan straight out of its wrapper. It would be a pre-loved van for us.

The next decision we had to make was where to buy from. We wanted to go to a dealer rather than a private sale. Why? Even though this route is a little more expensive, most dealers give a year's warranty, whereas private sales are usually sold as seen. I also wanted to shop locally, in the central belt of Scotland, if possible.

My next consideration was size. Mr M told me in no uncertain terms that if I was going to get a campervan, then I had to be sure I could drive it, as he didn't think his dodgy knees would allow him to drive a large vehicle for many more years. And it was my dream, not his. OK, so a massive house on wheels was out of the question.

In my defence here, I feel I need to let you know that I'm not a nervous driver. I passed my driving test in the 1980s and happily drove for miles around the Lake District, Yorkshire Dales, and Wales. Moving to Scotland, I had a job that involved driving across the whole of Scotland, from the Borders to the Highlands and even across to the Isle of Skye. Another claim to my driving skills is that I have a full motorbike license. In my biker-chick days, I owned a beautiful black and chrome Triumph Bonneville 790cc and was even a motorbike instructor. So I can drive without panicking!

We also wanted a campervan that would fit in our driveway rather than have to be parked on the street. Our car insurance is cheaper because we park in our driveway. But we still needed the space for our car. We didn't want to have to park our car on the street just because we had a campervan. The insurance company for the car wouldn't like that.

At last, our options had become a little clearer.

I don't know what our neighbours thought we were up to when we measured our driveway with my sewing tape measure, which blew about in the wind as I crawled on my hands and knees up and down the drive. Mr M was a lift engineer for over forty years, and the house is full of his old tools, including metal retractable tape measures. But could I find them that day? No. Or had they been squirrelled away by Mr M? I wonder.

With the driveway and car measured, we now knew that our van could be no longer than seven metres and no wider than three metres.

Now that the size of the campervan had been decided, we needed to agree on the features we wanted. Again, these are personal choices, but here's how we decided.

What about a toilet? That would be my all-time essential feature. You know how it is on campsites when the toilet block is a mile away from your pitch and lit only by a 30 w light bulb that sometimes works but mostly doesn't. When it does work, it only acts as a light beam to highlight the clusters of spiders lying in wait for their next victim as you run into the toilet block, desperate to pull your knickers down after the mile run from your tent, trying not to trip over your boot laces that you didn't have time to fasten, and their shadows are massive, making you think giant arachnids are waiting to pounce on you. I know I'm an outdoor girl, but I have a severe arachnophobia!

Essential number one – a toilet, preferably spider-proof.

While discussing the bathroom, I could ask for a shower. That would be great on trips away. However, when you're on holiday, you can guarantee that most people you meet will be strangers. When they catch a whiff of your not-so-pleasant body odour, they don't know who you are, and the chances of bumping into them again are remote.

Away back in 2012, Mr M and I did a five-week cycle tour of Scotland with all our belongings squashed into two panniers. With limited clothes and washing facilities, we sometimes had to wear the same T-shirt for more days than I like to admit. I hasten

CAMPERVAN CAPERS

to add that we each had a T-shirt. We didn't care, and we never had any complaints from anybody, or if they did, they did it out of earshot. By the time we reached our accommodation each night, we were too hungry and exhausted to care what anyone thought about our smelly clothes.

So, whilst a shower is not essential, it would be a great luxury.

Then we needed to think about food. How would we cook? It would be a priority for Mr M because he likes having his mealtimes planned. Woe betide me if breakfast is after 8 am, dinner after 11.45 am, or tea after 5 pm. Yes, I'm a Yorkshire lass, so we have breakfast, dinner, tea and supper. Not breakfast, lunch, dinner and supper. And before you start that arguing, what is the main meal on Christmas Day? Christmas Dinner. Not Christmas Lunch. It's dinner, even if it is only 1 pm!

Mr M will wail, "I'm starving. I can't think straight. I'm dehydrated," which is quite funny as he does most of the cooking in our house, so late meals are his fault.

For me, a cooker in the campervan is a must-have. There has to be some form of built-in appliance with a hob to boil water. With one hob, you can make a whole manner of meals – stew, porridge, soup, potatoes and even cinder toffee, should you need a sugar hit or want to appear to be the perfect campervan host. Add in a grill, and your menu starts to grow. Throw in an oven, and you're living in luxury.

Hang on a minute; I can hear you screaming. You don't know what cinder toffee is.

Debra Murphy

Mother Murphy's Cinder Toffee

In Yorkshire, we call this cinder toffee, but you may know it as puff candy, honeycomb, hokey pokey, sponge candy or even sea foam. If you've never heard of any of these, think of the inside of a Cadbury Crunchie bar, and you'll get the picture.

I thought I'd treat you here to a recipe from my first book, *The Magical Tearoom on the Hill*.

A word of warning here. You're dealing with boiling sugar. Don't be tempted to make a bigger portion in the pan in your van, or once you add the bicarbonate of soda, you'll have boiling sugar pouring out into the campsite.

Once your cinder toffee has cooled, you can make it even more delightful if you break it into chunks and dip it in melted chocolate. Leave to set on parchment paper and pop a few pieces into sweet bags for a lovely handmade gift. You'll be the most popular camper on the site when you make this.

CAMPERVAN CAPERS

Ingredients

1 teaspoon bicarbonate of soda
75 g caster sugar
2 tablespoons golden syrup

Method

1. Put the sugar and golden syrup in a large, heavy-based pan. Allow to melt slowly over a low heat, stirring gently until all the sugar grains have melted.
2. Once melted, turn the heat up and allow to boil until the mixture changes colour and becomes a deep golden brown (not black!). This will only take a couple of minutes.
3. Take the pan off the heat and stir in the magical bicarbonate of soda. The mixture will explode into life like a volcano. Quickly mix to ensure all the bicarbonate of soda is blended, then pour the mixture immediately into a baking tray, roughly 14" x 10", lined with parchment paper.
4. Leave to cool and set for about 15 minutes. The final cinder toffee will be very crunchy or a little bit chewy, depending on how hot you were brave enough to get the melting sugar.
5. If making this extra indulgent, break some chocolate in a bowl over a pan of gently simmering water on a low heat on the hob until the chocolate starts to melt. As the chocolate begins to melt, turn the heat off. Once nearly all the chocolate has melted, take the bowl off the hot water and allow the heat of the chocolate to melt the rest.
6. Break the cooled and set cinder toffee into chunks, dip in the chocolate and place on a piece of parchment paper to set.
7. Store in an airtight container or pop into little sweet bags as gifts for friends.

Back to my wishes. I wanted my campervan to have a two-ring hob, with a grill and possibly an oven. Who knows, if I had the van linked up to an electric supply, I might even be able to use a microwave, but I still needed to research this. I wasn't sure if I could use all these appliances at the same time.

I know 'Mr Health and Safety' will find that out for me.

In my camping years, I managed perfectly adequately with just a one-ring camping stove. There is something quite soothing about hearing the click of the gas canister when you connect it to the stove. OK, your meals were limited as you could only use one pot at a time, but you could still make a mean-cooked breakfast in a large frying pan.

There's nothing quite like the smell of bacon frying on a camping stove outside the tent, sizzling away, making your mouth water as you cuddle your cup of tea to keep your hands warm.

Shortly after I met Mr M, he declared that, yes, of course, he would like to go camping with me. I now know that he was still trying to impress me by proving his love of the outdoors, but as I soon found out, he is, in fact, a camping hater.

Spurred on by the false hope that my new soul mate shared my love of camping, I arranged our first trip together. We would go to the Isle of Skye...in March.

We packed the car with my tent, a new super double sleeping bag, an extra duvet, and pillows, and we set off. It was cold. Well, it was only just officially the end of winter, and we were in Scotland.

It had been a few years since I'd put my tent up, but as Mr M was an engineer, I surmised that it would not be a problem as he'd be able to help me.

That was another wrong assumption I made!

Finally, a few hours after arriving at the campsite and having one of our first arguments (we were still a new couple, remember), the tent was up, with us providing the entertainment for the other campers on the site. We ate at a local pub and retired for a peaceful, cosy night, cuddling up in the tent.

"It's cold. I can feel the floor. I can hear the wind," moaned Mr M. All night!

Nevertheless, we survived, and I woke up early, eager to make breakfast. I turned over to see Mr M snuggled up inside the sleeping bag and most of the duvet – clearly, he was neither too uncomfortable nor too cold to sleep.

Sneaking out of the tent, I was amazed to see the distant mountains covered in snow. Not only the mountains. Our tent, car, and everywhere around us had a lovely white dusting.

I soon rustled up some fabulous porridge with my one-ring camping stove, followed by scrambled eggs on thickly sliced buttered wholemeal bread. We didn't have the luxury of a toaster.

Mr M sat on a camping chair, wrapped in numerous layers of clothes, muttering something about the breakfast being nice, but his hands and feet were still numb.

We have not had very many camping trips since that one!

Continuing my thoughts about food, I wondered if we needed a fridge. During my camping years, I never had such a luxury. In the olden days, we just had blue freezer blocks that you would put into a cool box, along with your food, and you hoped for the best. Camping was usually on a farm or field. The site owners often had a communal freezer where you could put your thawed freezer blocks to re-freeze. It was a risky business as you couldn't guarantee your freezer blocks would be there for you on your return; it was just the vain belief that scrawling your name on them made them secure.

Years ago, we didn't worry quite so much about best-before-dates. If truth be known, I'm not sure we even knew about sell-by-dates; if we did, we ignored them. But we survived.

One of my favourite campsites was Chapel Stile, in the heart of the Lake District. There were minimal facilities, just a couple of toilets, a hand basin, and a tap to fill your water container (usually just a kettle or pan, unless you were posh and had a proper water carrier). However, the site was situated in the Langdale Valley, overlooked by Langdale Pikes. There is no better view, in my opinion.

By the way, another one of my dreams is to own an original oil painting of Langdale Pikes by William Heaton Cooper.

It was on a camping trip to this site that I decided children could survive on anything after I caught my two-year-old son, Benjamin, eating sheep poo. He's fast approaching forty now and over six feet tall, so it clearly did him no harm.

Anyway, we would keep the milk cold by putting it into a river running through the campsite, creating a perfect fridge. Sniffing the milk told you if it was safe to use.

The ever-safety-conscious Mr M, however, is a little more cautious with food and likes to keep things as safe as possible. So, a fridge would be great. A freezer section within a fridge would be a luxury.

Now, a bed is the real reason you want a campervan, isn't it? Without a bed, well, it's just a van!

I wasn't too fussed at the position of the bed so long as I didn't need ladders to get into it. I still remember the pain in my feet as a child, climbing up the ladder to get on the top bunk bed. I always wanted the top bed because if I slept on the bottom bed, there was always the risk of catching my hair on the springs of the bed above me when I woke in the middle of the night and forgot where I was.

I wonder if there has been research on the association between bunk bed ladder use in children and plantar fasciitis in adults.

The other type of bed I knew I didn't want was one in a campervan's sloping pop-up roof section. I imagine this would feel like sleeping in a coffin.

And, as the lovely Mr M would be coming along with me on my trips, I wanted a double bed, not a single!

CAMPERVAN CAPERS

My next essential equipment consideration came as a bit of a shock. Do you know that not all campervans have fitted seatbelts on the rear passenger seats? Can you believe it? It's against the law to have a dog travel in your car unrestrained, but you could have two people in a campervan without a seatbelt who could fly over the driver's seat in an accident!

I was so alarmed to discover this that I had to do some research. At the time of writing this in 2025, I found that in campervans/motorhomes manufactured after 2006, you must identify any seats designated as passenger travel seats. The campervan/motorhome must have seatbelts for all passenger-designated travel seats, and passengers must use them at all times while the vehicle is in motion. It is also illegal and dangerous for anyone to sleep in the bed while the vehicle is moving.

Another alarming discovery was that of side-facing seats, which are now deemed as unsafe as seatbelts on these are ineffective in a head-on collision. Therefore, it is illegal for children under 12 years of age to travel on side-facing seats. You must adhere to the laws on car seats for children in your campervan/motorhome. All this means that vans manufactured pre-2006 might only have factory-fitted seatbelts for the driver and front passenger.

I wanted to ensure that if I were to take friends, family, and grandchildren out, even if only for a day trip, they would not be that elephant crushing Mr M or me in the front of the van in crash conditions. Not that I was planning many crashes, of course.

Another essential for me then was two front-facing rear passenger seats with factory-fitted seatbelts.

My list of desired features was complete: a vehicle smaller than seven metres long by three metres wide, a toilet, a shower, a cooker (with grill and oven preferably), a fridge, a double bed, and two forward-facing rear seat-belted passenger seats.

Full of excitement, I logged back on the internet to look for vans meeting my new requirements. There were still hundreds to choose from. But let's not forget that Mr M still had to make his views known regarding what we needed. He decided to join the debate, announcing that if he had to spend nights and holidays in a campervan, he demanded a permanent bed rather than one that had to be made up each night by rearranging the furniture. Ever the doom and gloom in a party, he said he wouldn't be able to manage that every night as he got older.

Once he had cast a shadow of doom over the bed situation, I thought about it and found myself agreeing with him. A ready-made bed would be great, rather than making a bed up every night.

So, another essential was a permanent double bed. I could live with that.

"And whilst I'm getting my say," continued Mr M, "I want a table to sit at for my meals. I don't want a couch where I need to balance a tray on my knees. I'm getting too old for that!"

I could see his thinking. When my children were younger, I ensured we ate our meals around the table, providing quality family time. We would chat about what was happening at school, and they learned manners that followed them into their adult lives. Now, it is the grandchildren who sit at our table. So why wouldn't we want to do that in a campervan?

Back on the internet, I could see that our choices were much more refined. With our list of essentials and budget, only two or three vans met all our requirements. Whittling it down even further, I searched for dealers in central Scotland.

Now we were getting somewhere.

Chapter 4

Finding My Dream Campervan

Before Mr M could make any more demands, I booked another slot (COVID-19 restrictions still applied) at the campervan dealer we'd recently been to.

This visit was again a revelation. At least we had more of an idea of what we were looking for. Yes, we looked at the new super-duper ones, but only because they are lovely to look at. Who doesn't like looking at posh new things, even if you know you can't have them?

What we didn't like was the lack of customer service at this place. We were there on our second visit, hoping to choose a campervan, but they could barely muster an acknowledgement that we had arrived.

With our list of essentials, it soon became apparent that we were looking for something on the lines of a converted transit van or an auto sleeper and one that would sleep two to three people. A couple were of interest, but without even discussing it with Mr M, I already knew that we would not be buying a campervan from this company. Both Mr M and I believe that if you don't treat each person like your most valuable customer, you don't deserve their custom. We felt the same when we had the tearoom, always trying to make each person who walked into the tearoom feel special, even if they only came in for a takeaway coffee.

We took our leave and set off back home, disappointed but a little wiser, and trundled our car down the road, discussing the pros and cons of the vans we'd looked at. I was alarmed that only a few weeks earlier, I'd viewed my pot of money as a life-changing amount, but now I realised that it was just a drop in the ocean in the world of campervans.

We chatted about whether we were doing the right thing. By now, I sensed that even Mr M now seemed hooked on us becoming campervanners.

Back on the good old internet, I found another dealer selling what I believed might be my ideal van. The price of it would even leave me some spare cash in the bank for essential repairs. An Adria Twin, that's what I wanted, and this dealer had a lovely-looking one.

I phoned the dealer and told the very friendly salesman, Steve, "I'd like to come and see your Adria Twin, please."

Steve, the salesman, booked us to visit that weekend and told us when to come so we would have plenty of time to look inside the van.

Saturday morning arrived, and we packed a picnic. It doesn't matter where we're going; we try to build in time for a picnic. You can't beat a flask of tea, homemade sandwiches, and some extra treats. Mr M always tells me just to put a KitKat in for him, but his eyes light up when he sees all the extras I squeeze in, especially my Fab Slices, which are like posh flapjacks.

We bundled Beatrix, our Border Collie, into our Aygo. She loves the car, especially when she sees Dad making a flask of tea. She knows that this means there will be food on the trip at some point. Beatrix has very few essentials in her life: food, stones, sticks, a dry place to sleep and to be near us. Her essentials are probably in that order, too! The campervan was going to be our home from home, so it was important that Beatrix liked it. I can, hand on heart, say that we both knew that if Beatrix didn't approve, we wouldn't buy it.

CAMPERVAN CAPERS

We were soon driving back up the A9, past the unfriendly dealer, to the dealers, Struans, on the other side of Perth (Scotland, not Australia).

Adhering to COVID-19 restrictions, we wore our face coverings and maintained social distancing, with Steve, the salesman, standing outside the van. Beatrix, of course, didn't need to wear a face covering.

I immediately fell in love with the van and knew if I were to buy one, this was it. This van met all our essential requirements, was within our budget, and came with a twelve-month warranty. It had low mileage and only one previous owner. Both the inside and outside were immaculate.

Steve, the salesman, showed us the massive bundle of paperwork that contained over ten years of MOTs, service history, receipts, and manuals for every single item in the van, which made Mr M's eyes light up. Our house is full of receipts, most of them for food we've eaten or things we've bought but no longer own. Mr M likes to keep them all, just in case.

More importantly, Beatrix didn't need encouragement to jump into the van and barged her way in before Mr M and me. Maybe she thought she needed to check this new place out for any danger, you know, like mass murderers or strange smells. She sniffed around and immediately looked content, lying in the aisle for a snooze.

It was paramount that Beatrix would be comfortable and safe when travelling long distances. I was delighted to note that the spare seat belts would allow us to clip Beatrix's harness onto them, letting her lie down on the floor in the van but still be safe, preventing her from flying into the driver's lap if she saw a cat or a cyclist en-route, but still give her enough freedom to move about to shift her position if she wanted to.

I was in love. But I knew that the next hurdle was whether I could drive the van.

"Can we have a test drive today?" I asked Steve, now my favourite salesman, as he talked more with Beatrix than with us!

"Let's see your driver's license and national insurance number," he said, waving the van keys at me.

Now, I'm one of those people who can remember which cakes people like and whether they have one or two sugars in their tea, but could I remember my national insurance number? Not for the life in me.

Steve, the salesman, sighed,

"You can't take it out on the road, but you can have a drive up and down in our grounds if you like."

"What about all the other caravans and campervans parked everywhere!" I gasped, already starting to panic.

Steve, the salesman, assured me that he had every confidence that I could drive a vehicle up and down a car park without crashing into other stationary objects.

Oh, the stress! Not only was Steve, the salesman, prepared to hand over this campervan to me, but he was letting me loose in the van by myself.

"Go for it," Steve, the salesman, said, smiling.

Once I'd got myself settled in the driver's seat, I turned on the ignition. After a few deep breaths, I was ready to take my first-ever drive in a campervan.

My initial observation was that the handbrake was on the right-hand side, down by the foot well, which meant I had to reach down to use it. Who decided this was a good place for a handbrake? However, I was pleasantly surprised at how much you can see in the wing mirrors, and my confidence was boosted a little to note that you can get a little glimpse out of the rear window. Driving a campervan might not be too bad after all, I thought.

A few minutes later, I was both proud and surprised that I had indeed managed a little car park tour without hitting any of the other lovely new vehicles around me. I'm sure I saw Beatrix, Mr M, and Steve, the salesman, standing at the top of the grass bank, well out of my way, though. Did I see them covering their eyes? I wondered.

CAMPERVAN CAPERS

I begged and pleaded with Steve, the salesman, not to sell the van to anybody else and arranged to return the following morning for a proper test drive.

Shall I tell you another reason Steve became my favourite salesman that day? He never once tried to rush our purchase or tell me that loads of other people were coming to see the van and I might be too late if I didn't buy it right now. He never offered me a deal if I secured the purchase that day. I remember somebody saying something about buying in haste and repenting in leisure.

Telling Steve, the salesman, about our picnic and needing a place for Beatrix to play, he directed us to a lovely park half a mile from the dealers called Noah's, where we could sit and eat our lunch, and Beatrix could run around. Before long, we had parked the car and were settled on a bench enjoying our picnic, and Beatrix was zooming around to her heart's content, chasing her stick and a tennis ball, coming back to us now and again for a bite of a sandwich or a biscuit.

Then, it was back in the car for what was quickly becoming a regular journey back down the A9.

The following day, we were again travelling on the A9, all the time looking at lay-bys in a different light; that would be a good place to stop, but, oh no, not that one. Like we already knew what we were talking about!

Arriving at the dealers, I spotted my van. Yes, I'd already started to feel like it was mine. Despite my successful tootle around the car park the previous day, I didn't feel confident driving the van from the dealers for our test drive. I had already visualised the traffic lights, roundabouts, and dual carriageway and was beginning to panic. Mr M agreed he would drive from the dealers, but I would have to take over at a suitable place.

Following Steve, the salesman's suggestion, Mr M drove along a narrow road to Gloagburn Farm Shop and turned the van around in their huge car park.

Debra Murphy

We swapped over, and I climbed into the driver's seat. My palms were sweaty, my T-shirt felt clammy, my mouth dry, and I genuinely believed that everyone in the car park knew it was my first time in the driver's seat of this ginormous motorhome. Was I their lunchtime entertainment? I wondered. Had Steve, the salesman, phoned in advance announcing that there was another one coming for a test drive and for them to get their seats arranged for a good view?

Get a grip, Debra, I told myself. You're a good, confident driver. OK, the van is a bit bigger than you've driven before, but no larger than some of the other vehicles you've just seen on this very road.

Then I was off. First gear. Oh no! A right-hand turn straight away. Somehow, I managed it. Apologies to the drivers behind me that day as I made my way back to the dealers, gingerly going through traffic lights and more right-hand turns. I think I did manage to get into fifth gear at one point. I was mightily glad to get back to the dealers in one piece but knew I had a huge smile on my face, Mr M wasn't hiding his eyes, and Beatrix was nodding off in the aisle. This was going to be OK!

And so, the Adria Twin became ours (on paper anyhow). The next task was to arrange when we would take delivery of her. Yes, I'd decided my van was a she and would be called Evie. I'd originally planned Eva after Eva Cassidy, but Mr M said Evie sounded much better. It's not often I do, but I agreed with him.

And that day, a white, 13-year-old Ducato van became Evie, our new campervan.

COVID-19 had cancelled our usual Lake District holiday cottage stay in June 2020, which was then re-arranged to June 2021 and eventually became August 2021. Not wanting to pick up Evie and leave her all by herself on our drive as soon as we collected her, we arranged to pick her up after our holiday.

CAMPERVAN CAPERS

Meanwhile, I set about sorting the insurance and breakdown cover as I wanted to have everything in place before we set off to the Lakes to ensure there was nothing I'd forgotten. One of my fellow dog-walking friends has a motorhome, and he advised us to join the Caravan and Motorhome Club. I'll admit to being a bit hesitant and wondering whether I really wanted to be part of a 'gang'. Well, it's the best thing I could have done, because for something in the region of £50 a year membership, you get access to their website, a whole host of information, tales and guidance, a list of campsites and approved sites, and, as a member, you receive a discount on your bookings and motor insurance.

I got lots of price comparisons for insurance, and secured an excellent quote with a company recommended by the Caravan and Motorhome Club, for which I received another discount. I was also pleasantly surprised to find that there are times when maturity has its benefits. Both Mr M and I have had our driver's licenses for many years and have a good no-claims bonus on our car insurance that the company would consider. It also worked in our favour that I'd chosen a van that could be parked in our driveway and not on the street (well worth considering). The membership also gave us a discount on breakdown cover and, as a bonus, covers both of us in any vehicle, meaning we could cancel our existing breakdown package on the car. However, check your breakdown restrictions; not all breakdown companies include campervans and motorhomes.

Chapter 5

An Epic Bus Journey

With everything organised for collecting Evie, we could finally enjoy what would probably be our last cottage holiday in the Lake District for a few years. If everything went to plan, we would spend our holidays in Evie for the foreseeable future. This trip to April Cottage in Grasmere was long overdue, thanks to the COVID-19 lockdown.

During that long-awaited two-week holiday in Grasmere, we parked our car outside April Cottage, and it never moved until it was time to drive home again.

Driving in the Lake District is a lovely experience, but finding somewhere to park is a nightmare and often involves a bank loan for parking fees. However, the bus network there is fantastic and includes the 599 open-topped double-decker bus that runs every 20 minutes from Bowness to Grasmere. It's my all-time favourite bus journey because, being prone to travel sickness, I can sit on the top deck, admiring the scenery and feeling the breeze blowing on my face, listening to the tourist information playing through the loudspeakers next to each seat. The sound system gives the same information every trip, every year, but I never tire of hearing it. Even in the rain, I sit on the top deck, with Beatrix keeping me company. Mr M usually sits downstairs to stay warm!

CAMPERVAN CAPERS

As an extra bit of information, if you ever choose to take the 599 Stagecoach bus from Bowness to Ambleside, the tourist information audio recording tells you that near Brockholes, you are approaching what is reputed to be the bus stop with the best panorama in the UK. On a good day, you get the most magnificent sight of Langdale Pikes. Sitting on the open-top deck of the bus, this view is every bit as brilliant as standing at the bus stop. I'm biased, I know, because this is my favourite vista of the Lakes. I've already told you of my desire to have one of the original oil paintings of Langdale Pikes by William Heaton Cooper from the art gallery in Grasmere.

During this holiday, we searched for campsites to stay with Evie on our new campervan adventures. On a day out to Coniston on the single-decker bus from Ambleside, I used the journey as a learning curve for future adventures. This bus goes from Ambleside to Coniston and has a scenic detour through the sleepy village of Hawkshead, including the steep, narrow Hawkshead Hill. I was already worrying about whether I could drive my vehicle on the narrow roads in the Lake District, but I decided that if this huge single-decker bus could get along these roads, my shiny new girl would have no problem. Do you see my logic?

Well, what an experience! We've been on this bus before, and I've cycled this road many times over the years, but I'd never really paid attention to the road, being too busy soaking in the views of the hills and fells. On this particular day, as we got on the bus, we noticed a driver who looked about 12 years old and, standing beside his cab, was a woman in uniform, obviously his supervisor. From the word go, it was clear it was the first time this boy had ever driven a bus along this road. Initially, I felt slightly embarrassed for him as the woman was letting all the passengers know she was there because it was the boy's virgin drive on the route, and she began telling him what to do from the minute the bus set off.

However, this woman guided the boy over every inch of the journey, telling him when to move in, when to wait, when to take the whole road for the bend and how to own the road over bridges. There were a few tight sections when the bus had to pass a massive timber lorry coming in the opposite direction, and when the driver of a car panicked up the notorious Hawkshead Hill and their passenger had to take over the driving. Clearly, the bus drivers along this route always try to wait at a specific spot at a set time because they know the road is only wide enough for two buses at particular points. The same applies to the timber lorries; the drivers all know the times of the buses and wait at designated places.

It was as this bus pulled into a small passing place a mile or so outside Ambleside that I noticed a bus stop was situated right by the gates of Skelwith Fold Caravan Park. Interesting, I thought, and made a note to investigate this campsite further. Maybe this could be a new location for our summer holidays in the Lake District.

I listened to every bit of this woman's advice and etched it all into my memory. Always toot, toot at a blind bend. Remember to breathe and keep smiling.

I can tell you there was no chatter on the bus from the passengers during that journey. At different points in the trip, we all laughed, gasped, and prayed for the boy to get us to Coniston without mishaps.

When I first realised this woman was training the driver, I felt slightly irritated that she was making it obvious he was learning. But within the first 10-15 minutes, I felt relieved, not only for us as passengers but also for the young lad, that she was his guide for this route. I doubt any other bus driver could have given the fantastic insight, patience, and support the woman gave him that day. I was in awe of her skills and how she guided the boy on his first arduous journey.

When our bus finally arrived at Coniston, all the passengers cheered and congratulated the driver on his skills and thanked

CAMPERVAN CAPERS

the woman for her amazing training skills. I genuinely believe that this boy grew into a man on that day.

Did this experience fill me with confidence that I could drive Evie on these roads? Not exactly, but it reassured me that it is possible to easily fit an Adria Twin campervan onto them. Only time will tell if I can show the same skills as the young boy when it is my turn to drive my campervan in the Lake District.

*****

Refreshed after our long-awaited holiday in Grasmere, we returned home with the anticipation of collecting Evie the following Saturday.

However, even with the best-laid plans of mice and men, a rogue faulty tap in Evie's bathroom that needed to be replaced still hadn't been delivered to the dealers. COVID-19 got the blame for this, too. Much to my disappointment, Evie's pickup day was rescheduled to Saturday, 28 August 2021.

Soon, we had our plans made. We would drive our car to Croy Station and get the train to Perth, where lovely Steve, the salesman, would pick us up (including Beatrix, of course). I'd drive Evie home, but I felt I needed to have Mr M with me for moral support.

As I chatted with Mr M over tea the night before pickup day, I discussed everything I'd have to think about, highlighting all the new things we had to consider when driving a campervan.

With a chuckle, Mr M remembered Croy station's car park.

"Will Evie fit under the barrier?" he asked, smirking.

We had so much to learn.

Chapter 6

Evie Pickup Day - 28th August 2021, Daytime

Today, my lifelong dream was about to come true. We were collecting Evie, our new campervan. I had quickly whittled my inheritance down by more than a pound or two, but I didn't care.

As you will recall, Mr M stipulated that if I bought a campervan, I had to be able to drive it. I knew that, but I wasn't confident enough to drive Evie home from Perth alone for my first proper drive. So, I smiled nicely at Mr M and gave him *the* look that Beatrix had taught me so well, and he agreed that for my first journey, he would accompany me, but I still had to be the driver.

Our pickup day plan was to leave our car at Croy train station, get the train to Stirling, and then take another train to Perth. Steve, my favourite salesman, had agreed to collect the three of us at Perth station and drive us to Struans so he could hand over the keys for Evie to us or, more precisely, to me.

I would then drive Evie, with Mr M and Beatrix acting as the support team, to Croy Station, drop Mr M off for him to take our car home, leaving me to have a short five-mile solo trip from the station car park to our house. Beatrix would stay with me to offer moral support. Girl power!

When we arrived at Perth train station, Steve, the salesman, was waiting for us. I remember being so anxious and excited that

CAMPERVAN CAPERS

I could hardly talk. Once we were in his car, Beatrix was sitting in the car's footwell, wondering why we were in a strange vehicle and if we would ever have the picnic she had seen Dad making at home.

I was fully aware that there was so much for us to learn about the ins and outs of owning and using a campervan before we could even start enjoying the experience. Being a writer, I had my trusty notepad with me, and I also planned to take lots of photos.

Steve, the salesman, gave us a tour around Evie, showing us how to work the gas, electric, fridge, awning, and toilet, all of which I knew I had immediately forgotten.

By the look on Steve, the salesman's face, he knew it too!

With the luxury of a complimentary full tank of diesel, it wasn't long before I was finally taking charge of my very own campervan and turning on Evie's engine.

Was I nervous? You bet I was. Mr M asked me if I wanted him to drive. No, I was going to do this. Was that a touch of disappointment I could see in his eyes? I wondered if he was just as excited as me about becoming a campervan owner and desperate to have a drive.

With Beatrix strapped in the aisle, Mr M climbed into the passenger seat, and I settled myself in the driver's hotspot. We fastened our belts. I adjusted the wing and rear-view mirrors, then adjusted them again, just to be sure. Mr M looked at me, and we both smiled. Well, we grinned at each other. We had a campervan. Our own campervan! And we were off.

As we'd already had a couple of trips to Struans, I was now familiar with the nearby road junctions. They all had traffic lights, so I'd be fine. Wouldn't I?

I felt like everyone at Struans was watching me slowly edge my new campervan out of their car park. Beatrix sat in the aisle behind me, looking concerned, and Mr M patted my knee.

"You'll be OK, Debbie," he said. He only ever calls me Debbie when he wants to distract me from my thoughts.

Debra Murphy

Perhaps he knew that just at this moment, I did indeed need distracting from the fear that was probably etched on my face.

I calmed down a little once I'd negotiated the numerous traffic lights and junctions heading out of Perth. I hesitated a few moments at the Broxburn roundabout, feeling like a learner driver who didn't know when to pull out. Well, I did have to cross three lanes. Eventually, I edged onto the roundabout, and we soon safely headed down the dual carriageway.

I trundled my way down the A9, not exceeding 55 miles per hour, but this time I definitely got into fifth gear. I reminded myself to breathe and to relax as my shoulders and back were already aching with the tension. When did driving become so stressful? I wondered.

"Will I ever enjoy driving Evie?" I asked Mr M.

The drive home from Perth isn't long enough to warrant a picnic stop, but today was a special trip. It wasn't long before I noticed a large lay-by for us to pull in and have a break. I needed it! Looking out onto the glorious hills and mountains of Perthshire, parked in a lay-by, we had our very first picnic in our very own campervan. I felt like a kiddie in a sweet shop: my own campervan, Beatrix, my husband, and a wonderful picnic.

Of course, once refreshed, fed, and watered, I had to negotiate pulling back out onto the dual carriageway in my new campervan, which suddenly seemed as big as a juggernaut. The stream of traffic in both lanes was relentless, and all the vehicles appeared to be travelling at well over 70 miles per hour. I wondered if they had all been waiting for me to try to rejoin the road. Eventually, once I'd stopped my leg shaking on the accelerator pedal and noticed a suitable gap in the traffic, I was once again on my way.

"Well done, Debbie," said Mr M, mopping his brow. Was he mocking me?

Once we passed Stirling, I even negotiated leaving the M9 and joining the M80. It was only then that I started mentally

CAMPERVAN CAPERS

visualising the roads I'd be driving once off the motorway, and I could feel my hands beginning to sweat already.

The challenging drive started as we left the motorway and joined the B802. Suddenly, this road seemed very narrow! Slowly, I made my way to Croy train station to drop Mr M off so he could collect our car. Of course, I had noticed when we dropped the car off that morning that despite Mr M's frightening tactics the night before, there was no barrier at Croy Station. Perhaps ScotRail had heard about me!

I manoeuvred Evie into a parking space, or two or three, near our car, and Mr M climbed out.

"You'll be fine, Debra. I'll be right behind you," he said, almost skipping away from the van and getting into our car.

Anyone would think he was relieved that he was no longer my passenger.

Then, I began my first solo drive, with Beatrix for support, to gingerly make my way to our house. There was one T-junction where I had to take a right-hand turn. On a hill! Honestly, I was transported back to being an 18-year-old girl learning to drive a car. At least then, I had an instructor who could put his foot on the brake if I did anything stupid. Surprising myself, I managed this without any rolling back. Go, Debra, I told myself.

We had already decided that to keep Evie safe and secure, we would park her on our driveway and put our car behind her so that if anybody thought about stealing her, they would have to move the car first and then reverse Evie onto the street.

Driving onto our cul-de-sac, I could imagine all our neighbours watching to see how I would manage to manoeuvre a campervan. So, I did what any self-respecting Yorkshire girl would do. I stopped on the road outside our house, pulled on the ridiculously located hand brake, popped Evie into neutral, and jumped out, leaving Mr M to do the honours. Practising parking in our driveway could wait for another day.

I had earned a cup of tea and a biscuit.

Chapter 7

Sleeping On Our Drive - 28th August 2021, Nighttime

Long before we collected Evie, I had decided that on the day we brought her home, I would spend that night in the van to see if I liked being a campervanner. I chatted with Mr M about this and told him my first night in Evie would be in our driveway. That way, I could familiarise myself with everything in the van but feel safe wrapped in a security blanket, knowing I would only be a few steps away from home should anything go wrong or, heaven forbid, I didn't like it. In the worst-case scenario, if I absolutely hated sleeping in the van, I could take Evie back up to Steve, the salesman, and hand her back. Not that I told her that.

So, with the van safely parked on our drive, we took a trip out in the car to the local retail park to purchase a duvet and pillows for our new bedroom.

During that shopping trip, I realised that having a campervan is a talking point, and you have long conversations with people you've never met before. As I spoke with the salesman about the reason for my purchases, it transpired that he had had caravans and motorhomes all his life. I could feel his excitement about my new journey into becoming a campervan owner as he guided me to the best duvet, pillows, and duvet sets. By the time we left the store, he had shared many wonderful

CAMPERVAN CAPERS

memories of his various camping adventures, and I had spent a small fortune on bedding. This campervan life is not cheap!

Then, it was back home to spend a few hours preparing Evie for her first guest, me.

Fortunately, we have an external waterproof 240 v socket fitted on the side of our house, meaning we can plug Evie into this to use her electrical stuff on the mains rather than rely on her 12 v leisure battery.

I have learned this is like connecting to the EHU (Electric hook-up) on a campsite. So, I really do now have a campsite in the drive outside our house.

We also have a cold and hot water tap fitted outside, so I will be able to wash Evie without having to carry buckets of water from inside the house.

Despite my copious notes and photos taken on our tour with Steve, the salesman, around Evie and her features, once back home, we couldn't even remember how to get the electrics to work.

And so, the phone calls to Steve, the salesman, began. He laughed and told us again which switch to press. Hey presto. We had light. I could visualise Steve, the salesman, and his colleagues sitting around his desk having tea and biscuits with his phone on loudspeaker, enjoying the entertainment of us trying to get everything to work.

Nevertheless, with new bedding, the bedroom area soon looked quite homely. Fitting a duvet cover in a campervan is a day's exercise. I soon realised that opening the van's back doors would allow me to pull the bedding tight to make it snug. I hate wrinkled sheets and duvets – but not so much that I need to iron bedding.

Initially, the plan had been for me to spend the night in Evie, with Beatrix looking after me. Thinking about the consequences of this, I realised I didn't want to announce to the whole neighbourhood that I was in the van overnight, so Plan B had to be put into action. Beatrix is an excellent neighbourhood watch officer and barks to let everyone know if somebody walks down the street, a strange cat looks at her, a leaf blows across the pavement, or, as sometimes happens in winter, any deer wander along the road. No, Beatrix would have to stay in the house, leaving me to experience a solo night in the van. A good test for me, a chuckling Mr M told me.

That evening, my first campervan night began. I locked myself in, turned on the lights, drew the curtains, and closed the skylight blinds. I had a bit of a dilemma about what to wear in bed. Now, without giving you too much information here, I sleep in only my birthday suit at home. Would I be safe doing that in Evie? What if somebody broke in and found me? I told myself I was being ridiculous and that nobody would break in, and if they did, they would run away once they saw a person in bed. Hopefully! To put my mind at ease, I opted to sleep in pyjamas.

That would keep the burglars away, I told myself.

Along with a kettle filled with water, tea, milk, and biscuits, I had the essential item for any adventure: a large bar of Cadbury Dairy Milk Chocolate.

And that, as I sat alone in my new van, was the exact point that I knew I'd made the right decision buying Evie the Campervan. I'm not quite sure how to explain it, but I felt a release of tension and a sense of freedom. Campervan life really was for me.

I spent the evening cosy in my pyjamas, drinking tea, eating my snacks and writing the beginning of this book. I was slightly concerned that I had no running water, which meant no toilet, but Mr M agreed I could have the keys to the house, and there would be no charge for using the facilities! Cheeky!

After a last trip back into the house to use the bathroom, I returned to Evie, locked the doors, and tucked myself up in my new bedding.

CAMPERVAN CAPERS

How did I feel? Most importantly, I was comfortable, warm, and felt surprisingly safe. I even opened the roof blind to look out into the night sky for a while.

This was the life I thought as I reflected on the past few years. We've had immense joy mixed with times of trouble, sadness, and illness, but here I was, sleeping in my very own campervan. Another of my life's dreams was unfolding, and to be honest, I felt blooming good.

I didn't have a solid night's sleep as, quite understandably, I heard every single noise outside Evie. I didn't wake properly until 6 am when I crept out of the van, took myself back into the house, and slithered into our bed beside Mr M.

"You're freezing," he said, rolling over and going back to sleep. Clearly, he'd been concerned about me out in the van by myself!

Success. My first night in my very own campervan with no mishaps. OK, so I didn't really do anything other than write, drink tea, eat biscuits and chocolate, plan improvements to Evie's decor, and sleep. Tiny steps.

I made a few notes that night of things I'd already learned. It will be interesting to see how this list grows as I continue working on my book over the next few years. I'm betting that I will learn many lessons and make mistakes, which will be added to the book for your enjoyment.

Debra Murphy

A Newby Campervan Woman's First Lessons Learned

Check Your Views
Be sure to adjust your rear-view and wing mirrors, then tweak them again just to be sure.

Remember to Breathe
Breathing makes driving and living easier and much more fun.

Look for the Obvious Switches
There is a switch just inside my van above the cab to turn on the electrics. There will probably be one in your van, too.

Open the Back Doors
The easiest way to make the bed is to open the two rear doors of the van and sort it from that side. Enlisting the assistance of a second person helps, too.

Get Your Sewing Kit Out
The first sewing jobs I identified were to make a cover for the log sponge, currently serving as a headboard, and new curtains for the dining area. I might have some campervan material somewhere. I liked the idea of making Evie's interior look unique.

Chapter 8

What I Need. What I Really, Really Need

After my successful night in Evie, I was keen to get our first campervanning adventure organised. Over the next few days, we gathered bits and pieces that we both felt were essential for a road trip in Evie.

Following lots of internet searching, reading the different manuals and documentation in Evie and scrolling through YouTube videos, we finally worked out where the jack was stored and how to remove its snug, very tightly fitting storage box from under the passenger seat. We also identified the spare wheel under the van, but both felt it was frightening to think of jacking it up ourselves and that an emergency puncture repair foam would hopefully sort out any immediate problem in a remote location. We would, of course, always have our Green Flag membership card with us!

I've read about campervans being stolen nationwide and that thieves will even steal them from under your nose. We discussed how to keep Evie safe. In the driveway at home, we will always position her close to the side of the house and then park our car right behind her so that would-be thieves would have to move the car and then also need to reverse the van out of the driveway. We thought this would help to a certain extent and possibly act as a deterrent.

We felt we should also purchase a steering lock. There is so much choice - steering locks and wheel locks of all different shapes, sizes and prices – who knew there were so many to pick from? The trusty people in Halfords told us that all the locks probably worked equally as well as each other, and if somebody were hell-bent on stealing your van, they would. Locks act only as a deterrent. So, we opted for a middle-of-the-range steering lock with a red sensor for added effect. I wondered if the red light would seem bright in the van at night, but maybe we wouldn't need to put the steering lock on if we were sleeping in it.

I began wondering. If you were wild camping, would you avoid using the steering lock when you were asleep in case you needed to escape from would-be thieves, vandals or villains quickly? I figured by staying at a campsite, I wouldn't have my new fear tested.

As Mr M will agree, I'm one of those people who can hear noises that others don't even notice. I was worried that all our pots, pans, and other essential kitchen equipment might rattle about in the cupboards and drawers as we travelled around the country, driving me mad. I found a roll of non-slip matting in Flying Tiger in Glasgow for the tiny sum of £1. I was convinced I'd found the buy of the year, only to find that it's readily available from Tesco for, yes, £1. I'm sure it's available in many other places, and I'm even more confident that somebody will tell me I can buy it cheaper than £1.

Well, I was happy with my purchase and was soon busy cutting pieces to fit in all the drawers and cupboards. Time will tell if it really was a good buy.

Then there is something called a thermal windscreen shield. This is a work in progress. Looking at all the bits and pieces we had acquired with Evie, I was pleasantly surprised to find a thermal windscreen cover. This discovery, of course, came with so many questions. Where did it go? Inside or out?

CAMPERVAN CAPERS

How did it fasten on? When should it be used (obviously not when driving)? Was it needed or just something else to find a space for in the van?

YouTube is now my favourite app on my phone. So far, in my research on thermal windscreen shields, I've discovered that some go inside, but others go outside. Some tie on, but others are magnetic. Some people say they cause condensation; other people say they prevent condensation. There are some people who love them, but other people say they hate them. Some people say they are an essential piece of kit, whilst others think they are a waste of time and money.

What I did discover is that they're designed to keep the van cool in the sunshine (limited use in Scotland, then) and warm in winter. They're reported to prevent condensation on the inside of the van, although this is apparently easily fixed by sleeping with a window open. Who doesn't sleep with some fresh air coming into the room? I can tell you that a van with two people and a Border Collie will have at least one open window. Which thermal windscreen shield did we have? I have absolutely no idea. Maybe one day I'll camp next to somebody who knows all about this stuff.

Along with researching steering locks and thermal windscreen covers, I'd been looking for campsites near us. I decided that our first trip should be no more than an hour or so away, so we would have more time to get set up and learn how to use all the different gadgets in Evie.

It was September now, and the weather was hotter and drier than it had been for the entire summer in Scotland. I booked a two-night trip to the Immervoulin Caravan and Camping Park just beyond Callander. Not all the facilities would be open thanks to COVID-19, but we would have mains electricity and water. What more did you need?

Still on the hunt for essentials for our adventures, we had an exciting trip to GO Outdoors. Before too long, our trolley was piled high with plates, cutlery, dishes, cups, glasses, a collapsible washing-up bowl, a folding step for inside the van to get up to the bed, and a ground sheet for outside so we don't trail mud into the van.

Then Mr M decided we needed a set of screwdrivers and spanners. Next, we added a watering can to top up the water tank if the van was not connected to the water supply. Mr M, in his wisdom, also put into the pile of goods a couple of different hose connectors just in case the ones we had didn't fit the campsite taps. Finally, we added some chemicals to go into the toilet.

It's not the most exciting or fun research I have ever done, but before setting off on our shopping expedition, I googled the use of toilets in a campervan to determine exactly what we could, couldn't, or shouldn't do. Your campervan or motorhome toilet will be specific to your unit. Evie has a flushing toilet. The toilet has a cassette that holds all the waste products, water and paper.

This waste has to be emptied somewhere. Firstly, it's recommended that you use a green chemical in the toilet cassette to help with the odours, break down the contents, and keep the toilet smelling fresh.

You must never empty your chemical toilet waste anywhere except for the designated area in the campsite. If you're not on a campsite, you cannot simply empty the contents of your toilet cassette into the bushes or fields before you drive away. This is one of the complaints people make about campers along the NC500 route in the north of Scotland because they are dumping (excuse the pun) their waste anywhere they want and harming the environment. You will need to find a chemical waste disposal point; some garages and campsites will allow you to use their facilities, usually at a minimal cost.

For the holding tank in the toilet in Evie, we bought Thetford Aqua Kem Green Concentrate. We also purchased some of their Aqua Rinse to put in the toilet as we flushed it – this is supposed to help with a cleaner, smoother flush.

I'm guessing that new solutions will be created all the time to eliminate any chemicals being used.

Phew! What a subject.

Looking at our laden trolley, I wondered if there would be room in Evie for all our new bits and pieces, two humans and a dog!

Next, I did something I never usually do. I made a shopping list for the supermarket. Who'd have thought I'd ever write a list and actually follow it?

We planned our breakfasts, lunches, teas, and snack treats. Somehow, we decided we needed a new cafetière to keep Mr M happy with a supply of coffee. We opted for a double insulated stainless steel one rather than glass so that even if I struggled to drive smoothly, the cafetière would survive. Next to be added to the trolley were black bin liners, cleaning supplies, and, of course, a large bar of Cadbury Dairy Milk Chocolate for emergencies. It was doubtful that the chocolate would survive long enough for the trip, as I felt I could create some kind of emergency right then.

It's funny how Evie the campervan was making me see things in a different light already. The way our house is situated, we get the sun in our back garden until mid-afternoon, when it crosses over the roof to give the front of the house evening sunshine. I usually bemoan the fact that I miss the setting sun, as I don't like to sit at the front of the house and be on display to the neighbours. That evening, 1st September, at 8 pm, I sat writing in Evie, with the side door open, watching the sunlight on the Campsie Fells creating striking orange, bronze, yellow and gold colours on the hills.

The day before we were due to set off on our first adventure, we decided to fill up the fresh water tank to familiarise ourselves with how the taps, shower, and toilet worked.

Using the external tap at our house, we connected the water hose to Evie and filled up the tank. A little rocker switch inside the door (next to the switch that turns the electricity on!) tells you how much fresh water you have in the tank.

We were soon looking forward to having our first cup of tea in Evie, using water from the tap and boiling the kettle on the gas stove.

I turned on the tap in the kitchen.

Nothing.

I turned on the tap in the bathroom.

Nothing.

I flushed the toilet.

Nothing.

"Are you sure you filled the tank right up?" I asked Mr M.

He rolled his eyes, and we started working through the different manuals to determine why the water was not flowing through the taps.

Mr M found some information on the internet that suggested sometimes the fuse in the toilet cassette unit can become a little rusty and furred, which might stop things from working. He located the fuse, sanded it, cleaned it, and popped everything back together.

We tried the toilet again.

Nothing.

"What if the toilet and water system were broken when we bought Evie, and we didn't realise it when we collected her because Steve, the salesman, didn't show us everything?" I moaned, almost crying at the possibility that we had been sold a faulty campervan.

So, I phoned Steve, the salesman.

"Oh, hello, Debra," he said.

Was he laughing already? I wondered.

"We can't get the taps or the toilet to work. We've filled the fresh water tank and cleaned the fuses, but can't get it to work, and we're going away tomorrow," I cried.

CAMPERVAN CAPERS

"Have you turned the water on?" Steve, the laughing salesman, asked.

"Oh, is there a switch for the water?" said I sheepishly.

"Yes, next to the one for the electricity and the one that tells you how much water you have in your tank," he laughed. "Then you need to open both taps and flush the toilet a couple of times to get any airlock out of the system. I can guarantee everything will then work for you."

Of course, once we did all of this, water gushed from the taps and the toilet flushed like magic.

And just like that, I had the subtitle for my book.

Debra Murphy

Further Desires Of A Would-be Campervan Woman

Cadbury Dairy Milk Chocolate
An essential piece of kit for any adventure.

Cafetière
Keeps the non-campervan-loving folk happy.

Chemicals for Your Toilet and Tanks
Research these and find out which ones you prefer to use. Try to go as green as possible. You can't just dump your waste anywhere.

Collapsible Washing Up Bowl
Anything that folds up in a campervan is perfect.

Emergency Puncture Repair Foam
Find out where your spare wheel and jack are. Get a puncture repair thingy. The Green Flag breakdown membership card is far less frightening.

Steering Lock
The choice is yours. Your insurance company would probably like to know that you had one in place if your van gets stolen. Remember, the lock may only act as a deterrent.

Thermal Windscreen Shield
Work out what sort you have and toss a coin to determine whether you will use it.

Chapter 9

Let The Adventures Begin - 2nd September 2021

Immervoulin Caravan and Camping Park, Strathyre, Perthshire, Scotland

The following day, Evie was packed with everything we thought essential for our three-day adventure. It will come as no surprise to you that the Dairy Milk Chocolate didn't survive. The cool box was filled with food, our clothes were in the cupboards above the bed, and we were ready. Hopefully, I'd packed things securely enough with tea towels, the non-slip matting, and nifty positioning so that nothing would rattle or break in transit.

Of course, the first thing we noticed when we set off was the rattling of the grill. Next time, I will do better!

My first task was to reverse from our driveway. I jumped into the driver's seat and selected reverse, but looking at next door's car alongside Evie, I quickly lost my confidence, so I gave this job to Mr M. I could learn that skill later.

Once Evie was off our driveway, I resumed the role of driver and gingerly set off, feeling the eyes of the world on me.

As I eased us around the end of our cul-de-sac, our lovely neighbour, Chris, the fireman, pulled alongside me in his car and gave me such a huge smile and a thumbs up that I felt my confidence grow.

Then we were off. Me, driving my own campervan. Once out of Kirkintilloch, we joined the M80 motorway and settled into a gentle drive, sitting at 50-55 mph.

I quickly began enjoying the drive, taking my time to get used to the different view when driving a van rather than a tiny Toyota Aygo.

We were soon on the M9 motorway, and the turnoff to follow the A85 to Callander was a welcome sight. All was going well. This road was plenty wide enough for me and other vehicles. Going at a steady pace (some might call it crawling), I pulled into lay-bys at every opportunity to allow any traffic behind me to get past. To be fair, the road speed limit varied between 50 and 60 mph, and I was travelling at a reasonable speed. Anyone drumming their thumbs impatiently on their steering wheel would probably feel exasperated whatever speed I was travelling at just because I was a campervan.

Being the cause of other drivers' frustration is something that we quickly had to get used to. As the driver of a campervan, you'll have to accept that you will feel the fury of drivers when they find themselves behind you in your van. How dare we drive a campervan on a road?

I panicked at the thought of the bridge going through Doune, where vehicles usually have to wait to allow oncoming traffic. I soon realised that sitting high in Evie's cab, I had a much better view over the bridge than in the car, and there were no problems at all.

Beyond Callander, the road twists and weaves a little, and I had to breathe in once or twice, especially when faced with a timber lorry coming in the opposite direction on a particularly narrow bit of the road.

I must have been relaxing a little, though, as I could now appreciate the fabulous views as the sun burned through the clouds, revealing Ben Ledi and the surrounding hills. Loch Lubnaig looked amazing as ever, and I even started to imagine myself swimming in the loch once we were parked and settled.

CAMPERVAN CAPERS

A couple of miles down the road, we reached the campsite sign, and I drove slowly down the track, thankful for the lack of major incidents.

Excitedly, I parked Evie outside reception, turned off her engine, jumped out of the cabin and closed the door behind me. Well, I closed the door on me! Yes, my thumb was still inside the door.

Quickly opening the door again, I looked at my hand, expecting to find my thumb missing. It was still there, just gushing lots of red blood.

Feeling light-headed and sickly, I sat on the bench outside reception and took some deep breaths. There was a moment when the campsite owner and Mr M discussed how much sympathy they should give me. By the time I'd listened to Mr M telling her I was too clumsy for words and the campsite owner declaring her pride in me for my lack of crying or shouting at my injury, I felt a little better. Still, I let Mr M manoeuvre Evie to our allocated pitch.

Thankfully, we had packed our first aid kit into the garage, so a plaster was found, and I soon forgot my injury and wandered around, just taking in the scenery. The sun had come out, the mist disappeared, and the hills and silence surrounded us.

This was why I wanted a campervan!

Between us, Mr M and I worked out how to connect Evie to mains electricity.

With some fumbling, harsh words and eye-rolling, we somehow managed to pull out the side awning and even level the legs. We decided that we would put it back away at night-time because we didn't know if it was safe to leave it out overnight.

The camping table and chairs were quickly assembled, and our two-day home was sorted.

We were all set, as we had already filled Evie's water tank before we left home and put the required chemicals in the toilet.

Debra Murphy

The great thing about being on a campsite is that you're surrounded by like-minded people who love to chat. It didn't take us long to get to know our neighbours, and we enlisted them to help get the fridge working. Within the first half an hour of being there, we had learned so much.

Our first discovery was that not all sites have a fresh water tap alongside each pitch, meaning unless you're lucky enough to have an extra-long water hose (which we did thanks to Steve, the salesman), you might have to carry water to your van. I didn't even look at Mr M because I could already read his mind, gloating that he told me to pack the watering can.

Once we had learned how to fill the fresh water tank onsite, we then learned how to empty it. Now, in our van, this is the most awkward thing in the world. You have to take off the top of the bench seat, unscrew the large blue twist top and, reaching down into the water tank, pull the bung from the bottom. Another job for Mr M to do later, I muttered to myself.

We soon discovered that fabulous though our fridge was, it was much smaller than we realised, and our large carton of milk needed pouring into various receptacles, because they wouldn't fit in the fridge door—smaller milk cartons required for next time.

Both Mr M and I are reasonably clever people, but it didn't occur to us that the waste water would need to be stored somewhere. Thankfully, we were advised by a seasoned campervanner that we needed a container to drain our waste water into.

Looking around at the different campers, I could see that there was indeed an array of containers. Most of the other vans seemed to have one of some sort, and even though they were of various shapes and sizes, all appeared to have wheels. It quickly became obvious to us that only having a small plastic tub to drain our waste water was, well, plain silly. My first job when we got home was to buy a waste water container.

CAMPERVAN CAPERS

Once we were all set up, it was time for our first campervan meal. It was hard to believe it was the end of September, with the sun now beaming down. We had a problem getting the hob ignition to work, but thankfully, we had packed a battery-operated candle lighter (because Mr M doesn't think I can be trusted with matches).

That teatime, we had the best-ever meal of chicken curry with boiled rice, naan bread, poppadoms, and mango chutney, finished with mugs of tea and biscuits. I even enjoyed doing the washing up!

This is the life, I thought. And I'm sure Mr M was equally at peace that evening, although it didn't last long before we needed to get out the citronella candles and Smidge for the midges, but it was a small price to pay.

Beatrix seemed equally content in what I'm sure she thought was her new home. To be fair, I think Beatrix is happy so long as she is near us. Sharing our biscuits is always a plus for her, too.

We had a blissful couple of hours wandering down the riverbank towards Loch Lubnaig. I realised that we were way too far down the river to walk to the bit of the loch where you can swim, but I wasn't bothered in the slightest.

Returning to the van, we got ourselves settled. That feeling of being in my own campervan with my husband and Beatrix couldn't be bought. Well, actually, it had, of course, but you know what I mean.

Before too long, the doors were locked, the curtains closed, the kettle was back on the hob, and I was in my pyjamas. Supper was enjoyed by all, and then we went to bed. Beatrix decided she would sleep under the table.

We debated which side of the bed we would sleep on. I opted for the side closest to the back doors because I knew Mr M would feel the cold, and I'm a tough Yorkshire girl who is never cold.

Debra Murphy

How did our first night go? It was a bit strange, and there was some cursing when I needed to get up during the night for the toilet and clamber over Mr M. But, we both agreed that it had been a very peaceful, quiet night on the site. We really did believe that we had made the right decision buying Evie.

The following day was gloriously sunny and hot, and we enjoyed our breakfast sitting outside Evie - porridge made on the hob how it should be, slowly so that the milk is soaked up by the oats, bringing out the natural sweetness. Of course, with Mr M and Beatrix being creatures of habit, she was pleased that this new home of hers served hot buttered toast.

As the shower blocks were closed due to the COVID-19 restrictions, I decided today was the day to test Evie's shower. We had worked out the hot water system the night before, but were unsure how much water the shower would use.

The bathroom in our van is very snug. The toilet swivels so you can move it out of the way when using the shower. The tap from the sink pulls up and hooks onto the wall to make the shower head, and a shower curtain pulls right across the bathroom concertina door.

Before too long, I was having a wonderfully hot shower. Thankfully, I'd not taken as long as I do at home because the hot water ran out just as I washed away the final bits of soap from my body.

Did I enjoy the shower experience? If I'm honest, probably not enough to repeat it. Although it's designed as a wet room, it took longer to dry the bathroom than having a shower. However, we now knew it worked, and I'd experienced it. I think that under normal circumstances, the shower blocks would be open, so we wouldn't need to use Evie's tiny bathroom. Who needs a shower every day on holiday anyway?

Let's talk more about the bathroom facilities. Not only were the shower blocks on the campsite closed due to COVID-19, but so were the toilets, which meant only one thing.

CAMPERVAN CAPERS

Evie's toilet had to be used. Yes, for more than just a wee! That was an experience for both of us. I'm guessing that if your stomach is now churning at that idea, then campervan life might not be for you.

To give credit to Mr M, he was the one who did the honours of taking the toilet cassette to the chemical waste disposal and emptying the contents. I like to think he was on a learning curve, and he could advise me on how he managed the task later, and I didn't ask too many questions!

The Immervoulin Caravan and Camping Park is situated just outside Strathyre, and we decided to treat ourselves to lunch at the lovely Broch Cafe just down the road. You can walk most of the way off the main road, but be aware that there is a short section, 50 metres or so, where you have to walk at the edge of the road. Something to consider if you have young children or dogs who are afraid of traffic. The Broch Cafe serves delicious coffees, meals, and cakes. As it's one of the few places along this road, it's popular with hill walkers and cyclists, and, being right on the national cycle route, it can get very busy, so be prepared to wait for your food and drink. It's worth it, though. Funny enough, this cafe is built in the same place where the public toilets used to be!

Fed and watered, we enjoyed chatting with different people at the cafe, and then we headed back to the campsite. We noticed a man fishing from the riverbank, and soon, Mr M and the fisherman were chatting away. Meanwhile, I discovered that some people were swimming in the crystal clear water further down the river. That was it. I was back to Evie and into my swimming costume, beckoning Mr M to come and keep an eye on Beatrix as I took a dip.

It was cold but not freezing, and really only just deep enough to swim in a couple of places. I did lift my feet, so I can now say I've swum in the River Balvaig. Beatrix had a paddle next to me, with Mr M watching and taking photos.

Debra Murphy

Perhaps I should have saved the shower to have after my dip in the river. I'll know for future trips.

That second evening passed peacefully, with us enjoying bolognese and pasta, followed by lemon drizzle cake and hot custard. Perfect.

We chatted more with our neighbours and discovered that many campers on this site have seasonal pitches and spend most of their summers here. We were lucky to get booked for one of the last few weekends when the site was open before closing for the winter. That was something else I learned as I assumed that all sites would be open all year round.

The following morning, it seemed to take us hours to get ready. Washing up, packing dishes, pans and crockery back into the cupboards and finding a space for everything was like trying to pack a suitcase at the end of a holiday.

Our long orange electric power cable is heavy and took up so much room, but I watched others wrap theirs onto a cable reel, so we had another essential tool to buy now. This would keep the cable tidy and take up less room in the garage.

We now knew that the waste water from the sinks and shower is referred to as grey waste water. It cannot just be dumped anywhere on the ground. It has to be emptied into a drain. Between us, using our ridiculously small plastic tub, we eventually had all the grey waste water emptied from Evie. The fresh water, so long as it has not been contaminated, is safe to dump on the ground, obviously avoiding flooding campsites and areas where other campers walk. We decided that just in case we needed water on the way home, we would empty the fresh water back at our house on our drive.

After checking that everything was packed away and that no windows had been left open, we were on our way home. Mr M said he would drive as my thumb was still sore, but I suspected he just wanted to drive. On the way home, he decided we should call at his brother's house to let them see Evie. And I thought it was just me that was proud of her!

CAMPERVAN CAPERS

Later that evening, we were back home. Evie was unpacked, locked up, and ready for her next adventure, and we were exhausted. It's surprising how energy-zapping new adventures can be.

Alas, we had found a problem in Evie. When we initially ordered the campervan, I was so worried that I would struggle reversing her that I asked for a reversing camera and parking sensors to be fitted. Unless the parking sensors needed activating somehow, these were not working. So, on the Monday morning after our trip, I was back on the phone with the ever-patient Steve, the salesman.

After a few minutes of looking through notes at his end, he confirmed that, although we had indeed paid for the parking sensors, they had in fact, never been fitted. As I'd now driven Evie a couple of times, I decided that the reversing camera was quite sufficient and asked for a refund for the missing parking sensors. At the same time, I discussed with Steve, the salesman, the possibility of getting a spare gas cylinder from Struans as, due to COVID-19, they were in short supply. I wanted a spare full one so we wouldn't need to worry about running out of gas on an expedition. In the gas storage area in Evie, there is room for two large 6 k gas cylinders to be safely carried. Steve, the salesman, worked his magic and told us we could collect a spare full gas cylinder at our convenience.

Chapter 10

Accordion Lessons - 16th September 2021

Maragowan Club Campsite, Killin, Scotland

Following our first adventure in Evie at the Immervoulin Caravan and Camping Park, I felt a little more confident in our journey to becoming seasoned campervanners. Just a little!

We had been fortunate on our first adventure because the weather had been perfect, but both commented how it might have been different if it had rained. With two people and a wet dog, how would we have kept the seat covers clean?

I hunted through the house and found several blankets to cover the bench seat and a couple of extra ones for the driver and passenger seats once we arrived at our destination. What I wanted to do was to make some covers, and I decided that could be my winter project.

The biggest thing I've learned so far on my campervan journey is that owning a campervan is not cheap. We thought we had bought all the essentials before our last adventure in Evie, but now we needed another shopping trip. I know you can buy most things online, but I prefer to physically see things before I purchase them and try to do so whenever possible.

A couple of days after returning home from our first adventure, we once again found ourselves at GO Outdoors.

CAMPERVAN CAPERS

Perhaps we need to move house so that we don't live quite so close to this store of temptation. Shortly after going through the shop doors, we had in our trolley a 38-litre Wastemaster tank roller. We could now collect our waste water and then easily roll the container to a drain to empty rather than using our silly little plastic container that held less water than a kettle.

The next item into the trolley went a doormat. This was essential, I told Mr M, because it had a picture of a campervan on it!

Something else I'd learned was that although some campsites declare themselves dog-friendly, dogs must be on the lead whilst on the site. So, we purchased a large dog leash screw to attach Beatrix's extending lead to it, meaning she still had the freedom to wander around the outside of Evie but would be tethered securely.

Eager to keep up our learning curve of campervan life, I scoured the Caravan and Motorhome Club website for another adventure. We'd tried an independent site for our first trip, and now wanted to experience a club one. The site that jumped out and called to me to stay was, of all locations, the Maragowan Caravan and Motorhome Club Campsite just outside Killin, below the infamous Ben Lawers range. For those who have not read my other books, it is the Munro that I had to be airlifted off when I had a heart attack in 2019.

But I survived, obviously!

I'd also now discovered the benefits of membership with the Caravan and Motorhome Club. I've already said that I like to physically see things before I buy them. Well, I also want to talk to a real person rather than book things online. With the club booking system, you can do this. One of my qualities that others may see as a weakness is that I never pretend to know about something if I don't. After admitting to the very friendly woman on the other end of the phone that I was feeling a bit (OK, a lot) like a fish out of water, she gladly gave me lots of valuable information about the different types of pitches available on the club campsites. And there was me thinking you just chose a pitch.

The very basic pitches are known as eco or economy. This means you have a place to park for the night but no access to electricity. You still have access to fresh water and dedicated waste areas to dispose of your grey waste water and chemical toilet waste. The site will probably not have a toilet block, so you will need to be self-sufficient.

Then, there are standard service pitches. On these, you can access mains electricity and fresh water. The electricity connection is close to your pitch, but the fresh water tap is not necessarily right beside you, so you still need to have some way of carrying water to your van. The site will have grey water and chemical toilet waste areas, and usually has toilet blocks and showers.

If you're looking for a bit of luxury, there are superior pitches. On these, you have mains electricity, a fresh water tap and grey water waste drain at your pitch. These cost more, but are more convenient. The site itself will have chemical waste areas, toilet blocks, and showers.

It's worth noting that not all pitches are hardstanding. Some are on grass. For the moment, still finding my feet as a campervanner, I decided I would always try to book hardstanding, so I wouldn't have to worry about getting stuck on a boggy grass pitch in bad weather (not unusual in Scotland!)

Another thing to be aware of when you book your pitch is whether you'll be using an awning or not. If you book a pitch with an awning, these are wider than the other pitches, and you may pay extra.

Some sites have motorhome service points where you can drive your campervan or motorhome over a drain to deposit any waste water from your unit before travelling home. I have since realised you can also fill your fresh water tank at these.

CAMPERVAN CAPERS

As I'd already discovered, not all sites are dog-friendly, and if they are, they usually have a limit on how many dogs you can have in your booking. Some dog-friendly sites also charge extra for dogs, although I'm not sure why. Also, as we have learned, dogs are not free to roam on the site and must always be on the lead. A long leash and a stake to fasten them to (the leash and not the dog!) outside on your pitch is very handy. Just remember not to make the lead so long that your dog can run into the road or pester the people on either side of your pitch. Not everyone likes dogs, and not all dogs like people!

The Maragowan site has hardstanding serviced pitches, meaning they have electric , but the fresh water tap might not be right beside the van. Knowing this, we would just put some fresh water into Evie at home before we set off and then top up when we arrived. Good job that Mr M thought of the watering can!

With our next adventure booked, I phoned Steve, the salesman and arranged for us to collect the spare gas cylinder and the remaining refund for the missing parking sensors. Going to Perth en route was not too much out of our way.

Being fully aware that Mr M is not the biggest fan of camping and would probably have adventures in Evie under sufferance, I thought that I could enhance his enjoyment by equipping him with some new fishing gear to re-ignite his love of fishing. Some of the campsites I'd seen, including Maragowan, are close to rivers, and you can purchase fishing permits, with some even having free fishing. You need to check on the different fishing seasons and times, though. There are times and dates fishing is not permitted, and not all places allow you to keep your catch. These might be different outside Scotland, too, so make sure you check.

That did, of course, involve a second trip in one week to GO Outdoors. Before too long, a smiling Mr M had waterproof fishing trousers, jacket, and hook things in the trolley. I was slightly concerned when he told me he would need to buy some live bait the day before we set off to Killin. I asked where he would keep these wiggly things (I kept my hands over my ears as I didn't want to know that he had planned to keep them in the fridge along with our food, but I knew, really).

Packing Evie didn't take long this time, as many of the essentials can be left in her between trips. Fresh food, cooked the night before, plenty of chocolate, and a couple of pairs of clean knickers each were all we really needed.

The most difficult items to pack were Mr M's fishing rods. He'd bought a long plastic tube container to keep them in because I didn't want smelly fishing rods on the bed. Yes, that was the best place I found for the rods: on the bed, snuggled up to a couple of cushions so they didn't fall onto the floor during transit. Mr M agreed the rods could live under Evie during our stay at the campsite.

The morning arrived for us to set off to Maragowan at the same time as one of my migraines, so Mr M took charge of the driving. With a picnic and flask of tea packed and all the other essentials, we detoured to Perth and Struans to collect the spare gas cylinder and remaining refund for the missing parking sensors.

"That will pay for tea and cakes at the cafe in Killin," said Mr M, smiling.

We had hoped to get a few more tips whilst at Struans on how to use things in the van properly, but the technical guy was away, moving house. We were struggling to get the ignition to work on the hob and the grill, so a telephone consultation had to suffice. That was just typical for 2021 – Zoom meetings, telephone calls and anything except meeting real people. Over the phone, he informed us that the reason we couldn't get the ignition to work on the cooker was because our model didn't have one. The ignition was only for the grill and not the hob.

We still needed to find out how to drain the boiler in winter, as this seemed to be beating Mr M, the engineer, and everyone else in the campervan showroom. We knew this was

CAMPERVAN CAPERS

vital because if you don't drain the water from the boiler in winter, it could freeze, risking frozen and possibly burst pipes.

Shortly before lunchtime, with the spare gas cylinder secured in its holder and the remaining refund in our bank account, we left Perth and were on our way to Killin. My super-duper migraine tablets had kicked in, but Mr M continued as my driver. We stopped just outside Callander for some lunch because we could. I love our campervan picnics, even if they are only in a lay-by.

Both Mr M and I are familiar with the road to Killin, including the very tight bridge over the Falls of Dochart, so I was mightily glad Mr M was driving. I was shocked at how many pedestrians were standing on this narrow bridge, trying to get a good view of the waterfalls below, even though they could see a campervan trying to drive along it. I resisted the temptation to wind my window down and push them off the bridge

Once safely across the bridge, we looked out for the campsite flag. It's worth noting that if you stay at Maragowan, your sat-nav might try to take you down a little road just before the campsite. Fortunately, I'd studied all the fabulous information in the welcome email and made sure Mr M ignored this road and took the correct entrance to reception.

For me, part of the fun of a new adventure is arriving at your destination and discovering the ins and outs of everything. At the reception, I was informed that I could pick my pitch from any available that had white posts with numbers on. We had to find a suitable pitch and then park between the two small white posts on the pitch and not on the grass between pitches at any cost.

Collecting Mr M's free fishing permit to fish in the river that ran alongside the site, I wondered if we would be having trout for tea.

Selecting an empty pitch that looked quite level, we soon had Evie connected to the electricity. Fortunately, the pitch was close enough to the tap, and our extra-long water hose reached it, so we didn't need to use the watering can. I was ignoring the fact that I now had live bait in my fridge, telling myself that as they were in a sealed container that was double wrapped in cling film and plastic bags, they could not escape.

Our new grey waste water container only just fitted under Evie, but with a bit of shuggling about, we had it positioned so that it could catch the waste water. We discovered the following day that, despite having wheels, a full waste water carrier is cumbersome. It's worth remembering to empty this before it gets full. This can be emptied down the drain by the tap, so we didn't have to go too far to manoeuvre ours.

We even managed to put up the awning without much difficulty this time, having learned how the legs work.

To our delight, despite being told there was no ignition on the cooker rings, the grill ignition was now working like a dream. We now know our hob has no ignition, but the grill does. I also learned this trip that hand-held battery-operated candle lighters don't work quite so well if you drop them in a sink full of water. Mr M does despair at how clumsy I can be.

I popped the kettle on the hob, and Mr M set off to play at being a fisherman. He certainly looked the part in his new gear. As for me, I was soon enjoying a mug of steaming hot tea and a piece of my homemade coffee cake and Beatrix a rich tea biscuit.

As I sat under the awning on a camping chair, the mist created a gentle drizzle, enough to need a jacket but not enough to cause a calamity. There were no views of the hills because of the low cloud, but the mist and the late September days ensured I was not plagued by midges.

Initially the campsite seemed devoid of people, and I was able to enjoy the peace and listen to the chirping birdsongs. I could hear the traffic on the road to Kenmore. As I had chosen a site just off the main road, that's OK. And it's not a major road, so it's not like a motorway sound. There was a soothing drip, drip, drip of rain from the awning. Beatrix was soon

CAMPERVAN CAPERS

asleep, learning that under the awning was better than in the drizzle.

I spent the next hour watching other new arrivals setting up caravans as big as houses. I was enthralled watching them manoeuvre their massive tourers with a hand-held remote control, as I had expected them to manually push these giants. Watching it was amazing, but I was glad it wasn't me.

Yet again, we found that people on the campsites eagerly pass on their advice, guidance, opinions, and expertise. Mr M returned from his fishing expedition (without any fish) and disappeared to get fresh water for Beatrix, appearing half an hour later, accompanied by Peter Knight and his accordion. Only Mr M could achieve this. A pleasant half-hour passed as Peter gave us a few tunes and shared some tips for Mr M, who has been learning to play the accordion for ten years but only ever got as far as taking his out of its case.

We also chatted with some of our neighbours about levelling blocks. Some people use them, others don't. We were given lots of advice about which ones to get, how wide they should be, how strong they need to be, and how they can make an enormous difference to your comfort in the van if the pitch is on a slope—something else to buy.

Then, it was time for the serious work of cooking tea. Before too long, I had a curry bubbling away on the hob and the rice boiling in another pot. It smelled delicious, and my mouth was watering.

"You can't park there," said a man in uniform who seemed to appear out of nowhere.

I was a little confused, but it transpired that we had not followed the exact instructions and were not parked perfectly between the two white posts on our pitch.

I tried very hard not to roll my eyes and asked politely why it was such a big issue. I was very sternly informed that the grass between the pitches is a firebreak, and by law there should be three metres between your van, car or awning and the next pitch's equipment. Once I realised this, I fully understood the reason for this request to move our van to the correct position. The uniformed man was very friendly and helpful, chatting away and telling me that it would be OK to finish our meal before we moved our van.

I want to add a note here - just to confirm what I had been told about fire risks; a few months later, I read in a Caravan and Motorhome Club magazine about a fire that had broken out in a caravan on one of the club sites that had not been able to spread to other pitches or vehicles because of the correct fire break distance being adhered to.

A lesson well and truly learned.

The Maragowan site is in a lovely location, and there are plenty of walks nearby, either into the village of Killin or along the riverbank and nearby fells, giving plenty of opportunities for dogs to get off the lead and have a good run around.

One of the benefits of a Caravan and Motorhome Club site is that the shower and toilet blocks should be of a certain standard. You don't need to use your gas to heat the water in your van for a shower, and, of course, the site facilities are bigger than our tiny bathroom. Following the Immervoulin adventure and toilet experience, we decided that using the onsite toilets for major events would be much better than having to empty the results from the toilet cassette. And you've paid for the facilities with your site booking, so why not use them

This site also has laundry and washing-up facilities. Not something we needed on this visit, but it's worth knowing if you're planning to stay away for prolonged periods of time.

That evening, we decided that as the breeze had turned into more of a wind, we would rewind the awning in because we didn't have any pegs or guy ropes to fasten it down. We could already hear the fabric blowing and thought it better to put it

CAMPERVAN CAPERS

away rather than have to do this in the middle of the night. Perhaps we were a bit over-cautious, or maybe not being over-cautious is being naïve.

Next on our learning curve was to get the gas central heating working. Yes, as small a van as Evie is, she has her own gas central heating. After reading the manual over and over again and a fair bit of fiddling about with the boiler settings, we eventually got the heating to work. Then, once it was working, I realised one vent was right next to where Beatrix lay, and I didn't want her to be subjected to the hot air blowing on her, so I turned it off again. We now knew it worked, so if we needed it, we would be able to use it.

"What we need is a portable electric radiator," announced Mr M. "It's going to be cold in this van without heating soon."

More expense, but as Mr M pointed out, if we are paying for the the electricity on the site, why use our expensive gas to keep us warm? Of course, I'd need to do a bit of research to determine what we can and can't use in Evie onsite.

On our last trip, we struggled to work out how to close the concertina blinds across the inside of the windscreen. They certainly feel a bit flimsy, and you have to adjust the rear-view mirror to get them to close. Once you've mastered it, they are quite easy. Opening them again and locking them so they don't close as you drive is a little fiddly, but it seems easy after you've done it correctly once. These things are worth practising in your van before you start your adventures, and certainly before it's dark.

The other windows in our van all have blinds, and they also have an insect screen. Your blinds will be specific to your vehicle, but for ours, you pull a catch together to close the blackout blind and wiggle the catch a different way to pull up just the insect screen, allowing you to open the windows even during a midge attack. I wondered why there isn't an insect screen on the large sliding door, then realised that the cooker is located along that door, so a midge screen might act as fire fuel.

After a pleasant night's sleep, we awoke to find the weather had taken a bit of a turn for the worse. There was not much wind, but the drizzle was now gentle rain. However, this didn't bother Mr M as he donned his fishing gear and set off to catch lunch for us.

Beatrix and I walked down to the village to see the Falls of Dochart. This tourist attraction differs from most other waterfalls as they are not in a remote location but run right through the village. This means there can be congestion on the bridge, as we discovered the day, before when traffic is trying to negotiate the narrow road across the bridge and has to fight with pedestrians taking photos. I've seen these falls with hardly any water in them at all, and on other occasions they have been mightily impressive. Today, the river was pretty low, but the rocks looked very slippery, so I decided not to risk climbing down onto them.

Killin itself has a lot to offer. There are several cafes, pubs, inns, hotels, shops, and a small Co-op. It's worth noting that your site booking at Maragowan gives you discounts in some of these places, so remember to take your booking receipt with you.

Wandering back to the campsite, I wondered how Mr M had fared with his fishing, but he was already back in Evie. He was wet and cold and had caught no fish.

It didn't take much to persuade him to get changed out of his wet gear and take a stroll back down to the village with Beatrix and me for some lunch at a cafe. Of course, being still in the throes of COVID-19, we had to sit outside the cafe, under shelter, but still wolfed down some tasty homemade soup and a lovely latte.

Despite the social distancing, we enjoyed a good couple of hours there and chatted with different people. Beatrix is such a stunning and well-behaved Border Collie that she attracts attention wherever we go.

Once back at the campsite, it was time for the kettle to go on again. Well, we didn't have any cake at the cafe, so afternoon tea and a sweet treat inside Evie was quite justified.

CAMPERVAN CAPERS

I've already found that one of my pleasures of campervanning is to watch the other people on the site. There was a couple in a motorhome next to us who appeared to have been in exactly the same position in their van all day. I wondered if they worked remotely as her phone seemed glued to her ear. Personally, I'm always pleased when I can't get a mobile signal, so I can just put my phone away for a few days.

Looking around the site, there were satellite dishes, awnings, and clothes dryers with many assorted designs, ideas, and lifestyles. Who knew that campervan watching could be so much fun and so informative?

We watched a traffic jam build up on the site as a couple of people tried to leave in their caravan, and a new campervan arrived. It was soon sorted, and the huge caravan looked like it turned on a sixpence. I even started to believe these big caravans with their remote controls seemed easier to manoeuvre than Evie!

A second very peaceful, cosy night in Evie was enjoyed before it was time to get packed and ready to leave. Each site will give you a time that you can arrive and also a time by which you must depart. We did seem to take an awfully long time to get packed up, but we were still learning and knew that before too long, we would have this mastered to a fine art.

Overall, our campervanning life was going well, and we have had two wonderful adventures in Evie.

Debra Murphy

Would-be Campervan Woman's Pitch Rundown

Eco or Economy
Virtually nothing there for you.

Standard Serviced
You can access mains electricity and fresh water, just not right at your pitch. There will be grey water waste drains, chemical toilet waste areas, and usually toilet blocks and showers.

Superior
More expensive, but you have electricity, fresh water, and a grey water waste drain at your pitch. The site will have chemical waste areas, toilet blocks, and showers.

Hardstanding
Beware of grass pitches that can become like a bog and will try to swallow your campervan.

With or Without Awnings
Decide if you need a pitch large enough for an awning, but remember, you might have to pay extra.

Motorhome Service Points
These are where you can fill your van with fresh water and deposit any grey waste water.

Dog-Friendly
Not all sites are dog-friendly. Check the site rules before booking, especially if you have more than one dog.

Fire Break
Park on one of these at your peril!

Chapter 11

They're Not Wide Enough! - September 2021

During our Killin adventure, we noticed that even if the van is on a slight slope, it can cause problems. Fortunately for us at that campsite, it was only a tiny tilt, making our heads higher than our feet, which was better than the other way around, or worse, making one of us fall out of bed. It did mean the water couldn't drain fully from the sink.

As always, we looked around the site at people's different setups with their vans. Some had snazzy automatic levelling kits that dropped from the van's undercarriage. We noted that only caravans appeared to have this facility. Lots of other people were using levelling blocks, and, of course, I now needed to investigate these and decide if we should purchase some.

Returning home, I was soon on the internet and bamboozled by the different choices. After researching and talking to other campers, I decided the Fiamma brand was my first choice. Maybe this was psychological because our canvas pull-out awning was a Fiamma. I knew we had to make sure we bought levellers that were both strong and wide enough for the weight of our van and size of our tyres. The advice is that you should ensure you have enough spare width to allow the tyre to sit fully on the leveller.

Debra Murphy

All things considered, I ordered a pair online, which arrived promptly and came with a nice bag to store them in. Mr M volunteered to try them out on the drive at home, and I nervously watched as he drove Evie onto these creaking, plastic blocks. He was a star, I have to admit. But, alas, we both agreed the blocks were too narrow. A few days later, a second, wider, stronger pair arrived, which was much easier for Mr M to drive Evie onto. I am still not brave enough to do this.

This new set has three levels and is easier to position under the tyres. I'd not be so keen to do this by myself without anyone to guide me. Mr M is now a dab hand at this, and if required, we use these. Usually Mr M drives up one level on them, and occasionally has gone up to the second, but never the third, as we are scared Evie will topple over the end of them.

Perhaps being confident enough to use levelling blocks is an indication of whether you're a real campervanner.

Soon, I'll try this. Soon.

We now have a spare pair of small levelling blocks sitting beside the thermal windscreen shield in our shed at home. One day, I'm sure I'll meet somebody who will be happy to take these off our hands.

Chapter 12

But She's Called Foxy! - October 2021

Evie was already 13 years old when we bought her, but there had been only one previous owner. The day we collected her from Struans, Steve, the salesman, told us that her previous owners, Mr and Mrs Bowler, would be happy to meet with us and discuss any questions or problems we had.

Did Steve, the salesman, chuckle?

So, on 2nd October 2021, we arranged to take Evie to meet Mr and Mrs Bowler. I baked cakes to take with us, as they had already invited us for a cup of tea and a chat. It's a well-known fact that you must have cake or at least a biscuit with tea. One day, it will be the law.

With their address keyed into our sat nav, we set off. I knew driving Evie was becoming more enjoyable as I sang along to Van Morrison's 'Brown Eyed Girl'. This, by the way, was the first song I danced to with Mr M on our blind date all those years ago. I don't often dance or drink alcohol, but when I indulge in the latter, then dancing usually follows. Maybe it was my dancing skills or my ability to drink copious amounts of Guinness that day, but Mr M seemed to quite like me and proposed only a few weeks later.

What a fabulous time we had chatting with Evie's previous owners. I was a little concerned when Mrs Bowler looked close to tears as we parked Evie in her drive, saying, "It's lovely to see you again, Foxy."

Foxy? Was that her name? Oh no! I felt guilty admitting that Foxy was no more because she was now a van called Evie.

It was evident that this couple still had great affection for their old campervan, and I asked them why they sold it, given they appeared to love her so much. They told us the only reason was to get a caravan with more room. Indeed, a gigantic caravan was parked in their garden.

Was that a tear I saw in Evie's headlight?

For the next couple of hours, we listened to tales and adventures that this lovely couple had taken Evie (Foxy!) on. They were eager to share valuable tips and advice with newbie campervanners. I made lots of notes, of course.

How to stop the rain from soaking the bed when the back doors are open has already become one of my concerns. Mrs Bowler gave us the simple tip of putting a piece of plastic over the bed. Such a simple, obvious solution, but if you don't know, you don't know. Not only does this prevent the rain from soaking the bedding, but it also allows you to use the bed as an extra shelf during the day to store dishes, plates, and other items, rather than relying solely on the small kitchen area.

Evie's gas central heating works incredibly well, but if you're already on a site where you've paid for your electricity, you don't need to use your gas. Portable electric radiators work perfectly well in campervans. Mr and Mrs Bowers showed us the ones they always used when Evie was Foxy. So long as the heaters are below 1500 kW and you don't use other large electrical items at the same time, you should be OK on most sites.

We learned everything there is to know about the boiler in Evie. A frost control button releases any water in the boiler if the temperature drops below three degrees centigrade. Mr Bowler demonstrated how to release this button, reset it, empty the boiler, and refill it. If you want to use hot water or central heating, you must turn on both the bathroom and kitchen taps fully once you have filled the fresh water tank. Doing this allows you to get water running through the whole system, including boiler, and to remove any air locks before you turn the boiler on. If no water runs through the system, the boiler trips the system, and a red light shows, and it needs to be reset. We now know how to do this, too.

We should get a low-wattage electric kettle so that we can have ample cups of tea without using any gas. I could see the logic of this, but I do like my kettle that whistles when it boils on the gas hob.

Mr Bowler alarmed me by reminding us to get a pest repeller. I knew we might get insects in the van, but I'd turned my mind off to this. I know we get beasties in the house, but I seem to have survived in Evie without any major trauma, although there have been occasions when I've threatened to leave home because the spiders were so large that they wore clogs. It never occurred to me I had to protect Evie from larger pests, such as rats, mice, and rodents. Apparently, these creatures, cute as they are, like to make their homes in campervans, especially during the colder months, and will happily munch their way through the campervan interior, along with any wires and cables they take a fancy to.

I didn't like the idea of killing all these creatures, but Mr Bowler told us about plug-in devices that work on repelling the beasties with ultrasonic sound. These emit a disorientating pulse, which is reported to make these pests scramble to find a way out of your campervan. This type of repeller is safe and eco-friendly, with no chemicals, smells or radiation, and there's no need to clean dead bodies from your vehicle. Most importantly, they are safe for humans and pets.

I have now ordered a pest repeller.

It was a brilliant afternoon and well worth the drive to listen to Mr and Mrs Bowler sharing their experiences. If we have as many happy years with Evie as they have had, I will be one lucky woman.

Over the next few days, I thought of ways to make Evie, our campervan, different from others. The first thing was to make new curtains for the dining area. Evie already had dining room curtains, which were perfectly adequate but beige. I knew I had some campervan material in my stash at home. Yes, I have a material stash – not as large as my wool stash, but still quite extensive. My original plan was to use the existing beige curtains as a template for my new creations. Then I decided the beige material would work perfectly as a lining for my new curtains.

A few hours later, I had a lovely new set of lined curtains hanging up in Evie. They were finished off nicely with some blue ribbon tiebacks, for which Mr M felt obliged choose the colour. All this upcycling without spending a penny. Even Mr M was impressed, but he still sighed and rolled his eyes when I said,

"I told you my craft stash would come in handy one day."

From our first few trips in Evie, I realised how much things rattle when we were driving, so next on my list was to minimise this – both for my sanity and to prevent things from getting damaged. The first thing I needed to do was to make something to hold the cutlery safe and secure. I looked at a few options online but decided I could make myself a cutlery roll. Once again, I hunted through my stash for suitable material. I wanted to make it hard-wearing and waterproof. I found some lovely thick cotton material with an old-fashioned sweet design and lots of oilcloth.

My sewing machine came back out, and a couple of hours later, I had a pretty roll for the cutlery and a second one, slightly larger, for the other utensils – bread knife, scissors, tin opener, and wooden spoons. Mr M said they were perfect. He was even more impressed when I surpassed myself to make a third for the new spanners and screwdrivers. The cutlery rolls used the very same oilcloth that we had in the tearoom as tablecloths, which made me smile.

CAMPERVAN CAPERS

I also cut two larger pieces of oilcloth to cover the bed during the day. Now, rain will not come in when the back doors are open, and we have an extra work surface – all without getting the bedding dirty.

Evie is becoming ours.

Before I end this chapter, let's take a moment to discuss oilcloth. When one of my proofreaders from the Black Country in the West Midlands (you know who you are) read this chapter, she told me that not everyone would know what oilcloth was. She said she couldn't understand how I was using it for my creations as she thought oilcloth was something you put on the floor.

"No!" I exclaimed. "That's Lino!"

Then began the great oilcloth debate of 2024. Mr M joined in. Would he agree with me? No.

Would my friend's husband agree with me? No!

They all declared that oilcloth went on the floor. Mr M said that the word I was looking for was 'fablon'.

"No!" I exclaimed. "That's sticky-back plastic."

To prove that I was correct, I consulted the internet. An online fabric retailer site states:

'Oilcloth is a much-loved fabric because of its durability and ease of cleaning, as well as its bright and cheery colours and patterns. It's available in a variety of prints and solids. Oilcloth is often associated with retro, classic, and novelty patterns. It doesn't fray when cut, so hems aren't required. It's waterproof with a shiny and smooth surface that can be easily wiped clean.

Oilcloth was originally a cotton duck or linen fabric that was coated with boiled linseed oil to make it waterproof. Then, in the 19th century, it began to be replaced with waxed cotton. In the 1950s, oilcloth fabric became synonymous with the printed vinyl that we know today. Distinguishing itself from laminated cotton or flannel-backed vinyl, oilcloth continues to captivate with its rich history and modern-day charm'.

Told you!

Debra Murphy

A Quickly-Learning Campervan Woman's Improvements

Keeping The Rain Out
A simple sheet of plastic covering the bed stops the rain from coming in when the back doors are open and also provides an extra worktop.

Gas Central Heating
Your van might have this, but consider investing in portable electric heaters for when you are on campsites where you pay for electricity.

Boiler
Learn all about your boiler – how to fill it up, the different settings for heating and hot water, and how to empty and reset it.

Electric Kettle
A low-wattage electric kettle saves you from having to use your gas, but then you lose the joy of hearing a whistling kettle.

Electronic Pest Repeller
You need to discourage rats, squirrels, and other beasties from making their home in your van.

Curtains
Soft furnishings really do make your van cosy.

Cutlery Rolls
Make something (or buy) to stop your cutlery and other bits and pieces rattling as you travel from place to place.

Chapter 13

Happy Wedding Anniversary, Mr M - 8th October 2021

The Trossachs Holiday Park, Aberfoyle, Scotland

Somehow, I managed to convince Mr M that there would be no better way to celebrate our wedding anniversary than a long weekend away in Evie. I told him I'd found a campsite only 40 minutes away from home, so we wouldn't need to spend all weekend driving, giving us more time to relax, and added that he could fish nearby.

The Trossachs Holiday Park is situated just off the A81 on the way to Aberfoyle. We've passed it many times on our cycle rides, but never needed to investigate it until now. I was so excited looking at their website, which boasts superior pitches, so there would be no need to run electric cables for miles or carry water to fill up Evie's fresh water tank. Once on the pitch, Evie would be connected to electricity, fresh water, waste water drain, and the TV aerial. I guess an aerial would be important for those who like to while away the hours watching in their caravans or campervans. As we don't have a TV at home, it's no surprise that we don't, or intend to, have one in Evie.

Getting ready for this trip, I was alarmed to find a pool of water on the bathroom floor in Evie. The only place it could have been coming from was through the ceiling vent. We had just had some wild weather – torrential rain and high winds, so I wondered if the rain had forced its way through the vent. I made a phone call to Mr Bowler, Evie's previous owner, and asked if this should happen. He assured me it certainly should not.

Yes, you guessed it, I was back on the phone with Steve, the salesman, and booked Evie back at Struans for the following week after this next adventure. I did have the foresight to take photos of the leak and send them to Steve, the salesman, as I could be sure that when we got Evie to them, there would be no rain or wind!

Taking the advice of Evie's previous parents, we had now invested in a small portable electric radiator to plug in when connected to mains. I know Evie has gas central heating, but as I've now discovered, why use our gas if we can use the electricity that we've paid for onsite? Also, I feel much happier using an electric heater rather than having gas running through Evie. We do have two carbon monoxide monitors, just in case you were worried.

I'd also purchased a pair of wellies to slip on outside the van. That was an ordeal finding wellies to fit over my calves. I wouldn't say I have exceptionally large calves, but I have struggled all my life getting wellies or calf-length boots to fit me. Now, I have a very large, size nine half-wellies that flop around my feet as they are too big, but my 'fat' calves stop me from walking out of them.

Along with all the food and clothes we had for the weekend, we had now discovered that one-litre bottles of milk fitted perfectly in Evie's fridge.

At this campsite, you can check in after 11 am, so with only a 40-minute drive from home, we didn't need an early start. I told Mr M that I would do all the driving as I needed to get to a point where I felt I could drive Evie as easily as I did our car. That day, the rain seemed horizontal, so my driving skills were most certainly tested.

CAMPERVAN CAPERS

"Just look at the rain. It's going to be a wet weekend," Mr M kept telling me. Like I didn't already know!

With no mishaps, I soon parked Evie outside the campsite reception. When I booked the pitch, I had confessed on the phone that I was still a novice and asked for an easy pitch to park in. The lovely woman told me she had booked us onto the pitch nearest the reception, so they would be close by if we needed any help.

It was indeed close to the reception but up a bit of a hill to get to it. Mr M watched with amusement as I spent some considerable time manouevring Evie onto the pitch. It may have taken me a few attempts, but I managed it. And for all you readers mocking my reversing skills, you may recall from your own driving test that you don't actually have to do a three-point turn. You are required to turn the vehicle around using forward and reverse gears without touching the kerbs on either side of the road. Well, I did that, and I didn't hit anything.

Evie's engine was turned off, the handbrake applied, steering lock attached, and we were at our new home for the weekend. With the electricity and water right next to Evie, it didn't take us long to have everything connected.

It was still raining, and I was almost pleased to be able to test my design for keeping the bed dry when I had to open the back doors to get things out of the garage. The oilcloth worked perfectly.

One of the extra pieces of kit that Mr M had decided was essential was a tap adapter, just in case our water hose connection didn't fit the tap at any site we visited. I could almost sense his sheer joy when he realised we needed to use it on this campsite.

What we discovered about our fabulous new grey waste water container was that Evie is quite low to the ground, and this container is deep at the wheel end. We improvised and have this sitting under the pipe catching the waste water, but it sticks out from under the van. We will just have to be careful. I'm not spending any more money on another container!

We have been researching all the different chemicals available for the grey waste water, toilet, and fresh water as we would like to use the most environmentally friendly brand, whilst at the same time staying safe. This is ongoing research, but we found some campervan loo rolls in the campsite shop. Who knew that was even a thing! Apparently, this is better for portable toilets as it dissolves easier and helps to break down the nasty bits.

When I found this lovely campsite online, another thing that caught my attention was an onsite cafe. Once set up on our pitch, we made our way to the cafe. Sadly, there were no gluten-free cakes - I was on a gluten-free diet at the time for my arthritis - but there were plenty of biscuits and cuddles for Beatrix. Our beautiful Border Collie captured the heart of Claire at the reception and cafe as soon as she saw her. The staff there were very friendly and helpful, and nothing was too much trouble for them.

I'd promised Mr M that he could do some fishing close by the site and we would purchase a permit when we arrived. Alas, it transpired that the fishing season on this river finished the day we arrived. Oops. But then, Mr M, the fisherman, should have known that, so I didn't take any responsibility for that error. It's also worth remembering that there is no fishing on a Sunday for some fish species in Scotland. Some sites have free permits, others charge by the day, and you can also buy a yearly license.

We eventually managed to drag Beatrix away from the cuddles and biscuits and returned to Evie. I smiled to myself when I realised that tasks I get out of at home – cooking porridge, boiling the kettle, listening to its whistle, cooking bacon, washing up and making the bed – I actually love doing in Evie. There is something comforting about pottering around doing basic tasks in your van. It feels like the complex problems of real life get put on hold during a trip in a campervan.

Then, there is the excitement of finding an immaculately clean shower and toilet block, brushing your teeth, and having a hot shower. As I've told you earlier in the book, although Evie has a shower, it's tiny. Why have the bathroom soaked when I can use the facilities I've paid for?

Now I discovered a new major problem - how will you carry clean clothes to the shower block without getting them wet? There's so much to prepare for a simple shower. You will need to do a recce at each different campsite. Is there a chair in the shower cubicle? Are there any hooks to hang your things on? Is there a screen or curtain to keep your clean things dry? How will you keep clothes off the floor? How will you avoid standing on the floor with your bare feet? What will you wear on your feet in the shower? Have you got everything: shower gel, shampoo, deodorant, a clean, dry towel, and something to stand on when you get out of the shower? In my case, these will be the sandals I use for cold water swimming.

But this planning is all part of the fun.

Once we were settled, fed, and watered, we took time to look around the campsite, which is situated in the Loch Lomond and the Trossachs National Park. Looking around from Evie, we could see the top of Ben Lomond to the right and the Campsie Fells to the left. It was strange to see the back of these hills as we are used to seeing the other side from our house.

The site is close to Sustrans National Cycle Route 7, so cyclists can easily join this and head towards Aberfoyle, Loch Katrine or Balloch.

We discovered a lovely woodland walk from the site where Beatrix could run off the lead. On their website, this is called the Famous Bluebell Woodland Walk, so the month of May would be a wonderful time for this.

I would point out, though, that if you're like us and don't like to move your campervan once onsite, you'll need to be self-sufficient for food as there are no shops, restaurants or eating places within walking distance. There is the cafe and site shop, but this sells only the basics, as most campsites do. The nearest village or town is Aberfoyle, and you could get a taxi for about £10-12. There is a bus stop about a 10-minute walk from the campsite to Aberfoyle too.

The following day, after a peaceful circular walk around the woods and forest, we headed back to the campsite cafe, armed with my gluten-free cakes. I shared them with Claire and the other staff members, and now they want me to supply their cafe with gluten-free cakes!

We whiled away a good hour drinking coffee and tea, eating my homemade coffee cake, writing, and listening to the comings and goings of people needing advice or help with problems. Again, nothing was too much for Claire and her staff. I got the impression that they thrived on issues that would test them.

Beatrix found her corner in the cafe and settled to watch the world go by. We could all learn a lot from the behaviour of dogs.

We eventually returned to the van, and I prepared to cook us a special anniversary meal. OK, it was a simple feast of fish fingers, boiled potatoes, and steamed vegetables, followed by some homemade lemon drizzle cake and hot custard. Bliss! It might not be Michelin star food, but oh boy, it was good! Even better, we ate this outside in the weak sunshine with our anniversary cards on the table—the height of sophistication.

The following day, we felt it only right that we revisited the cafe, and Claire was just as friendly. Everyone seemed so happy to talk and extremely helpful.

During this adventure, we encountered a strange problem in the van. For some reason, the water was not working correctly in the bathroom. The toilet flushed, but we had to turn on the tap in the kitchen to get the bathroom tap to work. Another trip to Struans was needed. Evie came with a 12-

month warranty, so we were trying our best to identify any problems now rather than later.

Our next learning curve was pulling out the awning and how to peg it down on a firm surface. It's OK not to have it fastened down when there is no wind, but there was a breeze on this day, and I was slightly concerned it would blow the van over. It was raining, but it wasn't cold, so we didn't want the main sliding door closed. Yes, we risked it and secured the awning legs out as much as we could with our little camping pegs. Of course, as soon as we'd secured the awning, the rain stopped, and the sun came out. Now, we were worried about putting the awning away wet.

My list of campervan worries is growing daily!

"Let's go for another walk. The sun will dry the awning, and then we'll pack it away before we go to sleep tonight in case this wind gets any stronger," I suggested, which Beatrix agreed was a great idea.

After our walk, we needed to wind the awning away before the rain came back and darkness fell as we still struggled to remember how the leg joints worked so it would sit snugly back in its rack on the roof. It still took us two or three attempts, which probably gave everyone around us a laugh. One day, I'm sure we'll be able to do it with our eyes closed.

It was evident on this trip that we needed to become more organised in how we carried things in Evie. The grey waste water container takes up a lot of space in the garage area. I read in a Facebook group that some people carry theirs in the bathroom when travelling, which makes sense as it would be clean and empty. We are only two people and a dog, but I felt like one of those hoarding families where you can't move for bags and clothes.

We needed some boxes, and to be more realistic about what we really had to take on a trip. After all, how many water carriers did we need? Evie has a large fresh water tank, so we can always fill it up with water at home if the site doesn't have any, which would be very unusual. We'd decided that taking a large bottle of drinking water would be a good idea, and we could refill it from the water tap onsite for drinking and for Beatrix. I'm not convinced that the water in the tank is fit to drink without boiling, and we put Aqua Sol in the tank to purify the water. I'm sure there are lots of different products to use, but Aqua Sol was the one we chose. This product purifies drinking water, kills harmful organisms, and eliminates tastes and odours. You simply add Aqua Sol each time you fill the fresh water tank.

From my research so far, some people say the water is safe to drink, while others, like us, boil the water first.

Everything needs to be planned and thought out in this campervan life. Things you take for granted at home are a major consideration; mealtimes have become an event, snacks are a work of art, and you need to plan everything.

A pleasant discovery was how quiet it seemed in the van. There's nothing quite like lying in bed looking out of the skylight windows as the sun rises and the clouds clear, or watching the rain bounce on the windows. The latter is the most common in Scotland!

It's equally cosy at night with the blinds closed and lights on for supper. That's what life is all about – getting up, breakfast, washing up, shower, dinner, tea and cakes, tea, washing up, supper, washing up, reading, writing, and then bed.

Of course, amongst all this, there would be time for more walks and cycles and hopefully cold water swimming once we'd become more accustomed to campervan life. For now, everyday tasks consume our time, but in a nice way.

We now know that the fridge has three settings – one for when on 240 v, one for 12 v and one for gas. When connected onsite, you should use the 240 v setting. You can turn it onto the 12 v to keep the fridge cool if you move from site to site. On our trips, we're happy to switch the fridge off, clean it out

CAMPERVAN CAPERS

and put any remaining food back into the cool box for the journey home. As we become stricter and more organised about what we need, we shouldn't find ourselves with lots of food to take home. In an ideal world, we would go home with no fresh food at all. If there is no electricity, you could use the fridge on the gas setting. There are some risks with gas, though, and you certainly shouldn't drive with the gas turned on. Remember that in some countries, it is illegal to travel with your gas turned on.

We now realised that a brighter light was needed for the front of the cab area. If you were sitting in the passenger seat, it seemed too dull to read. The existing ones on the ceiling above the seat run on batteries, so I wanted to source some rechargeable ones.

I also learned that crochet needs to be a small project. The Lion King blanket I was working on had multiple balls of wool and was already the size of a double bed, so it was not ideal for a small area.

We needed to establish some sort of order – a place for everything and everything in its place. That included people and dogs!

I was surprised to realise how many little lights there were in a small campervan. It's a bit like trying to sleep in a disco with lights flashing all night. Then, once you're comfy in bed, as much as they annoy you, you can't bring yourself to get back up to sort them. We now have the electronic pest repeller with two green lights and one red one. The main switchboard for monitoring power and water has a 240 v, 12 v, and a water light. When the campervan is locked, the dashboard has a flashing red light to show that the alarm is set. Just to add insult to injury, the shiny green light for the fridge is located just below eye level for the person who sleeps on the right-hand side of the bed, so Mr M sees this all night.

But there was not a clock in sight. So, when the disco lights woke me up, I didn't know whether I'd slept all night through the party or just nodded, which meant having to have my phone next to me to check the time. Of course, I was then tempted to see if there were important messages, texts, or social media posts to see, which is why I refuse to take my mobile upstairs with me at home when I go to bed. I suppose we could just get a clock to go on the wall in the bedroom area, but that would be another light.

If I thought living in the campervan needed good organisation skills, packing up to go home is an event itself. I decided to carry the bulky grey waste water carrier (now clean and empty, of course) in the bathroom whilst travelling. I packed around it with bags so it didn't bang and damage the toilet or the flimsy bathroom concertina door.

We still needed a cable winder for the electric cable to save it from getting damaged in storage. This has now been ordered.

Driving was definitely becoming more enjoyable, and leaving for home, I even reversed out of our pitch. Somebody told me I would not be a proper campervanner until I clipped something with my wing mirror. This day, to my horror, I clipped a couple of branches with the passenger mirror, but I'm pleased to say I didn't catch any vehicles with the driver-side mirror.

The drive back home was better for me to get used to driving Evie, as it was not just a wide, straight motorway. Apologies to the drivers behind me as I took my time, especially when I had to find the appropriate moment to overtake the numerous cyclists on my route. Even Mr M commented on how he felt more confident in Evie when I was driving.

Was that a compliment? I was not 100% sure.

Would I ever be fully confident driving Evie? I wondered.

Cleaning the van when you get home after an adventure is a necessary evil, especially when you have a dog sharing your small space.

CAMPERVAN CAPERS

I took all the carpets out, hoovered them, swept and mopped the floor and replaced them. Every hard surface in Evie was wiped down with an antibacterial cleaner, and any fabric sprayed with Febreze.

My idea of covering the bench seat with two blankets kept the original covers clean and fresh. I took these blankets off and washed and dried them, which was far easier than having to clean the seat covers themselves. I still planned to make some fitted covers for this area, though. Maybe I could even find some online and get an idea for a pattern. I wanted to make them myself and have unique covers rather than buy some that another van might have parked next to us. That would be like turning up at a wedding to discover somebody else has the same outfit on as you.

I also decided that I needed to design some covers for the front seats in the cab to protect the original ones from general day-to-day living grime because putting blankets over them didn't work very well as they fell off as we moved around.

Something else to remember is that if it's been raining at all during your trip away and you've had the awning out, you should wind it back out again at home to allow it to dry completely, much like putting your wet tent up to allow it to dry fully before packing it away. That way, you prevent having a rotten awning for your next trip.

We also needed to get some strong guy ropes and pegs for our next trip, so I wouldn't dream of becoming Dorothy from the Wizard of Oz blowing away in my campervan if the wind whips up the un-retained awning. I wanted one of those fancy full awnings like an enclosed tent on the side of the van, but these are so expensive.

An important point to consider is that some campsites don't allow you to pitch a tent next to your campervan unless it's an all-enclosed tent in the awning. So, if you plan to have family and friends camp next to you on a site, check out their rules and regulations regarding tents and awnings.

We'd now had three trips away in Evie. Was I enjoying campervan life? Yes, but it's my dream and not Mr M's. It's becoming evident that he likes campervanning slightly more than he enjoys camping, and I started to think I would have to be realistic about how often he had trips in Evie as there is only so much tension a small campervan could hold.

Did this mean that solo adventures might be on the horizon? I wondered, smiling to myself.

Debra Murphy

Cleaning Tips From A Cleaning Hater

Enjoy Your Holiday
Don't spend your precious holiday stressing over the small things.

Empty The Toilet Cassette Accordingly
You will know how many times you have used your toilet. Don't leave it too long to empty this on your trip, or it will be too heavy to carry. Make sure you empty it before you leave the site for home.

Grey Waste Water Carrier
This won't empty itself. Do this daily or, like the toilet cassette, it will be too heavy for you to carry or drag.

Fresh Water Tank
Empty this before you leave the site for home. Although this can be emptied anywhere, as there are no chemicals in it, and it is clean water, use your common sense. Don't do this at your pitch if there is no drain there, or you'll flood the campsite. Look for the motorhome service point at the site where you can drive over a large grate to empty this. You could even park at the side of the road and empty it down the drain.

Clean As You Go
Pick up things you've dropped. Wipe stuff you've spilt. Spray surfaces you've used. Wash up after each meal. Empty the bin daily.

Take Your Shoes Off
Simple things like making sure everyone removes their boots and shoes before they come into your campervan help to keep the interior relatively clean. A towel hanging by the door lets you wipe your dog's paws because, unless you are a better dog trainer than we are, your dog will forget to wipe their paws.

Buy A Small Swing Bin
We have a little plastic swing bin that we keep in the bathroom. This is lined with a bin liner so that rubbish is not gathered in the style of the Lady in the Van.

CAMPERVAN CAPERS

All-Purpose Cleaning Spray
Don't have separate cleaning products. Get yourself an all-purpose spray so the van is not full of a hundred and one bottles, sprays, and polishes.

Wait For A Dry Day When You Get Home
You can then give your van a thorough clean. Trust me, I don't know why, but cleaning your campervan doesn't feel remotely like cleaning your house. As we have a dog, we have a good wipe down of all surfaces, remove, shake and wash all the dirty seat covers in our washing machine. Then I lift all the loose carpets and rugs, shake them outside the van, and hoover them. I use a cordless Dyson (good for making the grandchildren think you are hoovering the drive) and hoover the fitted carpet in the cab area. Then I mop the floors, leave everything to dry, and replace the carpets and covers. A liberal spray of Febreze and Carpet Fresh does no harm, either.

Don't Forget The Fridge
Make sure you have turned off your fridge so that it doesn't run on the 12 v battery when off-grid, or your van will have a flat main battery in no time. Be sure to remove all food from inside the fridge and wipe it down. Leave the door open for a few minutes to let it dry before locking it closed again.

Dry Your Pull-Out Canopy and Awnings
If you have had any rain during your trip, get these back out and let them dry out fully before packing them away, or they might disintegrate before you get to use them again.

Plan Your Next Adventure
With your van now clean, get yourself a big pot of tea, a plate of biscuits, and plan another trip.

Chapter 14

Frost In October! - 15th October 2021

Today, I headed back up to Struans for them to sort out Evie's faulty plumbing so that we don't need to turn on the tap in the kitchen to get the bathroom one to work. They were also going to look at the leaking vent in the bathroom ceiling.

Getting ready to set off, I was panic-stricken to find a great pool of water under the van but was relieved to discover it was from the frost protection valve in the boiler. The previous evening had been unusually cold, and the temperature must have dropped below three degrees centigrade. I should have realised because there was frost on the car and Evie's windscreen.

It was a good lesson to learn because it highlighted to us that if it's getting anywhere near cold enough outside for frost, then the water system in Evie should be emptied and the boiler drained when not in use. Thankfully, our frost valve had worked perfectly, doing what it was meant to do and dumped the water before it got the chance to freeze in the flimsy pipes of the campervan. It no doubt alarmed the neighbours seeing the water draining from Evie as, although I knew it was clean, unused water, they didn't know that and would probably imagine I was draining all sorts of liquids onto our drive.

My confidence in driving Evie was growing, and I enjoyed my solo drive to Perth. I was amazed at the early autumn tint colours on the trees and hills. My only disappointment was that I was listening to Ken Bruce on Radio 2, and as I arrived at Struans at 10.30 am, I had to miss Pop Master. Not that I ever got many of the questions right, but I still liked to play along.

Leaving Evie at Struans was like leaving my child in a hospital. However, I had an enjoyable hour's walk into Perth and along the banks of the River Tay. Another leisurely hour was spent indulging in tea and scones in a cafe and even doing some Christmas shopping. My bargain of the day was finding a pair of 50p flip flops for in the shower at campsites and a pair of slipper boots for Mr M's cold feet before I returned to Struans in a courtesy taxi.

The vent in bathroom ceiling was sorted and had been resealed but the tap needed replacing and would have to wait until the parts arrived. Apparently, campervan parts were still difficult and slow to obtain with the long-lasting effects of COVID-19 restrictions.

Would we ever be free from the effects of this pandemic? I shuddered.

What I hadn't anticipated was that the relaxed day I'd had in Perth would result in my drive home coinciding with peak-time traffic. Funnily enough, I relished this as it was my first time driving in a traffic jam, so I practised my slow control for a very long time. It took me nearly three hours to get home on what would usually be an hour's journey.

The following morning, I decided the outside of Evie needed a good clean. We'd bought some Fenwick's Motorhome Cleaner, which can be used on all areas of the campervan exterior, including the wheels. Washing Evie made me realise I needed to buy a taller, safer ladder, as I couldn't reach Evie's roof. Soon, with the help of Mr M, Evie was gleaming, and the awning was out drying just to be sure I'd not managed to get it wet. We'd even cleaned the car at the same time. The neighbours would probably have laughed as it was the first time they'd seen me do anything to my car in all the years I'd lived here. But I loved washing Evie.

It was becoming more evident that campervan life was not just about setting off into the sunshine. Now that Evie was part of the family, I could see both her beauty and her flaws. The back of the cooker and sink cupboard is open to the elements when the sliding side door is open, meaning that if it's raining, this unit gets wet. Clearly, this had happened before, as the wood here has a slight water stain at the bottom. Not wanting this to get any worse, I decided to make a waterproof cover. Out came my oilcloth stash again, and making a crude pattern, I soon had a slide-on cover. Now, when the side door is open during the rain, this unit, the sink, and the cooker will stay dry.

Chapter 15

Let's Go Back to The Trossachs - 30th October 2021
The Trossachs Holiday Park, Aberfoyle, Scotland

With the campervan bug consuming me, I had decided to get away as often as possible to justify buying Evie. Being busy people, we only had a couple of free days left in October, so I needed to find a campsite close to home. Another trip to the Trossachs Holiday Park was the perfect solution.

It was lovely to go to a campsite for only the second time and find that we were already seen as part of their campsite family. We even had the same pitch as our last visit, so it was like going home. If this were an audiobook, I could have Mark Knopfler's *Going Home*, the soundtrack from the film *Local Hero*, playing at this point.

This trip was definitely about identifying things we could do better or things we shouldn't do.

For this outing, we now had winders for both the electric cable and water hose. These were perfect, and the cable and hose took up much less space in the garage when rolled up.

If I could, I would change the position of the grill in Evie, which is at knee height, right next to the bench seat beside the table. As I enjoyed a lazy cup of tea after a meal, I wondered why my legs felt warm. Then I noticed I'd left the grill on, still burning gas. It was a good job that I noticed it before we went out and left the gas burning away, or even burning Evie!

The van has an electric retractable step below the sliding side door. This had been working perfectly well since we got Evie. Now, Beatrix is a stone-obsessed Collie and constantly brings us little stones as presents. Unfortunately, I'd not noticed she had popped a small pebble on the electric step, only realising this when the step jammed as I tried to wind it in. Fortunately, after lots of sighs, moans, a bit of shuggling, and shaking, Mr M managed to free the stone, and the step mechanism seemed to have survived. Would it have been a total disaster if the mechanism had been damaged beyond repair? I'm not convinced it would. We'd just remove it and get some free-standing steps that I have seen outside lots of caravans. I can imagine this is a common occurrence and too expensive to bother about fixing.

'Mr Doom and Gloom' now decided we needed a spare bung for the cold water tank.

"What if it breaks, and we have no way of keeping water in the tank?" he wailed.

I told him I'd search the internet later, but secretly, I wasn't in a major rush. I'd recently found a new group on Facebook for Adria Twin Camper Van Owners with countless daily posts full of advice and friendly warnings of what to do and what not to do. You can post a question, and before you have time to think, somebody is offering a suggestion. I've not yet seen any posts in this group reporting a problem with their fresh water tank bung!

My bargain flip flops were a great success in the shower, even though I had to have that nasty bit of plastic between my toes. My daughter reliably informed me that I needed a pair of sliders to wear in the shower. I'll definitely be in a rush to find some of those for my next adventure.

I decided that we needed a drive away awning. With a wet dog, two humans, two pairs of muddy walking boots, two wet jackets and two pairs of waterproof trousers in the van, it gets a bit crowded. Wandering through the campsite on our walks, we looked at what seemed like hundreds of awnings, all assorted sizes, shapes, and designs. If we had extra space in an awning tent, we could put all our outdoor gear in there, keeping the inside of Evie dry. I would ask the Adria Twin Camper Van Owners Facebook group for advice on the best type to get for Evie.

Now that the nights were drawing in, we really needed better internal lights. Sitting in the passenger seat, I found it was a bit dim for reading or writing.

You might also want to find out if there is any Wi-Fi on the campsite. On some sites, you need to rely on your own data, some provide free internet access, and others have Wi-Fi you have to pay for. That way, you can ensure that if anyone is not really feeling the love of campervan life, they can still get access to racing, football, social media, or anything else they need. You might even have a laptop to play DVDs or access a Netflix account for longer, darker, colder evenings in the campervan.

Now, I know some people might like gourmet food in their campervan, but I discovered by mistake the simple joy of tinned beans and sausages. These are not something I'd choose to have at home, but I bought them in error. They were a lovely breakfast surprise. We also decided that even though we usually grill bacon at home, in Evie, we'd fry it because grilling in the ridiculously positioned grill caused too much grease to splatter around it, which was then difficult to clean.

I've already told you we don't have a TV at home, but I was reliably informed I should watch Merton & Webster's Motohoming series and that I could get this on catch-up on my laptop. I wasn't sure I wanted to spend hours watching a whole series. It was surprising how short each episode was once I'd fast-forwarded through all the adverts, repeated sections from previous episodes and previews of future ones. Over the two evenings on this adventure, I watched the whole series.

Debra Murphy

I learned a few tips from the series but was somewhat disappointed that the programme skimmed over most things and didn't explain the little details at all. Watching this series made me revisit my draft of this book to ensure I was adding enough detail and interesting tales.

I hope you feel I did that. As the book progresses and follows my confidence growing, the stories become more about the trips rather than the simple joy of finding my pitch on a site and managing to get the electricity connected.

Debra Murphy

A Would-Be Campervan Woman's Thoughts Versus Merton & Webster

Why Are There So Many Fob Buttons and Keys?
Indeed. Evie's key fob is huge. It's not the first time I've spent five minutes trying to unlock or lock all the doors. There's a button to lock the side door, one for the front and one for the back. There's a key for the engine, which also works for the petrol cap, one for the toilet flap, one for the fresh water filler, one for the steering lock, and a house door key. If Mr M had his way, we'd also have keys for old doors, cars, and padlocks we no longer own.

Watch Out for Your Wing Mirrors
I've already learned that lesson. I have to say that I was slightly more concerned about catching my wing mirrors than Ms Webster appeared to be about the ones on her hired motorhome. Maybe that's why hire companies charge so much.

Avoid Grass Pitches
I'd already decided to pick hard-standing pitches whenever possible to avoid getting stuck in the mud and squashy grass.

Learn How to Connect the Electric
It's always good to know how things work before you actually need to use them. Getting to a campsite late at night and being unable to work out how to connect to the electricity or water is not ideal.

Read the Procedure Notes
I'm thinking of creating a checklist for things we need to do before setting off from home and when leaving a campsite. As I don't intend to hire out my campervan, I don't think I need written procedure notes

CAMPERVAN CAPERS

Ignore the Traffic Behind You
You can't do much about traffic building up behind you, so ignore it. Don't stress the small stuff. Be polite, though, and pull into lay-bys when possible to allow vehicles to pass you if you notice a long line of traffic following you. It doesn't matter how fast you drive; some people will want to get past you just because you are driving a campervan, motorhome or caravan.

Concentrate When Driving a Campervan
I would totally agree. I love driving, but being in charge of Evie takes up every bit of my concentration. I'm sure that as I gain more experience, I'll be able to really enjoy it. I'm equally sure that driving a campervan will always need a great deal more concentration than driving a little car.

Wild Camping Looks Amazing
Merton and Webster had an evening of wild camping when they were off-grid with no mains electricity or water and had to be self-sufficient in their motorhome. It looked quiet, peaceful, and very dark, with no light pollution, although I'm sure that the camera crew ensured they were OK and well-stocked with essentials. Wild camping is on my to-do list, but not yet.

Know Your Vehicle Size
It's vital to know how big your vehicle is for driving under bridges and on very narrow roads. We have a sticker on our cab visors showing the height and width of Evie in both metric and imperial measurements, so we don't have to remember. Our sat-nav knows our van dimensions, so it should not, in theory, send us down any roads or routes that she will be too big for.

Know How to Put Fuel in Your Van
It's never a good look to be standing at a petrol station trying to figure out how to open your fuel cap or wondering what fuel to use. This is something you need to learn about your campervan, as they will all be different. It's also something I still need to learn about Evie! We joke at home that diesel fairies live with us because our car always seems full of fuel whenever I need to drive it.

Chapter 16

Evie Goes To The Lake District - 12th November 2021
Skelwith Fold Caravan Park, Ambleside, Cumbria, England

It was time to take Evie on a longer trip before we tucked her up for the winter. Both Mr M and I agreed that during our honeymoon period, we wouldn't have any campervan adventures in winter when there might be snow or ice. We know from experience that the weather can change for the worse very quickly in Scotland. A road that is just a little narrow in summer seems to shrink to the width of a postage stamp in winter, with snow, ice, grit, and dead leaves hiding verges and ditches. We didn't want to find ourselves stuck somewhere trying to get to or home from a campsite. No, Evie would stay safe and secure on our drive throughout December, January, and February.

"Do you think we could take Evie to the Lake District?" I asked Mr M.

He looked up from his laptop, lifted his glasses, and rolled his eyes.

"You want to go to Skelwith Fold, don't you?" he sighed.

He knows me so well.

Taking his eye roll as a sign that Mr M thought this was a good idea, I jumped on the internet before he could change his

CAMPERVAN CAPERS

mind and booked us a three-night stay on a premium pitch. If you remember, we'd spotted Skelwith Fold Caravan Park during our visit to the Lake District earlier that year. I didn't think I was brave enough to drive Evie right through the Lakes on the narrow, twisting lanes just yet, but I knew this site was only just off the beaten track. After all, the single-decker bus managed it, so surely I could.

I love the Lake District and still dream of living there one day, so I was beyond excited about our next adventure. Over the next few days, I beavered away making bespoke covers for the driver and passenger seats using parchment paper to design some very crude patterns. I searched my material stash and found enough tartan pieces to make a Scottish-themed driver seat cover and a multi-coloured patchwork affair for the passenger seat. I didn't know what I was most surprised about: how I made them fit the seats, how great they looked, or how much Mr M liked them. Evie now looked very posh and even a bit hip. I was most impressed with myself.

Everything felt much more organised this time, as I had packed stuff differently. All the bits and pieces for the attachments for the water hoses and standpipe were now in a handmade roll-up wash bag in the driver door pocket, so we wouldn't need to search around for these when we arrived at a site. The grey waste water container was in the garage out of the way. Our new water hose and electric cable winders were perfect, and it was amazing how much less space these took up now.

All the essential food and drink were packed, including sachets of hot chocolate, marshmallows, Cadbury Flakes and some squirty cream. I was planning to indulge myself. As this would be a long journey, I also put together a tub of sweets for us to munch on. I don't know about you, but some chewy, chocolaty, fruity treats make the trip much more enjoyable.

Who am I trying to convince? I just like eating sweets!

We planned to share the driving down to the Lakes as I thought two hours of driving was enough for one person still getting used to campervan driving. Mr M would drive from home to Gretna, and I'd take over from there as I know the roads in England better than Mr M. To be honest, I was quite excited at the prospect of driving my campervan to one of my favourite places.

This was our first time travelling in Evie on a three-lane motorway. With the wind howling and rain coming down horizontally, I was glad Mr M was driving. It was surprising how fast 50 mph seemed, and the van was buffeted all over the place.

At Gretna Services, we stopped in the caravan parking area. I wasn't sure Evie would fit in a standard car space, and we just wanted to err on the side of caution.

It's worth noting where the different parking places are in the services, as there is usually a section specifically for large vans and caravans. Don't struggle to park your campervan in a car parking space, no matter how small your vehicle is. The spaces for cars are not really wide or long enough for a van.

We enjoyed our picnic lunch in the comfort of Evie without tackling the hordes of people potentially carrying the dreaded COVID-19 virus. I say comfort. This trip was awkward as Beatrix had a plastic collar on to prevent her from scratching a wound on her ear after a minor operation. She still managed to find her own space, even though she constantly gave us looks of disgust for making her wear that monstrosity. I'm sure if I'd been wearing shorts, my legs would have been cut to ribbons by the plastic as she barged her way past me.

Leaving the services and re-joining the M6, the weather had improved somewhat, and I was now driving, feeling like a pro, until I left the motorway and joined the A66 towards Keswick. I could sense that cars behind me wanted to get past just because I was driving a campervan. Or was that just my lack of confidence? Remembering Merton and Webster, I didn't let them harass me. They could wait.

CAMPERVAN CAPERS

Worse was to come.

Usually, I love the drive from Keswick to Grasmere along the A591. You get the most amazing views, including the Helvellyn range, Thirlmere Reservoir, Helm Crag and even glimpses of Windermere. It's a bit twisty and up and down along most of this route, and on this trip, I was again the slow driver. I was sticking to the new lower speed limit on this road of 40 mph; it just felt like I was holding everyone up.

This stretch of road has what must be the best but weirdest dual carriageway I have ever driven on. It only lasts a couple of miles, but heading towards Grasmere, the two lanes on your side of the dual carriageway are the old road as it used to be. As you drive along it, the opposite two carriages are out of sight over a rise, so to the unsuspecting eye (or stranger to the road), it's very easy to think you are driving a standard two-lane road and panic when somebody overtakes you on a blind bend thinking that a car might come in the other direction. Even though I've driven (and cycled) this road many, many times, I still can't bring myself to overtake anything. For some reason, the dual carriageway doesn't seem to give you this impression when you travel from Grasmere towards Keswick.

And if that road was bad enough, well, the road out of Ambleside towards Clappersgate and Hawkshead felt no wider than a pavement, and there were two narrow humpback bridges to negotiate. If you recall, I told you about this road in Chapter Five, *An Epic Bus Journey*. I breathed a sigh of relief that I was not going any further down this wiggly, winding road than Skelwith Fold Caravan Park.

Once on the stunning grounds of the site, I felt less stressed. A long red drive wound its way up through a forest. I wouldn't have been at all surprised if a herd of deer had walked out in front of us. This private road seemed to go on forever, but was really less than a mile. Before I knew it, I had parked in front of reception, checking in for my first campervan adventure in the Lake District. Could life get any better?

Skelwith Fold Caravan Park is stunning. There are static caravans, chalets, motorhomes, and campervans, although there are no facilities for tents. I booked us a premier pitch with electricity, water and a waste water drain. The pitch was hardstanding, huge, and large enough for a motorhome with a large, fitted awning and a second car. There was even a picnic table with benches. Perfect.

Once set up, we wandered around to familiarise ourselves with the facilities. Oh, my! Wait for this. There is a library. An actual library on a campsite! I was in heaven. In earlier chapters, I said I was worried that future generations would not experience the joy of writing on real paper with a pen or pencil. Another fear is that the joy of a physical book will be forgotten. Reading on a computer or tablet does not compare to experiencing a proper book's touch, feel, and smell. My evenings were now planned writing surrounded by paper words. At the time, I was writing my second novel, *Beatrix The Time Travelling Collie*, and felt this new location would be the perfect inspiration for some more chapters.

Next to the library, there are some immaculate shower blocks and toilets with underfloor heating. There is a large dishwashing area, coin-operated dishwashers, and a laundrette. Even the chemical toilet disposal area was spotless. Don't even get me started on the reception and shop. This must be the best-stocked campsite store I've seen in all my years of camping. Fresh food, frozen food, sweets, and bread are just a few of the delights to mention. It has newspapers, magazines, books, maps, and gifts. I've seen smaller and worse-stocked mini supermarkets than this place.

As we prepared tea in Evie, Beatrix made herself comfortable under a well-positioned bush where she could watch anything and everything, as Border Collies do.

Later that evening, we strolled up to the library. I typed away on my laptop, Mr M read, and Beatrix lay by my feet.

CAMPERVAN CAPERS

The only distraction was when people saw Beatrix and came in to say hello. She strutted around, knowing that she was a beautiful-looking dog. I think she thought she was the Queen that night, which, of course, she always was to us.

The following day, we made a picnic and wandered down the site's long and winding drive to catch the bus to Ambleside so Beatrix could run around in Loughrigg Park.

It was a magical walk down to the bus stop, admiring the magnificent trees. We really did feel like we were deep in the Lake District. What was most surprising was the heat. It was unbelievable that in November, we were walking in just T-shirts. Was it only the previous day that Evie had been blown about in the wind and rain on the motorway?

The bus only takes 10-15 minutes to get to Ambleside. During the journey, I noticed a path running alongside the road and thought this would be worth investigating on another day.

Once we were off the bus, Beatrix was pulling on her lead, and I'm sure she would have been able to find Loughrigg Park herself without us, as we'd been there so many times before on previous holidays. This park is a perfect place for dogs to run free without them pestering anyone. There are lots of benches around the edge of the park, so you can relax and watch the world go by. For those with children, there are a couple of play areas with swings, climbing frames and a miniature fort, all fenced off so dogs can't get in. If you're like me, you'll be pleased to know there are no amusements or noisy rides. Now I think about it, I can't think of anything like that anywhere in the Lake District. The nearest would probably be Blackpool Pleasure Beach.

Sitting in Loughrigg Park felt quite surreal. It was so hot. And I mean hot. We hadn't taken suntan lotion or sun hats with us because it should have been cold. It was November in the North of England, for goodness' sake. I thought about our cottage holiday in the Lakes in August, and I honestly don't think it was as warm then as it was this day. Global warming indeed.

I know we had a picnic and a flask of tea with us, but you can't go to Ambleside and not have a coffee in Zefirellis Restaurant and Cafe. So, in November, we enjoyed an extra treat, sitting in the sunshine outside one of my all-time favourite cafes.

I have so many wonderful memories spanning at least three decades of trips to Zefirellis, from discovering my love of garlic as a teenager, to treating my young children to gigantic mugs of hot chocolate, to enjoying coffee and cakes with my husband and Beatrix. When I first visited in the 1980s, this was a relatively new establishment with a small cafe, restaurant, and cinema. Now, 40 years later, it is still one of the most popular places in Ambleside. Many moons ago, I had my first date and walnut slice there, and I can confirm that these are just as good today.

Ambleside is not a huge town, but it has everything: a park, lots of cafes, bookshops, a fish and chip shop, a mini supermarket, a museum, and the most amazing outdoor clothes stores. Just remember your credit card!

Make sure you visit Bridge House, one of the most photographed buildings in the Lake District. This was originally an apple store, built over Stock Beck to escape land tax. It only has two rooms, one up and one down, but reportedly, a family with six children once lived here. And Mr M thinks our campervan is snug!

After looking at heaps of new walking boots and clothes that we neither needed nor could afford in Gaynor Sports, we strolled along to the bus stop for the short journey back to the campsite gates.

Now, the amble down the site drive seemed sublime that morning, but after a day wandering around in the heat, the walk back up the drive felt never-ending. And uphill. We were

CAMPERVAN CAPERS

not in any mad rush, so we took our time, again enjoying the magnificent scenery.

Was Skelwith Fold Caravan Park as good as I had hoped and anticipated? Absolutely.

Sadly, our short but very enjoyable stay came to an end, and we once again got ready to return home. Packing Evie up was getting easier each trip as we started to have a place for everything.

My claim to fame? I drove Evie through the Lake District and back home in one piece.

We stopped at Gretna Services again on the way home, pulling into the caravan park like professionals. It was lovely to have our own food in the comfort of our van, with a brief trip to the services for the loo, as we didn't want to use ours and have to find somewhere to ditch the chemicals. You can't simply put them down your domestic toilet at home.

By late afternoon, Evie was parked up at home, emptied, and I had the bedding removed for washing.

We were saddened when most of the UK was battered by Storm Arwen at the end of this month. This storm focused its power over the North of England, mainly Cumbria. Skelwith Fold Caravan Park was right in the centre of the destruction, and I cried when I saw the reports and pictures on the news. The wonderful winding road and woodland had been almost destroyed, with over 500 of the 150-year-old trees brought down, causing £500 k of damage.

Loughrigg Park also suffered, with trees that we had sheltered under from the sun a couple of weeks earlier now destroyed. One man sadly lost his life in this park during the storm. I couldn't imagine how the area was coping or how the people felt. All I could do was hope that nature would work her magic and turn her destruction back to beauty and that this area would once again flourish.

Chapter 17

Keeping Evie Safe Over Winter - 2021

This year has been a fantastic experience living my dream of becoming a campervan owner.

Do I love it? Every minute.

Was Mr M loving it? Sometimes.

Does Beatrix love it? Of course.

Now that I'd joined the Adria Twin Camper Van Owners group on Facebook, I received daily posts giving great advice and suggestions. One of the best bits was, *'Enjoy and don't buy the 'essential rubbish'; just work out what you really need, and wait a while to see if you really need it before buying it'*.

I was still debating the drive away awning idea. There were countless suggestions and so many to choose from.

During my research, I discovered that, despite my concerns over using the pull-out canopy in the rain and wind, people do this, but with the canopy tilted on a slope to allow rain to run off. You can also get sides to add to make an enclosed awning and use straps to secure it down in the wind.

The all-in-one awnings did look great, though, and seemed to give so much more room. I decided that I'd research this further before spending more money on Evie.

With the approaching winter weather, I was wondering what to do with the van's soft furnishings in winter. Would you listen to me? How grand did I sound! What I meant was, should I take the bedding and blankets out in winter? And what about the mattress? If I took these into our house, I'd have to sleep in the van as there would be no room for me. So, I opted to remove the bedding, duvet, and pillows, but leave the mattress, original cover, and, of course, our oilcloth pieces over the bed.

To be honest, we didn't know anything about how to keep the inside of Evie dry over the winter. Opinions varied on social media. Some people put them into storage and take everything out. Some people do nothing with them. Others leave the heating on a touch, along with a dehumidifier. I wondered whether we should cover Evie with the outside canvas cover that came with her, which has been sitting in the garden hut since we bought her. After more investigation, I discovered you must be very careful when covering your van or caravan for the winter. You need to ensure that all the dirt and grime have been cleaned away and that the van is completely dry. If not, the cover can do more harm than good. As we were not tall enough to clean the roof of Evie as well as we would have liked, we felt it would be better to leave her naked in the garden. After all, cars and vans stay outside all winter on garage forecourts and don't seem to suffer any adverse side effects. To be on the safe side, we left her plugged into the mains electricity and had the electric heater set just above freezing to hopefully keep the dampness away. With the plug-in pest repeller, we should still have a van come spring.

So, the garden hut is now bulging with a too-small set of levellers, an unknown type of thermal windscreen shield, and the van canvas cover. We are going to need a bigger hut!

Over our few trips in our first year of being campervan owners, we became surprisingly good at preparing excellent meals in Evie with just a two-ring hob and a grill. I've read campervan books where people cook long, complicated recipes on outdoor fires and barbecues. Including oysters. I'd like to know how the first person who found an oyster shell, opened it and said,

"I know; I'll sell this as an expensive delicacy and say it's an aphrodisiac."

Me, I'd no more eat the contents of my hanky than I would eat an oyster. But that's just my opinion.

For me, it's all about preparation. If you've made a stew, chilli, or curry at home, make an extra portion or two and freeze them. Then, you only need to use the gas to reheat and the other gas ring to cook rice or potatoes. I use a two-pan steamer in which I can put potatoes, rice or pasta in the bottom pan and add vegetables to the top steamer section.

Mr M loves his vegetables, and even if he is cold and miserable, a plate of steaming veggies can put a smile back on his face.

Pitta breads or naan breads can easily be warmed up for a minute under the grill. Using boil-in-the-bag rice makes for perfect portion control and no waste.

Lean, low-fat sausages, however, can be cooked very well on the grill. A good tip is to cut them in half lengthways midway through cooking to ensure they are cooked properly, which also stops them from rolling off the grill pan onto the floor if your van is not level. Beatrix thought Christmas had come early when this happened to me one day. She doesn't steal food usually, but if food is on the floor, she thinks it's fair game.

Now, I know not everyone is a cake and pudding lover. I still can't quite believe I'm married to somebody who doesn't have the same love for sweet delights that I do. Mr M tells me that I'm all the sweetness he needs! But I need sugary treats, and I certainly need them on my adventures. Take puddings you've made at home and some custard powder to make your own custard in the van. One tablespoon of custard powder, one tablespoon of sugar (or three sugar lumps) and half a pint of milk will make enough for two hungry people. If there's

CAMPERVAN CAPERS

only one hungry person, you're in for a treat. Or you can take pots of ready-made custard and heat these in a pan on the hob.

As you work your way through this book, I'd like to think you've started to see me as a friend. As that friend, can I give you some advice here? There must, under no circumstances, be any cold custard served at any time, on anything, for any reason. There is absolutely no excuse for this disgusting yellow monstrosity, and I will never be persuaded otherwise.

I now have a list of food supplies I like to have in the van. With these, even if you can't buy anything else while camping, you'll not starve for a few days.

Debra Murphy

The New Campervan Woman's Store Cupboard Basics:

I leave a stock of the following in the van between trips but never leave anything unopened, and I always take everything out over winter:

Baking foil	Parchment paper
Cling film	Freezer bags
Washing Up Liquid	Washing Up cloths/sponges
Vegetable oil	Porridge oats
Tea bags in a tin/jar	Hot chocolate sachets
Coffee – in a jar	Sugar - in a tin/jar
Juice/squash	Honey
Jam	Custard Powder
Tinned peas	Tins of Heinz Beans

Even tins of Heinz Beans and Sausage

The day I set off on an adventure, I add:

Bread – in a container	Potatoes
Fresh vegetables	Boil-in-the-bag rice
Pasta	Butter
Home-cooked meals	Home made soup
Cheese	Biscuits (lots) in a jar/tin
Bottles of drinking water	Milk in cartons
Cakes (umpteen) in tins	Cadbury Dairy Milk (loads)

The important thing to remember is that everything should be in either a tin, jar or container so that nothing can decide to come into your van and nibble away at it. Hopefully, your pest repeller will prevent this, but it's good to be extra cautious here.

Chapter 18

A New Year Of Adventures Begins - 22nd March 2022

Evie was finally going to get a new tap in the bathroom. Yes, that's how long it had taken to arrive at the dealers.

We were excited to get out in the van after the winter rest. It was a sunny spring day, so we packed our picnic, books, writing pads, and a ball for Beatrix.

I felt very relieved that Evie jumped into action as soon as the key was turned. It was like she was desperate to go for a drive, and she handled like a dream on the now-familiar road to Perth. Once at Struans, I handed over the keys to the van and left her, again feeling like I had left my child at the hospital.

We had a pleasant walk to the park at Noah's, with Beatrix pulling on the lead because she knew where we were going and that we had a picnic in the rucksack. Once there, we ate our lunch, Beatrix played with her ball, I wrote, and Mr M slept.

A stroll back down to Struans and Evie was ready, with her new tap installed and working.

It was my turn to drive home, and I was surprised at how comfortable I felt driving after the winter break. But to get home, I first needed to stop for some diesel. Mr M had told me it was a job I needed to learn how to do when he was with me. Oh, the stress! Which side was the fuel cap?

To Mr M's amusement, I discovered that the visual management system in Evie is wrong. You know what I mean by VMS? It's a system that conveys information without you having to search too hard for what you are looking for. Like when you go to the supermarket, if you look up, there are signs indicating what is down each aisle.

The vehicle's visual management system should show you easily which side the fuel cap is by having an arrow pointing to the side of the fuel symbol on your dashboard. This was incorrect in our van; Evie's VMS shows that her fuel cap is on the driver's side, but she is fibbing. It is actually on the passenger side.

Mr M had warned me that it was difficult to get the fuel cap off and that I had to be careful not to break the key, because this was the same key for the ignition. He also warned me that I had to be careful to get close, but not too close to the fuel pump. I had to be careful not to get diesel on my hands and should be careful not to spill fuel down the van.

"I have been to a petrol station before, you know," I snapped at him.

Very skilfully, I was able to stop the van in the right place next to the fuel pump and even managed to get the petrol cap off. I very nearly passed out filling Evie up, though. She was already half-full, and it still took another £74.00 to fill her up!

I wondered if we should just top up on-going in the future, which would probably be better for less weight as you drive, as long as I knew I had enough for my journey.

On this trip, I noticed that with the dining area ceiling blind open, the sun shone directly over Beatrix, who was lying in the aisle. So, another thing to remember before you set off on a journey in bright sunshine with a dog or young children in the rear seats is to close this blind so you don't cook passengers or pets as you travel.

Once home, it was time to re-pack Evie, ready for this year's first adventure back to the Trossachs Holiday Park.

Chapter 19

The Start Of British Summertime - 27th March 2022
The Trossachs Holiday Park, Aberfoyle, Scotland

As year two of my journey into becoming a campervan woman began, I pondered my progress so far. I loved Evie and hoped that I had many years of fun and excitement to come. But I didn't exactly feel like a confident campervanner.

In my head, I planned everything, from what we needed to take to where it would go in the van. Could I remember how to connect the electricity? Would Mr M be cold? Would the roads be wide enough? Would I be able to find my pitch on a new site? You get the picture. I was still a novice and knew it. So, for the coming year, I set myself a target to recognise my campervanning journey that I have already travelled and to make changes wherever I could to improve our comfort and enjoyment of adventures. I felt this was particularly important for Mr M as I was now fully aware that he would never be a campervan man by choice and was coming on adventures because he wanted me to be able to follow my dream.

And that's why Mr M is such a special person.

Over the winter, we bought a second small portable electric heater as the van does get cold when the outside temperature drops. Hopefully, on this trip, Mr M would be snug as a bug.

Debra Murphy

Keeping the bed dry when the back doors were open had become an obsession of mine. I'd already sorted the oilcloth for putting over the covers, and this was working reasonably well, but if the wind was howling, rain could still blow in and around the sleeping area. On the Facebook group, I saw that some people had purchased covers that fit over the back doors, but these were hard to find, not always the right size, and extremely expensive. Another suggestion was to use a shower curtain. Genius! I scoured the local B&M store and bought a waterproof shower curtain, which was nothing fancy, just a cheap and cheerful one to see if my idea worked. Of course, as everyone can guess, I left the store with far more than just a shower curtain. You can never go into B&M and only buy the item you actually need, can you? I screwed some hooks inside the top of the back doors and hung the shower curtain right across. It was perfect and long enough to hang down and cover the garage below the bed, too. When driving, I would be able to unhook the shower curtain from the top so that I could see out of the rear window and reconnect it from the inside once onsite. For the small investment of £3.99, our bedroom area was now completely protected from the elements if the back doors were open. Being more organised, we should only need to open these doors when getting set up and then packing away because five minutes of rain pouring into the van could result in a miserable adventure if the bedding was soaked.

I'm sure by the time you're reading this book, all campervans will come with some sort of factory-fitted rear door protector. Maybe Adria will see my idea and pay me to design one for them. Dare to dream!

The Trossachs Holiday Park is very handy for us, and I thought that going to a familiar place would allow us to settle back into campervan life and take stock of how we were doing things. So, with everything packed in the van, we were ready for the short journey. I did feel we were starting to get better at taking less with us.

CAMPERVAN CAPERS

Then, we were off on another adventure.

With a little knowledge, looking at the site facilities before you set off is certainly worth taking your time over. I knew that our pitch on this site would have water right beside us, so we didn't need to fill up Evie's fresh water tank at home and have to drive with that sloshing around and putting more weight in the van. We could do this onsite when we arrived, but we took a couple of large bottles of drinking water. I was still not convinced that I wanted to brush my teeth or drink water from Evie's tank, and we had decided that we would only use this water for washing up and flushing the toilet.

It was March, and in Scotland, the days were still short. After quickly getting everything connected on our pitch, we headed out for a walk around the forest by the campsite, and decided that closing the windscreen blinds and all the curtains and putting the electric heaters on low would ensure the van never dropped below freezing. It would be dark before we got back to the van, and it would be nice to return to a cosy place rather than a cold, tin box, as Mr M had described Evie in one of his 'I hate campervanning' moments. This would also prevent the boiler's frost control from kicking in and dumping all our fresh water.

Having the water attachments in the door well of the driver's door was working great as we no longer needed to go hunting in the containers in the garage area of the van.

Sometimes, when you're planning all these things, it seems like you're going over the top trying to be organised. Then when you see the difference it makes to these tasks, it's all worth it. You don't want to have to search through all your boxes of kit to find that one item that you need every trip, especially if it's raining.

The weather for March was lovely, and we could enjoy a few hours sitting outside. We now needed two comfortable chairs. We were using our old folding camping ones. You know, the type that folds up into a bag that you can put over your shoulder, is easy to put up and has a great little net pocket to put a drink in, or citronella candles to keep the midges away, but Mr M frowns on that, saying it's dangerous! The only problem with these chairs is that once you get in them, you sink into the bucket-type seat, and you have to stay there as you can't get back out unless somebody can give you a hand up. They are also not as high as a standard chair, so you feel like you are too low when sitting at the table. Plus, if we got flat-pack ones, they would fit more easily in the garage of the van.

I am not a list person, but I had started to prepare a list of essentials that we needed for our adventures, and I ticked these off as they were packed in the van.

Crocs are very handy to slip on in fine, warm weather, so you don't need to put walking boots on all the time on site.

I've said this before, and on this trip, I decided not to worry if I didn't have a shower every day. So, I didn't. Don't stress about the small stuff.

At nighttime, we now left the bathroom window open on the latch to let the air in. Two people and a dog! We did, however, leave one of the electric heaters on low overnight, and this worked well, keeping Evie at a temperature high enough not to lose all our fresh water. Of course, Mr M, who was closest to the bathroom, said he could feel a draught in bed. I, of course, was OK sleeping alongside the back doors. Choices!

To our joy, we also discovered that our choice of duvet last year was perfect and better than the one we had at home! It was worth the expense to get a good quality one.

I'm a fresh-air girl, and I like to have the windows open at home as often as possible. It's like a battle sometimes. I open them, and when I'm not looking, Mr M goes around closing them. It's the same in the van. I like to have the large side door open, especially with having a big, hairy dog sharing the van. But it can feel a bit drafty, so I make sure I pack a few extra layers and a blanket or two, and this can make the difference between being cold and miserable or snug and cosy.

CAMPERVAN CAPERS

Onsite, we don't move Evie, so with the driver and passenger seats swivelled around, there is some storage space behind the seats. This is where I now put a bag for dirty washing, which is much better than our old way of using a black bin liner, and the dirty washing can be tipped straight from this into the washing machine when we get home. I recommend using a bag with a zip to stop the smells from spreading through the van if the clothes are sweaty or wet and muddy from a day out in the hills or torrential rain.

On this trip to the Trossachs Holiday Park, we took a walk down to the River Forth. I thought it would be a gentle stroll in the quiet countryside. It turned out to be anything but. It's a lovely walk from the site along a single-track road that then becomes a good track, then a path, which finally disappears, and you have to find your own way to the river. Watch out for the ostriches in a field on the left-hand side of the track not long after leaving the campsite. I was amazed at how large they were, but didn't want to risk finding out how friendly they were towards dogs, so Beatrix was back on the lead as soon as I saw them.

Not five minutes further down this track, we stopped and chatted with a woman working on the foundations of a new house she was building from straw bales. She explained how she wanted to create a house that was as eco-friendly as possible and hoped to finish it by the end of the year. She invited us to pop along if we returned to see how she was progressing. I was so intrigued by this idea and was determined to go back and see it. Hopefully, later in the book, you'll find out if we returned and whether the house has been finished.

To get to the river, we crossed a couple of fields, making sure there were no 'Do not enter' signs anywhere. Although it wasn't the fishing season, Mr M wanted to have a look at possible fishing spots. I couldn't believe how fast the river was flowing and how deep and black the water looked in places. Mr M pointed out the best spots to catch salmon or sea trout, and where he would watch the flow. He explained how the dark, still water was very deep. Still waters run deep indeed.

After managing to drag Mr M away from the fast-flowing river, we meandered our way back towards the campsite. Except the field we had walked through now had the biggest bull I've ever seen in my life running through it. I looked at Mr M, he looked at Beatrix, and she looked at me. There was no way we were going in that field. Then, out of nowhere appeared a van towing a trailer. Farmer-type-looking people brandishing big sticks jumped out and started talking to the bull.

"Don't come any further until we've got him in the trailer. He keeps running away and coming to this field as it's his favourite place to run around," shouted one of the men. "He's harmless, really. A gentle giant."

I didn't need to be told twice! I'm sure he was a very friendly bull by the way the people were talking to him and laughing, but I didn't want to find out for sure.

As we waited for the beast to be lured into captivity once more, we watched with disappointment as black clouds marched towards us, clearly ready to deposit a big downpour onto unsuspecting people below them, including us. So, as we waited for the friendly giant bull to be captured, we stood, regretting leaving our waterproofs in Evie, watching as the rain clouds hovered above us and then pelted us with a torrent of rain. Once the beast show was over, and the humans and a Border Collie were soaked to the bones, the clouds continued their journey, and the sun returned.

"Let's go for coffee and cake in the cafe," I suggested as we changed out of our wet clothes in the van. Mr M didn't need much persuading.

Campervanning, like camping, takes a bit of organisation to be successful, and that includes packing up to go home. A

CAMPERVAN CAPERS

good tip is on the night before you leave the site, pack away everything you can, such as the outside table and chairs, so you have less rushing about in the morning, and you can enjoy a relaxing breakfast on your last day and still be ready to leave before your due departure time. Remember, if you're late leaving your pitch, you might delay the start of somebody else's holiday. How would you feel if that were you?

I was super organised on this trip for going home. As soon as I got up in the morning, I made the bed, covered it with the oilcloth and fastened the shower curtain back up. I could now pack everything back in the garage of the van without having to worry about the rain showers getting our stuff wet.

We still had hot water left in the boiler, so I cleaned the kitchen and bathroom while we were still onsite. I'd only have to dust and hoover the inside of Evie once she was unpacked at home. And clean the outside of the van, too!

You probably know now that Mr M is the world's health and safety monitor, and he was always telling me that I had to make sure I closed all the windows, locked the toilet cassette door, and pushed in the electric socket cover fully so nothing could get damaged in transit. Driving home from this adventure, I was keeping an eye out for rogue tree branches and glanced in my passenger wing mirror. What did I see flapping around? The toilet cassette cover. Who locked this, I wonder? I pulled in at the next available lay-by with Mr M asking what was wrong.

"I'm just going to lock the cover that's hanging down," I said quietly, giving him a sideways look.

Mr M looked a little sheepish. It was certainly a lesson learned that we both needed to check that things are secured. That could have been a costly mistake.

We still had a lot to learn.

Chapter 20

Evie Fails Her MOT - 11th April 2022

One of the drawbacks of buying a pre-loved vehicle is the dreaded MOT. Will the van that you've invested all your money, hours of your time and given your soul into making it your own, pass with flying colours, or will you find out you bought a dud?

We decided that although Struans had been fabulous with us, it's a good hour's drive away, so perhaps we should try one of the local garages now. Shop local, they always say.

I scoured the internet, found a local garage, and asked if they could do MOTs on motorhomes. The mechanic asked me the height of my van and assured me that, of course, he could, so we booked Evie in.

Test day arrived, and I tootled off to the garage, not feeling concerned as we had no problems with the van at all, and we had only done a couple of thousand miles since we bought her. All her previous MOT certificates were in her stash of paperwork, and each year, she had passed with flying colours, other than a couple of minor faults that had been sorted.

A few hours later, we got the dreaded phone call. Evie had failed, and it was a major fault. Almost reduced to tears, I listened as the mechanic told me,

CAMPERVAN CAPERS

"Your van has a big hole in the floor. It's a major failure, but I can easily solve it by welding a plate over it. Then we'll re-submit it for a re-test."

I conveyed this information to Mr M, and we both agreed it sounded a little odd. Surely, we would have noticed a hole in the floor. We solemnly drove to the garage in our little red car to look at our doomed van.

I asked the mechanic if he could show me the hole because, as Evie was still under warranty, I wanted to take some photos to show to the dealers.

Carefully creeping under Evie as she sat on the ramps, I was armed with my mobile phone to take pictures to send to the lovely Steve, the salesman. Mind you, I was not having quite so lovely thoughts about him at this point. Had he sold me an already corroded van? I wondered.

The mechanic gleefully pointed to, yes, a hole in Evie's floor. I looked aghast at him.

"But that's the gas vent," I told him.

"Well, it shouldn't be there. There should be no holes in the floor," he told me.

I pointed out the other vent (hole), and he said that was OK because it was in a different place, and that didn't count. I was mystified. How did that even make sense?

I showed the mechanic all the other numerous MOTs that had been carried out on Evie since she was born and that none of these questioned the hole in the floor.

"Well, love," he started.

The hairs at the back of my neck were standing up by this point. Love! I think the hairs on the back of Mr M's neck might also have been standing up, as he knows exactly how much I hate being called 'love'.

He continued, "All those other garages must have missed it. Do you want me to do the welding now, and then I can pass the MOT for you?"

Erm. No, I most certainly did not. I decided to take Evie home with me and speak to the dealers about this.

I drove Evie home and parked her on our drive, telling her everything was going to be OK. Of course, the first thing I did was contact Struans and Steve, the salesman, explaining the problem. I could almost hear him smirking.

"Leave it with me, Debra, and I'll speak to our engineers," Steve, the salesman, giggled.

Waiting patiently for Steve, the salesman, to return my call, I logged onto Facebook and the Adria Twin Camper Van Owners group and posted the news of my failed MOT, adding all the photos I had taken of the offending hole.

The politest suggestion I received about the mechanic was to ask if he was called Coco.

Meanwhile, Steve, the salesman, phoned back with the news that he'd spoken to two of their MOT centres and VOSA, who all agreed that this was not a failure. These vents are there for a reason and are factory-fitted when the van is made. Gas is heavier than air, so if there is a gas leak, it should drop, hence the vent.

With that, I drove back down to the garage (in my car, because Evie was going nowhere near that nasty garage again) and retold all the information I had received to the mechanic.

"They are all wrong. You can dispute it with VOSA if you want. Here's the paperwork," he mumbled.

Concerned now that Evie's MOT would expire at the end of the week, I had another phone call with Steve, the salesman, who assured me everything would be OK and booked us in at Struans the following day.

So, on 15 April 2022, we took Evie to Perth for a journey we had hoped to avoid by using a local garage. Evie passed with flying colours.

Next year, we will be taking Evie to Struans for her MOT!

Did I appeal to VOSA? No. I decided that I had had far

CAMPERVAN CAPERS

too many fights with different people in my life, and a dispute over whether my campervan should have a gas vent on the floor was just laughable. Members of the Facebook group were very concerned about Evie, and they said that I should name and shame the garage. I decided against it. I lived too close to them to risk anyone taking a dislike to me!

Interestingly, the garage that carried out the failed MOT never asked me for any payment. Silence speaks volumes if you ask me.

Chapter 21

Venturing Further Afield – 21st April 2022

Blair Castle Caravan Park,
Blair Atholl, Perthshire, Scotland

I know that I'm an adventure girl of sorts, but I'm also a bit of a creature of habit. When I go walking up the mountains and cycling around Scotland, I have my favourite routes. It would appear that I was inadvertently following this same pattern in my journey to becoming a campervan woman. I'd stayed in some campsites, and they seemed to keep drawing me to them. It was time to try some new places.

Wanting to venture a little further afield, I thought about different places we'd seen on our travels over the years. Thinking back to one of our cycle tours in 2011, I remembered the wonderful Sustrans Cycle Route 7 that we followed from Callander to Inverness, including a section from Pitlochry to Dalwhinnie. I have happy memories of this bit of the route when my son Benjamin joined us for a few days. I could visualise us cycling through Blair Atholl and past Blair Atholl Castle, and I was sure I could remember there being a caravan park there, too. I'm one of those people who can recall the tiniest of details of trips I've had, where I've been and what I've seen. I searched the internet for caravan parks at Blair Atholl, and I was right; there was one, the Blair Castle Caravan Park.

CAMPERVAN CAPERS

After the now-familiar routine of preparing some meals, shopping for essentials and packing Evie, we were off. The journey to this site from home is about two hours, and check-in time is from 1 pm. I decided that we would leave home at about 10 am, find a suitable place to stop and have lunch en route, and then when we arrived, we wouldn't be hungry, so setting up our temporary home would be much more enjoyable. There's nothing worse than not being able to concentrate because you're starving. Or, worse, Mr M is starving and moaning that he needs something to eat.

Not long after leaving Perth, the picnic had obviously started calling to Mr M, and he was already telling me he was hungry. Between Perth and Pitlochry, there are a couple of large lay-bys that have barriers separating them from the main carriageway. Perfect. I pulled into one of these, feeling quite safe even though we were on the A9, and we enjoyed our picnic lunch and flask of tea, and Beatrix had a stretch of her legs. It was lovely just to be in the moment and enjoy being in our campervan. We didn't need to talk and simply sat in a comfortable silence, allowing ourselves to relax. Yes, we were able to do that in a lay-by on the A9. Honestly, I wouldn't have believed it myself if I had not been there.

I had a good idea where the site was, and just as my memory told me, Blair Castle Caravan Park sits just within the grounds of Blair Atholl Castle. Just watch out for the little narrow bridge as you enter Blair Atholl that's only wide enough for one vehicle, but you can see what's coming the other way, so it's not really a problem.

Still on my learning curve for the different types of pitches, I'd booked a luxury superior pitch and even selected extra-large, so I knew we would have plenty of space, and there would be electricity, fresh water and a waste water drain right next to us. It seems that each campsite or organisation has their own way of categorising its pitches; you just need to check this out when booking.

Debra Murphy

Immediately as I drove up the short drive to the reception, I knew that I was going to like this site. There was a large area to park when checking in. The reception was well organised, and there was a great shop selling a range of frozen and fresh food, as well as various camping bits and pieces you might need. The staff were very friendly and helpful, checking if I'd been there before and fully explaining where my pitch was, how to get there and where the nearest shower block and chemical waste area were. They also reminded us that our check-in leaflet, showing our names and the date of our stay, gave us free access to the castle gardens and a discount on the entry fee into the castle itself.

We both laughed when we found our allocated spot because it was indeed very large, and we felt a little small compared to some of the other vans on the extra-large pitches.

One of the drawbacks of being on a hardstanding pitch is the lack of grass. This made pegging in the stay for Beatrix's lead difficult, so we dug it into the grass just beyond our pitch, meaning Beatrix was not quite as close to the van as we (or she) would have liked.

For this trip, we had two new chairs. They were quite cheap, but a couple of cushions on them (homemade, of course) from our garden chairs at home added some extra comfort. Actually, these were from our garden at home, but were originally on the seats in our tearoom. So, this is another memory for me of the years of Mother Murphy's Tearoom.

Whilst we were setting up, Mr M started on the task of filling up the fresh water tank, and I took the opportunity to try out the toilet blocks. As I returned to the van, I could see that Mr M was holding his head in his hands, bemoaning the fact that there was something wrong with the water tank as it was not filling up. I pointed out that there was a river of water pouring from underneath Evie. Problem solved. The frost guard had obviously been activated at home in the last cold spell that we'd

CAMPERVAN CAPERS

had two days previously. Something we again reminded ourselves we needed to be aware of.

With the frost guard activated, this meant we also had to find the reset button for the boiler. It's surprising the things you can find when you need to. Ours is in a little space in the garage of the van, with a push/pull button. There is also a cord hanging down that you can pull to reset it, but 'Mr Health and Safety' says we shouldn't use that as it will break the boiler reset button. I do wonder why all these things are created if they will break the things they are designed for. I wouldn't be at all surprised if one day Mr M tells me not to use the steering wheel in Evie in case I break it. But I kept my thoughts to myself.

Beatrix lay on the grass watching the proceedings, and I swear she gave me a knowing nod!

Going back to discussing the toilet facilities. These were great. Immaculately clean, with plenty of toilets and lots of shower cubicles. There is a covered dishwashing area, a laundrette and a chemical waste area behind the amenities. There are at least three toilet blocks dotted across the site, so if one is closed for cleaning, you can still access another.

Once set up, I had a craving for chips, so we went to the Atholl Arms Hotel opposite the caravan park and enjoyed an hour sitting eating chips, drinking coke and listening to Scottish Music. This was the life, I thought. Looking at the menu for evening meals, we decided that we would treat ourselves and go back to the hotel again that evening.

Learning from our last trip to the Trossachs, we remembered to close the blinds and put the electric heater on low in the van before going out for a meal at the Atholl Arms again. We enjoyed a lovely two-course meal, with the best sticky toffee pudding and hot custard I've had in a long time, before a gentle stroll back to the cosy warm van. We realised that we should have brought a torch with us, as it was very dark walking back to our van.

Debra Murphy

It was lovely and quiet on the site, with no traffic noise and very little light pollution. It really did feel like we were nestled somewhere special on the edge of the Highlands.

After a peaceful, cosy, comfortable night, we were both up early, eager to explore a little and find somewhere for Beatrix to run off the lead. There are plenty of places once you go through the campsite gates. Beatrix seemed to know where she was going anyway, so we just followed her. With our passes for the castle gardens, we wandered up to the castle and found a couple of little paths that seemed to skirt the campsite perimeter, so we knew we wouldn't get lost. We even managed to find a lovely track alongside the river, so Beatrix could play in the water. It's a beautiful area, but with only one day here, we didn't really get the chance to fully explore. We will definitely be back to this site.

Somehow, that night we found ourselves once again back in the Atholl Arms Hotel for our evening meal, so there was no cooking in the van this trip!

Reflecting on our trip as we drove home, we both agreed that two nights somewhere new is not long enough to explore properly because you really only have one full day there. The first afternoon is spent getting your pitch set up. You have the following day to relax, then you need to pack up again the next morning. However, the short trip did give us another chance to get our routine sorted for getting everything set up, working, and then re-packed ready for home.

But two nights away in my campervan is still an adventure, and I felt very lucky that I was following my dream to become a seasoned campervan woman.

Was Mr M loving it just as much as I was? I was not so sure.

Chapter 22

A Full Week's Adventure – June 2022

Skelwith Fold Caravan Park, Ambleside, Cumbria, England

How excited was I? We were going to have our first full-week adventure in Evie. And even better, it would be at Skelwith Fold in the Lake District. I was beside myself planning what we would need and what we could do when we were there. And this time, I was going to do all the driving.

Having been to the site before, we knew it had an excellent shop, and the nearby towns of Ambleside and Coniston also had plenty of food shops, so we didn't need a week's worth of food with us. Part of the enjoyment of my holidays in Evie was planning meals and deciding what we needed to buy from the supermarket or bake before we left. By the time we had everything laid out on the table in the kitchen at home, I did wonder if we had gone a little over the top with our preparation. It looked like we were catering for a whole army for a month, not just two people and a dog for a week.

As on our previous trip to the Lakes, we stopped at Gretna Services to allow Beatrix to do what she needed to do and for me to have a little break. I managed to persuade Mr M that we could wait for our picnic lunch and stop again once we'd left the M6 and joined the A66 towards Keswick. Mind you, when we stopped again, I was so excited because I could almost smell the Cumbrian Fells beckoning us that I gobbled up my lunch, and we were soon on our way once more.

On this trip, I thoroughly enjoyed the drive and felt my confidence was growing each time I set out in Evie. Travelling along the A591 from Keswick to Ambleside, I was even able to admire the Lakeland fells and pointed out the different mountains to Mr M. Mind you, I'm not sure why I do that because I know as soon as I've told him where we are, where we've been, or where we're going, he immediately forgets. Never trust Mr M's reply if you ask him for directions or where he has been on holiday!

Once through Ambleside, it was the anticipated couple of bridges on the road heading towards Hawkshead, over which I drove like a pro! I was very proud of myself.

Arriving at Skelwith Fold's entrance, it felt like we were going home. The red road up to reception and the pitches seemed to put their arms around us and welcome us. It was evident that many of the lovely ancient trees had indeed been felled, and lots of groundwork was still going on following last year's storm damage. The owners of the site had obviously undertaken the task and had worked like trojans to get it open again for the new season.

Once checked in, we picked an empty pitch opposite the one we had last year. Beatrix again found herself a comfortable place under the bushes and watched as we got Evie set up. With water and electricity at the pitch, we were soon ready for our week's holiday.

Mr M and I agreed that the van was a little tight for space when we were going away for any length of time and that it would be very nice to have one of those lovely spacious enclosed awnings that most people seemed to have on the site. We would look into that seriously once we were home again.

CAMPERVAN CAPERS

They were a lot of money, and we had to be sure it would be suitable for us and that we (I) could manage to put it up and back down easily.

Just as we were starting to cook our tea that evening, the inevitable happened. Evie's gas ran out. We both looked at each other.

"It's just as well we had a spare," said Mr M. "Can you remember how to change the gas cylinder?" he asked me.

"No, I've never had to do that. How would I know?"

That was how the conversation went on for a couple of minutes. Beatrix continued lying under her bush, watching the proceedings. Before things got out of hand and we had a proper fallout, I wandered across to reception and asked if there was anyone who could help us change our gas cylinder.

Within ten minutes, a warden came strolling down to us. He chatted away as he demonstrated how to change the bottle. The first thing we needed but didn't know we didn't have was a spanner that fitted the nut on the bottle. But the warden had one, so all was not lost—another thing we had to buy when we got home.

I'd seen that the site had a store for gas cylinders and asked if we could have our empty one swapped for a full one. That's when I learned that there are two types of camping gas: Calor Gas and Flogas. If you have Calor Gas, you can't swap your empty bottle for a full bottle of Flogas, and vice versa. This is because they are from two different companies, and the connectors are often different. We had Flogas, so we couldn't get a replacement at this site and would have to find a supplier near home. But our full bottle would last us a long time.

As we'd been on this site before, we knew our way around. The facilities were as immaculate as we remembered, and the library was just as alluring for me. I was still working on Beatrix's novel and was looking forward to spending a few hours each evening surrounded by books. There is nothing more inspiring for a writer than being in the presence of so many written words.

Skelwith Fold is perfectly located for me. A short walk down to the road at the bottom of the site takes you to the bus stop to go to either Ambleside or Coniston. This week, with more time to spare and longer daylight hours, we explored a little more and discovered that it is very easy to walk into Ambleside on the cycle track that starts right by the bus stop. I'm not sure I'd want to use it with my road bike as it is a bit rough, but walking along it was lovely, and Beatrix could run freely off the lead.

Shortly after joining the track, I was awestruck at the sudden perfect view of my favourite iconic mountains, Langdale Pikes. It took Mr M and Beatrix a good five minutes to realise I had stopped before they came back to see what the matter was.

"Look!" I cried, pointing.

Mr M glanced at the mountains. "Is that Langdale Pikes then?" he asked. He is learning well.

It's a lovely walk to Ambleside, and the route takes you through woodland, along the river, and past some fabulous slate buildings. The Lake District at its best. Just before Ambleside, we found the lovely Fresher's Cafe and thought it would be rude not to stop. It was hot, we were thirsty, and Beatrix certainly needed a drink. For the next hour, we sat outside under the shade of a canopy, enjoying lovely coffees and cakes, and Beatrix had some water and a snooze under the table.

For the last few years, we have spent our summer holidays in a cottage in Grasmere, and Beatrix seems to know and love this area as much as we do. One day, we took the bus to Ambleside and then walked to Grasmere on the cycle route, about a five-mile walk. Seeing your dog dashing to the lake to splash and chase sticks is wonderful. Beatrix absolutely loves water and would stand for hours in one spot waiting for you or

CAMPERVAN CAPERS

anybody to throw a stick to her. I managed to take a little dip in Rydal Water, too, but Beatrix didn't like me going out too far. Did she think I wasn't a very good swimmer? It's no surprise for you to discover that in Beatrix's finished book, there is a chapter about her visiting Grasmere and saving a young girl from drowning in the lake.

The week passed very quickly. Days were filled with open-topped bus trips, walks, treats in cafes, and dips in Coniston Water and Derwent Water at Keswick, and they were simply divine. I was in heaven. I was staying in my very own campervan in my beloved Lake District with my two favourite people. I know that Beatrix is a dog, but she doesn't!

How did Mr M manage in the campervan for a week? He absolutely loved it! Between us, we both enjoyed the peace and relaxation of the simple tasks of cooking, washing up, reading, writing and chatting to other campers. Other than the gas running out, there were no other traumatic events. The weather was great, and I think we could have both stayed for another week given the chance.

All good things must come to an end, and on the final day, we had a leisurely breakfast before packing everything up and heading back home.

Of course, a campervan holiday is not over until the van is emptied, cleaned and washed after an adventure. We were lucky and had a couple of dry, sunny days when we got home, meaning we could share the cleaning duties whilst enjoying plenty of cups of tea and biscuits in the sunshine. Well, it's hard work cleaning a campervan!

Now it was time to do some research into drive away awnings. Over tea and biscuits, of course.

Chapter 23

A Not-So-Perfectly-Fitting Drive Away Awning

After looking at hundreds of different awnings and tents on our trips away in Evie, we realised it was going to be a difficult task to decide which one to buy. I'd made my mind up that as I was now confident in my love for Evie and would, given the opportunity, spend all my time in her, the cost of an awning could be justified. Just about.

During our visit to Blair Castle Caravan Park, we chatted with two lovely women. Dogs, cycles, and an awning seemed to draw us together. They had a slightly larger motorhome than Evie but had a modest drive away awning. I'd watched them put this up and was intrigued by the inflatable poles. This idea looked much better than the old-style metal bendy things that you can never remember exactly which one goes where. I also observed how quickly they put their awning up. In no time at all, they had what looked like an extra canvas room attached to their motorhome.

We were soon chatting about cakes, dogs, cycling and awnings. They gave us a tour of their awning, showing us how it attached to the van. I could see that it was a very sturdy structure, and the inflatable poles were indeed very robust. I learned that this structure was called an Air Drive Away Awning, which allows you to attach the awning room to the

CAMPERVAN CAPERS

van with a little covered tunnel between the van and the room. You can then detach it from your van, leaving the tent still standing and the van free to be moved away; hence the name drive away. Of course, this wouldn't be needed for us as we never move Evie once we have arrived and set up. If you ask me, it's too much effort to re-pack things away to drive about. Never say never.

We discussed prices, and our new friends told us about the company they had used that seemed to have lots of similar products at reduced prices. I also discovered that you could pick up deals as ex-demonstration models.

I wondered how to get the right size and was told that it depended on the size of the van. The one our new friends had is available in small, medium and large.

Dunking digestive biscuits into our mugs of tea, Mr M and I agreed that a drive away air awning seemed ideal for us. I'd seen some that were huge and had multiple rooms, but I was being practical and sensible.

I soon had a list of my requirements: an air awning, the right size for our van, could be erected and dismantled by one person, the erected awning would fit easily onto site pitches, and most importantly, when packed away, it was light enough for me to lift and small enough to fit in the garage of the van.

Really, all I wanted was a little extra space to put wet coats and jackets, a table and chairs and a reasonably sized area to sit in if it was cold and wet rather than always having to be in the van with the door closed.

I began the hunt on the internet. YouTube was viewed millions of times, watching people put up drive away awnings in no time at all. I'm not daft, though, and realised they had probably done this hundreds of times and never in a howling gale or rain.

Prices I discovered ranged from £199 to over £1,000. How would I ever decide? Knowing the make of our friends' awning at the site in Blair Atholl, I visited Leisure Outlet's website and found the very one, the Westfield Hydra 320 Travel Smart Air Drive Away Awning.

The specifications told me it was a single-person pitch in twenty minutes. There is a tunnel between the van and tent with two doors, so you don't need to continually open the large main door. It has a panoramic view – meaning you can open windows on each side, making the tent a lovely place to sit and relax, with views all around. All the windows have blinds to close for privacy. It has a fitted ground sheet that seals all around with VELCRO®, so the tent is fully enclosed. It comes with a foot pump that only allows the poles to be inflated to the correct pressure. You can buy an inner tent as an extra if you plan to sleep in the awning, but that obviously makes the inside space smaller. It's lightweight and quick drying with a UV coating to protect it from the sun's rays (ha, ha), which will help prolong the life of the awning.

As there were different sizes and I was spending a large wad of money, I phoned the company and chatted with a real person about our van and which size to order. The woman gave me very clear instructions as to where to measure the height of the van. Once I had my measurements, I called her again, and she told me exactly which size to order.

A few weeks later, my awning arrived. I waited for a dry, wind-free day, then set about erecting my new toy on Evie outside our house. The first problem was that we have stone chippings in the front garden, and Mr M didn't want me hammering pegs in this, destroying the undercovering and allowing weeds to poke through. That was OK, I thought, as I only wanted to have an idea of how to put the awning up. It didn't matter if I couldn't peg it out fully.

Personally, I think these awnings should come with a warning as they can seriously damage a previously loving relationship!

CAMPERVAN CAPERS

Following the very basic instructions and tips I had seen on YouTube, I first connected the tunnel section to the main tent. All good so far. Next, I worked out how to fasten the awning onto our pull-out canopy. I thought the rest would be a doddle. I had a bit of a panic, thinking I had been sent the wrong connector kit because it was too thick to slide into the groove on our canopy, but then I realised it had two sides to it, different sizes. Phew!

Watching from the front room window, Mr M and Beatrix may have been smirking at each other. With the awning now attached, I spread the rest of the canvas out into what I felt was the correct shape. Mr M couldn't contain himself any longer and rushed out to take control of inflating the poles. We soon had the makings of an awning.

But no matter what I did, I couldn't get the awning set up so that the roof of the connecting tunnel didn't catch on top of the sliding door of the van.

"You've ordered the wrong size," Mr M gleefully informed me.

Sitting in the van, I phoned Leisure Outlet once more. An equally helpful person told me exactly how to measure the height of the van again. With that done, the woman confirmed that I had indeed ordered the correct size and that I should watch some online videos on how to correctly put the awning up.

I had a break for a cup of tea and a handful of biscuits (always works for thinking and problem-solving).

My engineer of a husband had no suggestions except to ask if I wanted more tea, and he was now engrossed in YouTube videos of people putting up awnings in less than 20 minutes.

Sitting back in the van, sipping my tea and munching on biscuits, I swore and glared at the awning. This clearly worked, and I had a light-bulb moment. With an air of confidence, I put my cup down, stepped back out of the van, and wound out the pull-out canopy on the van six inches. Hey presto, the awning was now the right shape and height, and it was not catching on the van door. It might not be the exact way to do it, but I told myself that if it worked, I was sure at some point I'd meet somebody with the same van and see how they had managed it.

Meanwhile, I messaged the two friends with their perfectly fitting awning and told them my dilemma, and I was relieved when they said they had seen this problem a few times with vans our size, and it didn't seem to give people any problems winding out the pull-out canopy a few inches.

And there it was. My not-so-perfectly fitting drive away awning. I couldn't wait to try it out. I'm sure I will have lots to write about on this subject over the next few chapters! Get yourself a big mug of tea and some biscuits, and settle down for the laughs.

Chapter 24

Two Weeks In A Static Caravan -July 2022

I was itching to use our lovely new, perhaps not quite so perfectly fitting, drive away awning for our two-week family holiday at Primrose Valley Haven Park on the East Coast of Yorkshire. I'd planned it would be my daughter with her family in one big static caravan, and Mr M and I could stay in Evie near them. But I was shocked to discover that it was almost as expensive to pay to take our campervan to the site as it was to hire a large six-berth static caravan, especially if we wanted a pitch with a space for an awning.

And that's why, for the second year running, Evie had to stay at home whilst we had yet another two-week holiday without her.

I apologised to her and explained everything, but I could sense her disappointment. More than that, I was worried about leaving her on our drive and somebody stealing her while we were not there to protect her, until our neighbour came to the rescue and parked his work's van behind Evie for the duration.

Another example of how being a campervan owner causes stresses you never even considered before.

Chapter 25

A New Oven - August 2022

I've realised that Evie is constantly on my mind. Is she OK on the drive in the cold weather and snow? Will our pest deterrent work and stop Evie from having her wires chewed or anything else nibbled if creatures crawl into her to escape the harsh elements? But that's what happens when you love something, isn't it?

I'm always thinking of things we can improve to make life more comfortable or easier on our adventures. One of the things I missed when cooking in Evie was an oven. With an oven, your choice of meals is vast – jacket potatoes, pies, pizza, warming up homemade lasagne and apple crumble. OK, so not always the healthiest of choices, but having a few walks during the day or some cold water swimming deserves extra treats, don't you agree?

We were a bit hesitant to use an air fryer in the van because they were still a relatively new product and had quite a high wattage. However, my son had asked for an air fryer for his Christmas present, so we went on an early shopping trip to try to hunt one down. Yes, I know it was only August, but I like to get all my Christmas shopping finished long before the December madness.

It appeared that everyone in the world was now buying air fryers, and there were none to be had. Looking at the empty

CAMPERVAN CAPERS

shelves in a department store, I saw something that caught my eye: a mini portable electric oven, only 750 watts. It said on the box, 'suitable for caravans and campervans'. Although I knew this wouldn't be a suitable Christmas present for Benjamin, I thought it would be perfect to use in Evie. I did the smiling nicely thing at Mr M and was soon the proud owner of a new oven. We popped into Tesco on the way home to buy a couple of Cornish Pasties to cook in it for tea that night.

Taking the new oven out of the box, we were slightly disappointed that it was very small inside, despite its outside appearance being the size of a standard microwave, but we popped the pasties in, and it heated them up perfectly.

One of the features of this new oven is that if you leave the door open, it then works as a grill, which would be much better than our existing gas grill in Evie, which is in a really awkward position and makes using it a safety issue if you're as clumsy as me.

Of course, for supper that night, the new grill function was tested by popping in some crumpets. Perfect.

By pure chance, the new oven fitted snugly into the top cupboard in Evie, which I believe was originally designed as a wardrobe. Why would you want a wardrobe to hang holiday clothes in a campervan? I'm not sure, but I'm glad Evie's previous parents made this adaptation.

The top of the hob and sink in the van have glass covers, which I didn't want to damage by putting the oven on them, so I dug out a spare plastic chopping board to protect them.

I couldn't wait to try it out on our next adventure.

Chapter 26

A Solo Adventure - 29th August 2022
Blair Castle Caravan Park,
Blair Atholl, Perthshire, Scotland

It had been a stressful August. We'd just returned from a fantastic, but exhausting two-week holiday at Primrose Valley and, although it was great to have the room in the large static caravan for my grandchildren to stay with us some nights and for my son to join us, I couldn't wait to get back to Evie.

Why was it stressful?

There were several reasons. Mr M had a bad accident on the last day of the holiday when Beatrix inadvertently pulled him down twenty concrete steps.

You can now read all about this in my book, *Beatrix The Time Travelling Collie*, Chapter 19, *"Is he dead, Mum?"*

I was sad to be away from my family again, and I'd also just started a new job supporting individuals with autism. On top of everything else, I'd made the tough decision to put Mother Murphy's Online Cakes on hold. I had diversified our business when COVID-19 restrictions forced the permanent closure of our tearoom. I soon realised that baking and sending cakes in cardboard boxes to people I didn't know was not for me. I wanted to sit down with people, share tea and cakes and chat with them. I need another tearoom!

CAMPERVAN CAPERS

Anyway, I'd decided we'd earned another trip to Blair Atholl to enjoy the peace of the Perthshire countryside. We had a new drive away awning and oven to try out.

Beatrix then had a bit of a scare with her health and had to have her spleen removed, so we needed to wait until the vet declared she was fit to go. (Another tale you can read about in Beatrix's book.) She still had her large plastic cone on to stop her scratching her wound, but at least we had a new awning for her to sit in during the day and evenings.

I booked an extra-large pitch again. Evie was packed, and all that needed to be done in the morning was to put in the fresh food. However, Mr M's kidney stones had other ideas. He decided he was too uncomfortable to have two nights in the campervan, but declared,

"As the pitch is booked and paid for, it will be a good learning curve for you to go by yourself."

Could I do it? I wondered. Of course I could, but maybe I'd leave the new awning until next time. My first solo trip would be stressful enough without trying to put this up, even though I had Beatrix as support. I'd definitely be trying out the new oven, though.

If you remember, on our trip to Skelwith Fold, one of our gas cylinders had run out, but they couldn't exchange it for a new one as we use Flogas and not Calor. Even though we had what was hopefully a full bottle left, I didn't want to take the chance and run out of gas completely. Mind you, I'm sure I could survive on an adventure living on Cadbury Dairy Milk if I couldn't cook anything. I'd sourced a Flogas supplier in Cumbernauld near our home and arranged to do a like-for-like swap on my way to Blair Atholl.

Mr M, even with his kidney stones, offered his support for me as I had to put diesel in Evie by myself and go to the building merchant for the gas cylinder. I managed both tasks and was soon waving goodbye to Mr M as he tootled back home in the car, and I went the other way up to the M80 motorway towards the M9 and Blair Atholl.

My only disaster on the journey was that I dropped my supply of sweets on the floor but left them there and didn't try to reach them, kicking myself for not putting them closer. Beatrix never touched them as they had mints in them, and she hates mint.

I stopped at our now usual barrier-protected lay-by for my picnic lunch. Picking up all the sweets, yes, I put them back in the sweet jar. I know the five-second rule had long gone, but they were my sweets, and I knew the carpet was clean. If my children can survive eating sheep poo, I was sure I'd survive eating sweets off my floor.

Sharing our picnic, we discussed how brave and excited we were at having our first all-girl adventure. OK, a dog and a girl, but Beatrix didn't know she was a dog.

Soon we were on our way again and finding our pitch at Blair Castle Caravan Park. I tried to be very systematic and do things one at a time, but fell at the first hurdle when I connected the electricity, and nothing worked. I remembered this happening before to Mr M and that he had to use a different socket on the site. I tried this, and, hey presto, I had electricity.

I soon had the fridge working, filled the fresh water tank, turned the gas on and even got the hot water system working.

Our pull-out canopy was now no longer a problem for me, and I soon had this setup, and I was ready to relax.

As it was my first solo trip, Mr M had suggested I had my evening meal in the Atholl Arms Hotel across the road from the site. Who was I to argue? That evening, popping the electric heater on and closing the blinds and the curtains, Beatrix and I set off in search of food.

It was busy in the bar, and there were lots of dogs. I had a very enjoyable meal, and Beatrix was by far the best-behaved dog in the hotel.

CAMPERVAN CAPERS

Returning to the site, I realised just how dark it was in Perthshire now that summer was coming to an end. Taking Beatrix out for her last walk of the day, I forgot to pick up either a torch or my phone, so it really was pitch black. What did I see? A faint glimmer of the Northern Lights (aurora borealis). I looked around to see if I could share this amazing sight with anyone, but I was completely alone. Rushing back to Evie, I phoned Mr M.

"Have you been eating magic mushrooms?" he asked.

Of course, this is a reference from the film *Local Hero*, and he knew I'd understand his humour. I grabbed my phone and jumped back out of the van to get a photo, but alas, they had now vanished. Had there been something magical in my meal at the hotel? I wondered.

Back in the van, enjoying our cosy surroundings, Beatrix slept at my feet, and I had a couple of hours of writing.

I wondered how I would sleep. Would I feel lonely without Mr M? Surprisingly, although I would have preferred him to be with me, I was very comfortable in the van alone, and I slept like a log. I considered whether to tell a little white lie and tell Mr M that I had missed him so much that I couldn't sleep, but I knew that's not really what he would hope for. Would he?

Waking up on the first morning of my solo adventure, I had a discussion with Beatrix about whether she'd be OK in the van alone for half an hour whilst I went for a shower. She looked at me and rolled her eyes, so I gathered all my stuff and headed off to the shower block, closing the van door but not locking it. If Beatrix needed rescuing for any reason, people would be able to get to her, but with the keys in my shower bag, they wouldn't be able to drive off with Evie.

I'm not entirely sure what other people do. I have seen dogs sitting on the seats looking out of their van windows. Were they waiting for their owners to come back from the shower block? Of course, Beatrix was too large and polite to sit on the seats, so she just sat under the table, waiting patiently for me to get back.

Returning to the van, freshly washed and changed, I made porridge, then I toasted my homemade waffles using the grill in the new oven and spread them with my raspberry jam. Beatrix approved, too, but I didn't put jam on her piece. Perfect. Just what campervan life is all about.

Over the next couple of days, I experimented with my new oven. Ever conscious of the power constraints in the van and not wanting to blow Evie's electrical system or that of the whole campsite, I unplugged everything, such as the electric heater, laptop, kettle and my phone, when using the oven. I might have been a bit over-cautious. Better that way, I guessed. Despite its small size, the oven was a great success. During my stay, I toasted more waffles and warmed macaroni cheese and roast potatoes. Meal options had now improved immensely. It was a bit of a faff having to move it around once I'd finished using it, but with my trusty plastic chopping board and oilcloth, I was able to put the oven safely on top of the bed to regain the space in the kitchen area to do the washing up and make a cup of tea. Sorted!

At this rate, I'll be writing a campervan cookbook. Maybe.

One of the benefits of having a Border Collie, even one wearing a large plastic cone, is that no matter what you plan to do, you have to go for a walk. Lots of walks. During our previous stay at this site, we had wandered quite a bit, but I knew there was much more to be explored, so I made a packed lunch and headed towards the castle. Beyond this, there's a deer farm, but Beatrix was way too interested in the lovely-looking animals for me to spend any time admiring them. At certain times of the day, these majestic animals are fed by the Atholl staff, and this is a great tourist attraction. Personally, I'd much rather see wild deer and not farmed ones, but then, what do I know about owning and looking after deer?

CAMPERVAN CAPERS

Moving on, I followed the signs and strolled towards Diana's Grove, expecting something relating to the late Princess Diana, I was wrong, of course. It's a large, wooded area named after Diana, the Roman Goddess of Hunting. This is an amazing space within the Atholl Estate where you can see some of Scotland's finest and tallest trees, including Grand Fir, Japanese Larch and Red Fir. The height and width of these trees are just amazing. I'd suggest getting somebody to stand in front of one of them when you take a photo just so the enormous scale of them can be appreciated later when you show others your snaps. These trees were planted by the Dukes of Atholl, known as the 'Planting Dukes' in the 18th and 19th Centuries because, by 1830, the family had quite astonishingly planted over 27 million trees in the Atholl Glens. Now, that is some planting.

On our previous visit, we had strolled around Hercules Garden and chatted with one of the gardeners. He had told us all about the different fruit trees and advised us to come back again in autumn and pick some of the delicious pears, apples, plums, damsons and cherries. The Atholl estate doesn't do anything with the harvest, so it just goes to waste if people don't pick it. Well, it was autumn now, so I had to go and investigate. Oh my! Everywhere I looked, there were trees straining with fruit. I had a spare plastic bag in my rucksack, so I filled it with some bounty. These would be turned into crumbles when I returned home.

Hercules Garden is a beautiful, tranquil place to wander around, all within high walls, so protected from the fierce winds that blow down the glens. It has been restored to its original Georgian design and is named after the mythological character Hercules, famous for his strength and adventures.

Just outside the garden, there is a magnificent statue of him, and I am convinced that Beatrix sat right in front of him for me to take her photo because she thought it was such a joy to see. There's so much more to tell about this place, but you need to be there to appreciate it. Walking around, there are lots of signs and information notices, and the Blair Atholl Estate website has some great information if you need more encouragement to visit.

With an afternoon's walking behind us, we returned to the van, and I popped the kettle on. Remember, originally, Mr M was supposed to be on this trip, too. To accompany my cup of tea, I was having some chocolate-coated teacakes. I know it was a pack of six, but fearing they might go off or entice some little beasties into the van, I did the best thing I could think of and ate all six! Well, I was busy writing, and I needed some brain fuel.

Of course, at teatime, I had a very healthy meal of cheese omelette and salad. I've got some new little omelette pans that needed trying out. It worked perfectly. Maybe using three eggs was a little excessive, though.

Returning from another walk around the castle with Beatrix, I was ready for some supper and enjoyed some Greek yoghurt and fresh strawberries. See, I don't actually live on Cadbury Dairy Milk all the time.

After another peaceful night, it was time to pack up and go home. I made a picnic for us to stop on the way back and soon had everything stored safely and securely.

It wasn't long before we were in Kirkintilloch, and Mr M, minus what was reportedly a huge kidney stone, welcomed us home with open arms.

Chapter 27

Mr M And COVID-19 - 25th September 2022

Blair Atholl Caravan Park,
Blair Atholl, Perthshire, Scotland

After the kidney stone episode last month, I felt Mr M deserved a few days away and knowing he quite likes the Blair Atholl site, I booked a new adventure for us.

The week before we were due to set off, I had taken a trip to Glasgow with a friend, and Mr M was complaining of a headache and sore throat.

"Take a couple of paracetamol," I told him and went off for the day. In my defence, he had been moaning for two days, and I thought he was just trying to get out of going away in Evie. As if he would!

Sitting in the cafe at John Lewis, tucking into my piece of Bakewell tart, my mobile rang.

"Positive! Are you sure?" I exclaimed when Mr M told me he had done a COVID-19 test.

I made a swift return from Glasgow, trying not to breathe any potentially COVID-19 germs on anybody on the train. At home, I looked sadly at his test, which clearly showed double lines. Mr M had indeed caught the dreaded virus. I quickly did a test myself, sighing with relief fifteen minutes later when it was negative.

Debra Murphy

Mr M took himself up the stairs and didn't come back down for what seemed like days. Beatrix was confused as to why he didn't come downstairs and why I did all the walks with her, even the late-night ones. When we met anyone, I told them to stay away from us, explaining the situation. I even had to make my own cups of tea. Honestly, I did look after Mr M, albeit from afar. I took drinks and food to him on a tray upstairs, but I wore a face covering, and I slept in the spare bedroom.

It was hard to believe that we had escaped this dreadful virus for so long, following all the rules regarding social distancing and face coverings. Heck, COVID-19 had even forced the closure of our tearoom. The only thing we could think of where he had possibly caught it was when we went to a Chris de Burgh concert at Glasgow Concert Hall a couple of days previously and, believing the virus was on its way out, we didn't wear face coverings.

A few days later, Mr M, looking as white as a ghost, slithered his way down the stairs. I sat at one end of the room, and he at the other.

"I think you should still go away in Evie this weekend," he said, in the most pathetic voice I've ever heard him use. His voice seemed to crackle, and what a cough he had.

"You're still negative," he croaked. "You need to be careful with your own health, and you don't want to catch this and pass it on to the vulnerable people you work with."

"I'll decide in a few days," I answered, worried he might have noticed the definite twinkle in my eyes.

A few days passed.

"Right, the fridge is full of meals for you, and there are plenty of snacks. You don't need to do anything. Just rest and get better. We'll see you in a few days," I said.

I did feel torn. Could I really leave him all alone again? If I'm honest, I was petrified of catching COVID-19 myself, and once I knew that he was over the worst of the virus, I'm sorry

CAMPERVAN CAPERS

to say, I just wanted to be away from it. Call me heartless, but that's what fear does to you. With my heart problem, I didn't know how I would be affected if I caught it, so I did what I thought was best. Would I have done that if Mr M hadn't suggested it? Probably not. Do I know for certain that Mr M would not have left me alone if it had been the other way around? Absolutely!

Anyway, rightly or wrongly, I packed everything, including my guilt, into the van and once again trundled up to Blair Atholl without Mr M. Pitching up at the campsite, we followed the usual routine, except this time I had a new air awning to try out. How difficult could it be? The website says it can be put up by one person in twenty minutes, I reminded myself.

This time, it wasn't too stressful getting everything connected and working in Evie, except for overfilling the fresh water tank. I did wonder where the water was coming from alongside the van, then remembered I'd not turned the tap off. Well, I wouldn't run out of water this time. It's not a problem overfilling the fresh water tank as the excess just pours out. No harm done.

Then, it was time to tackle the awning. Did I see Beatrix getting herself comfy, lying in the sun where she could watch me attempting this feat in what was now quite a brisk wind?

I easily connected the awning to the pull-out canopy on the side of the van, spread out the base of the tent to what I thought was the rough shape and started to inflate the poles. Then, the wind began to blow around me and the canvas as I struggled to control it. My task was made even more difficult because I was on a hard-standing pitch, so I had no grass to put the pegs into. No matter what I did, I couldn't seem to get the awning up how it should be.

Beatrix was watching me with interest and had even moved to get a better view, and I could feel the eyes of everyone on the campsite watching this lone girl attempting the impossible.

Nobody offered to help!

I huffed, and I puffed, and the wind blew the awning and guy ropes all around me. So, I unclipped it from the canopy and shoved it all in the garage of the van.

"Right. We're going to the pub for tea tonight," I told Beatrix, wiping away my tears.

The pub was packed out. We found a little table in the corner, and Beatrix got herself comfortable underneath. There were dogs everywhere: on the seats, on laps, under tables, and any other space they could find.

I was very proud of Beatrix because she never barked once and didn't get in the way of anybody. It seemed like all the other dogs were barking and yelping at each other. As Beatrix told me, Border Collies only talk when they have something important to say. Mind you, even the humans were noisy - laughing, shouting, and singing that night. We had a lovely meal and spent a good couple of hours whiling the time away, people and dog watching.

Taking Beatrix for a wander back through the campsite for her to do what she needed to do, this time with a torch and my phone, I looked around, but there were no Northern Lights to be seen. Typical.

Back at Evie, it was lovely and cosy; the lights were on, curtains were drawn, and the heater was warming the van up nicely. Perfect.

"Is it supper time?" I asked Beatrix.

Overnight, I contemplated my problem with the awning. What was I doing wrong? Then it dawned on me. I needed to fasten the ground sheet in place to the top section of the awning first. That's why I couldn't get the right shape. I could hardly wait to finish breakfast so I could have another go.

Pulling the awning back out of the garage of Evie, the first thing I did was to go around and fasten the ground sheet in place all around the four sides with the strong VELCRO® strips.

CAMPERVAN CAPERS

Things became much easier then. If only the videos I'd watched at home told you to do this.

An hour later, although not exactly perfect, I had a pretty good drive away awning set up. I put in my table, spreading a cotton tablecloth over it, placing my chair next to it, and popped the kettle on the hob.

Yet again, nobody offered to help me, but I'm sure Beatrix cheered for me.

Ten minutes later, I was enjoying a cup of tea and a celebratory biscuit with Beatrix. I did put a mug on the table for Mr M so we could imagine he was there with us.

Feeling on top of the world, I packed us a picnic, and we went for a long walk through the woods and along the riverbank, letting Beatrix paddle in one of the deep, clear pools now that her plastic cone had been removed and her wound healed.

Strolling through Hercules Garden, I once again picked a few apples, but only enough for me to make into some more crumbles for us. Then we had a lovely hour sitting on a picnic bench in front of the castle, which, despite the scaffolding around it, looked splendid in the sunshine.

I phoned Mr M and was pleased to hear he sounded much better and even happier to hear that his COVID-19 test was now negative. I have to confess to feeling a little teary that he was not with us to enjoy the moment, but I won't tell anyone if you don't.

To put a damper on my high spirits, it rained overnight, so I guessed I'd be packing the awning away wet and would have to put it up again at home to allow it to dry out. Just like a tent, you can't leave a damp awning packed away for weeks and expect it to still be in one piece when you pull it back out.

Inspecting the inside of the awning tent for leaks, I could see that there were gaps between the awning and the ground sheet as I had not correctly fastened it, so there were a couple of damp patches in the corners. I told myself I'd do better next time.

However, it was fine, dry and, much to my joy, windless the morning of our departure. Over breakfast, I made my plan as to how I would take down the awning and pack it away. To my surprise, my plan worked like a dream. I was even able to fit it all in its bag, zip it up and fasten the buckle.

I gave myself a pat on the back and posted photos on the Adria Twin Camper Van Group, telling them of my awning experience. They were full of praise, and all commented how horrified they were that nobody on the site had helped me.

Of course, I had a celebratory bar of Cadbury Dairy Milk. I think I deserved it.

With the rest of the van already packed, I put the awning (which now felt like a dead body) in Evie's garage and set off back home.

The weather wasn't great for a couple of days. With the next clear, still day, I erected the awning on our drive, using heavy boxes and the grey waste water carrier to fasten the main guy ropes to, as I couldn't peg them into our garden.

I also spent time going around the awning and correctly fastening the ground sheet into position. Immediately after this was sorted, the awning shape came together.

Another tip I learned was to remember to zip all the awning doors before making the final adjustments, or you might find you have the awning up but can't fasten the doors.

A couple of hours later, everything was dry, and I had another practice putting the awning back into its bag, much to Mr M's astonishment.

Does that make me a seasoned solo campervanner? Not quite, but I think I've got off to an excellent start.

This episode made me determined that I would always try to offer assistance, especially to a single person, if they looked to be struggling with anything. What's the worst they can say? No thanks?

By the way, I never did catch COVID from Mr M.

CAMPERVAN CAPERS

A Novice's Plan For Repacking The Drive Away Awning

- Wind the side canopy out a foot or so.
- Remove all the pegs.
- Tie the guy ropes up so they don't get tangled.
- Deflate the poles using the quick deflate button.
- Detach the awning from the van canopy. Find the four main corners of the ground sheet and use this as a base to fold everything.
- Fold the ground sheet in half over the awning.
- Put the awning bag alongside the short edge to check you have folded it to the correct size.
- Slowly roll the awning up, keeping all the bits inside the folded ground sheet, gently squeezing any remaining air out of the poles as you roll.
- Once it is all rolled up, put the awning bag over the sausage, and it should, with a bit of persuasion, fit in.
- Enjoy a celebratory bar of Cadbury Dairy Milk.

Chapter 28

I Need New Pegs

Following my struggle to get the awning pegs into the hard ground at Blair Atholl, I did some more research into what was available to make things easier for future trips.

I guess it goes without saying that the standard plastic pegs and even the thin metal pegs used for camping on grass are useless on hardstanding pitches. Looking at the different options, I found that there is a whole range of different pegs designed specifically for this. These are longer, thicker and stronger and can be hammered down without breaking. You can even get some that can be drilled in. I did consider those, but then I thought about having to get a cordless drill, find somewhere to store it and how to keep it charged, so I decided against it.

In the end, I found some very good ones at my now favourite outdoor store, Go Outdoors. We bought a couple of sets of hardstanding rock pegs that came with their own plastic case and a tool to remove the pegs from the ground when packing up.

There are way too many to choose from for me to be specific with this or tell you where to buy them from. A few minutes scrolling on the internet or visiting a good outdoor equipment store will give you a good idea of the options available.

CAMPERVAN CAPERS

We now have a good stock of these pegs. I have since dispensed with the bulky, flimsy plastic case they came in and just keep them in a couple of peg bags. It's well worth having more than you need because, despite the claims that they will not bend or break, they do.

Chapter 29

One Last Swim In Coniston - 17th November 2022
Coniston Park Coppice Club Campsite, Coniston, Cumbria, England

As soon as Evie came into our lives, I started writing this book, but I was also still penning my second novel, *Beatrix The Time Travelling Collie*. Some quiet time away with Beatrix for inspiration to finish the last couple of chapters was needed, and this had to involve a few nights away in the Lake District. I didn't really want to go to Skelwith Fold as that was our campsite, and it wouldn't be the same without Mr M. With narrow, wiggly, winding roads in that area, I wanted to make sure I wouldn't take myself down any routes I couldn't cope with.

On the Caravan and Motorhome Club website, I found the Coniston Park Coppice Campsite, just beyond Coniston Village, which was open all year round. From my trips and cycles around the lakes many years ago, I knew it was possible to avoid that epic road to Coniston via Hawkshead by sticking to the main A593. Calling this a main road is a bit of an exaggeration, but I was pretty sure it was more manageable than the Hawkshead diversion.

"I'm taking Beatrix away so we can finish her book," I announced to Mr M.

CAMPERVAN CAPERS

Looking rather alarmed, he cried, "It's November. It will be freezing in that tin box."

I noticed he seemed remarkably happy for me to have another solo adventure in 'that tin box' when I told him I wasn't expecting him to go with me. Tin box indeed!

The Lake District is not too far away from Halifax, so I always check to see if either of my children can come to meet me when I venture down that neck of the woods. This time, it was Benjamin who said he could have a couple of days away with me, and this seemed like the perfect opportunity to try out the drive away awning as an extra sleeping room. I'm sure that Benjamin loves his mum to bits, but he wasn't all that keen on spending a couple of nights in a tiny campervan with Beatrix, his own dog and his mum. But sleeping in the awning for two nights sounded like a good plan.

"Bring yourself an airbed and plenty of bedding, and you and Zeb should be fine," I told him. "You'll be able to have the electric heater in the awning too."

Full of excitement and with a bit of trepidation, I packed Evie for my first long solo trip down south. I was going on a writer's retreat in my own campervan in the Lake District. Never in my wildest dreams did I think that would ever be possible.

Mr M checked the tyre pressures for me and even filled Evie up with diesel, and bought me an extra big supply of Cadbury Dairy Milk, sweets and other treats to keep me going over the five nights.

"Take care and phone me when you get there," he said, giving me a hug. "Happy writing."

Did I notice an unusually beaming smile on his face as he waved us off?

The drive down to Cumbria was lovely and uneventful. I started my deep breathing exercises as I approached Ambleside, knowing that the driving would become a little trickier from then on. I was comforted by the fact that it was November, so there wouldn't be hordes of tourists on the little roads.

Debra Murphy

Once over the humpback bridge out of Ambleside, I laughed at the turn-off to Hawkshead and continued along the main road to Coniston. It's not quite ten miles from Ambleside, but that day, it seemed like a hundred. I trundled Evie along at probably no more than 30 mph all the way, feeling as though I couldn't enjoy the lovely scenery. I've cycled along this road many times, so I know it very well. Mind you, you don't need as much space on a bike as in a giant motorhome, which is how Evie still felt to me. The road was surprisingly very manageable, and visibility was good on most of the narrow sections. I took my time, and slowly but safely, I arrived at Coniston. Perhaps I now need to appreciate the progress I have made in my driving abilities in Evie rather than spoiling glorious journeys by worrying too much.

Having examined the map thoroughly before I set off, I knew that the site was just a couple of minutes through the village, but I didn't know what the road was like. Fortunately, it was traffic-free and had no nasty surprises, although it was a little narrow at one point. You need to keep an eye out for the signpost for the site on the left after the hill, as it can be easily missed. I was soon turning onto the drive down to Coniston Park Coppice Club Campsite. What a relief.

This site has a large area for arrivals to park as you check in at reception, which is always welcome after a long drive. The staff were very helpful, especially when I told them I'd be putting my drive away awning up and that I was still a bit nervous at the whole setting up thing. They assured me that if I got into any problems, they'd come and give me a hand. They also pointed out some nice pitches close to the shower block, telling me that the lower end of the site was closed over winter, but I could still walk through the site to the lake. I also took the opportunity to discuss the best routes to walk into Coniston with Beatrix.

Driving past the shower block, I easily found the lovely, secluded pitches as directed. Picking one that looked level, I manoeuvred Evie into the spot, remembering to reverse in so that the sliding door was on the correct side to give me plenty of space to put up the awning.

Despite the drizzle, I soon had the electricity connected and looked for the fresh water taps, but they were nowhere to be seen. I later found out that none of the Caravan and Motorhome Club sites have fully serviced pitches. They have electric hook-up ones, though you need to get water from the water station.

On further investigation, I learned that I could have pulled in at the motorhome service station by reception, where I would have been able to connect my water hose and fill up with fresh water before driving to my chosen pitch. Lesson learned. I was parked and connected to the electricity, so I wasn't moving Evie again. Thankfully, I had my trusty watering can in the van, and four or five trips later, I had enough water in the tank for my needs. After all, I had a six-foot-tall strapping son arriving in a couple of days, so he would be able to top the water back up for me, wouldn't he?

Then, it was time for the awning. I was in no rush, and there was nobody else on site watching me. Even though it was a hardstanding pitch, it was not too difficult to hammer the pegs into the ground, and it didn't take me long to have the awning up. The plastic windows were a little lopsided and not quite as tight as they should be, so I knew it wasn't perfect, but I felt like a star. I even think Beatrix gave me the thumbs, or paws, up.

After a well-deserved evening meal and a stroll down to the lake, it was back to the van for plenty of treats as I began writing the last chapter of Beatrix's book. I couldn't quite decide how it was going to end, and Beatrix didn't have any suggestions either.

Being out of the village and in the middle of nowhere, the site was very quiet and dark with no streetlights or other light pollution, but I felt surprisingly safe in this beautiful place surrounded by trees, knowing that the fells were just a stone's throw away. The Lake District really is my safe haven.

Waking up the following morning, the temperature had dropped, but the sun was shining. I made myself a bowl of steaming porridge, then shared some toast with Beatrix before we set off for a stroll into Coniston. From the site, there's a track that takes you alongside the road, and you start to get views of the hills and a glimpse of Coniston Water. I'd been told to go through a gate on the left at the top of the hill, then cross over the road to join a track that would take me the rest of the way into the village. Despite Mr M calling me the Pathfinder, I couldn't find this track, so I had to walk a mile or so on the road, which Beatrix was not impressed with. Thankfully, it's a quiet road, so we had no fast-moving traffic to contend with. I'd find the track on the way back, I told myself.

Beatrix seemed to sense that we were heading to the lake and pulled me all the way. As soon as we were at the lakeside, I was able to take off her lead, and she was in the water like a flash, waiting for me to throw sticks to her. There's nothing quite like watching her enjoy splashing around in water, especially after her health scare in the summer. It was like seeing her with a new lease of life. I wasn't going for a dip that day, though.

Coniston Water is one of the largest of the sixteen lakes in the Lake District. Here's an interesting fact: only one of them, Bassenthwaite Lake, is officially a lake by name. The others are meres or waters, Windermere being the largest.

The attraction to Coniston for me has always been the Old Man of Coniston, the mountain that stands 803 m (2635 ft) overlooking the village. It's a relatively easy trek up and down, but as with any mountain, the weather can change quickly, and things can go wrong.

I have had lots of adventures in my time and had a few near misses. The one that still brings me out in a cold sweat

CAMPERVAN CAPERS

when I think about it is when I was climbing this mountain with my children, who were probably around 6 and 11 years old at the time. Life was a bit mixed up for me, but I was still trying to give Benjamin and Chloe wonderful memories of us in the Lake District. They certainly still remember this one.

It was a spur-of-the-moment thing to go to the top of the Old Man. Once we could see the path up to the summit, we were all eager to climb it. It's a lovely hike, and the route I took was up through the old slate mines following the well-trodden zig-zag path. Once at the summit, the rain started, and I worried about my children slipping on the wet slate on the way back down, so I decided to take another route that I had done on previous hikes. For some reason, I started to panic on the way down, and I became desperate to get my little ones out of the bad weather. They had all the correct walking gear, but I was still worried.

That's how easy it is to get lost and take the wrong path or track. It only takes a lack of concentration or loss of confidence and one wrong decision. I realised very quickly that I had been leading my ever-trusting children down a rocky face.

Without trying to panic them, I sat us all down and looked around. In the distance down the mountain, I could see a man who had chatted with us earlier. Feeling like a total failure but rejoicing at the sight of him, I got out my orange survival whistle and blew on it with all my might. I knew the protocol when trying to attract attention on the hills: three loud, short blasts, each lasting three seconds, then take a couple of breaths before repeating. It took a few attempts, but eventually, the man heard me and waved to us, then held up his arms. I could imagine exactly what he was saying. Don't move! And we didn't.

The children were very good and listened as their mum explained they were in a bit of a pickle, and that help was on its way. We had a little wait until the man climbed back up the mountain, but then he appeared, took hold of Chloe's hand and told us to follow him. Before too long, we were back off the dangerous crags and onto the correct track.

As it happened, the slate was not too slippery to walk on, and the rain had stopped. This kind soul walked with us all the way back down the mountain until we were approaching the village once more. Thanking him and probably blubbering, I bundled the children into our car and drove off, with a sigh of relief, to the Ambleside Youth Hostel where we were staying.

The following day, I took Benjamin and Chloe to Zeffirelli's, and we had the biggest mugs of hot chocolate with cream and marshmallows. Was I bribing them not to tell anyone what had happened the day before? Possibly.

Another more laughable memorable occasion in Coniston was during one of my first holidays with Mr M, and I had parked our car by the tourist information centre in the village. For some reason, I think probably because card payment facilities in small places were still a hit and miss, and cash machines few and far between, we had taken out quite a bit of cash from the bank before we left home. Well, I had planned lots of coffee and cake events during our holiday, so it was necessary. Walking from the car, delving into my pocket to get some coins for the parking meter, I somehow managed to pull out my rolled-up notes. They blew out of my hand like confetti and started to float across the car park. Mr M was shrieking at me, passers-by were looking aghast. I was in kinks of laughter at the situation. Thankfully, I soon gathered my wits and was able to collect all my money. Mr M has never let me forget that and doesn't allow me to carry large amounts of cash at all now. He muttered something about how normal people would have a bag and keep their valuables safe. Some people have no sense of humour!

For many people, Coniston will always be associated with Donald Campbell CBE and his speedboat Bluebird K7 when, on January 4th, 1967, he was killed attempting to break the world water speed record on Coniston Water.

In 2024, the fully restored Bluebird K7 was finally returned to Coniston, and there were great celebrations in the village, which I was incredibly sad to miss. The photos of this magnificent speedboat being driven through the tight lanes of the Lakes on the back of a huge lorry were a sight to behold.

It's no surprise then that at the lakeside, there's a place called the Bluebird Cafe. I didn't venture into it that day, as Benjamin had already suggested it as a place for our lunch the following day when he joined us. Beatrix and I had a very pleasant lunch in a little cafe by the visitor centre, but I felt saddened for the owners that I was the only customer. I know from experience how difficult it is to cover your overheads in a cafe on busy days, never mind days when you only have a couple of sales. I was obliged to get myself an extra coffee and cake just to be nice. Beatrix lay on the floor, clearly tired from her swim in the lake. She didn't refuse any of my toasted sandwich, though.

The following year, sadly, this cafe was closed, and the building lay empty!

On the way back to the campsite, after wandering up a few of the lanes and tracks leading from the village and asking a local, I did indeed find the hidden track, and the walk back to the site was much better than on the road. I could imagine this being an old railway line, and it reminded me of the Strathblane Old Railway path I've often cycled on from Kirkintilloch.

The next day, Benjamin was coming to join us, so we had another wander into the village, this time walking down through the bottom of the site and taking the path that takes you into Coniston. This took a little longer than the other route, but it was very scenic and would probably be OK for pushchairs and wheelchairs.

I was pleasantly surprised to see that most of the places in Coniston were dog-friendly. Today's food treat was finding the amazing Herdwick Cafe. The cakes looked scrummy, and their home-cooked sausage rolls were the biggest I've ever seen. The mint slice! Oh my! And the coffees! This is a place I would be visiting again, I thought. I also convinced myself that I had deserved the ginormous treats because I'd done so much walking and had to walk all the way back to the site.

Beatrix, as usual, attracted lots of attention, and I chatted with a few people about the book I was writing, and they took details, saying they couldn't wait to read it. I'm not sure if I imagined it or not, but Beatrix looked very proud of herself.

We wandered back to the site on the high-level track, looking forward to seeing our visitors.

Once Benjamin and his dog, Zeb, had arrived, we discussed whether to cook tea in Evie or try one of the pubs in the village. As Ben offered to drive us, it was not a tough decision for me. I can highly recommend the Black Bull Inn. We had a fantastic meal in lovely surroundings before heading back to Evie. I was glad Benjamin had suggested driving because it would have been pitch-black walking with no streetlights. Don't forget to take a good torch with you if you're going to do this walk at nighttime.

That evening, we worked out how to get the electric heater in the awning tent by feeding the cable through the van's sliding door window. I always like to have a bit of air coming into Evie anyway, and with Mr M not there, I could do so without suffering the wrath of his moaning about the cold. It wasn't perfect, as the zip for the tent wouldn't close fully, so you could feel the cold coming in a bit.

Benjamin had brought a large battery-operated lamp and some twinkly lights, and we played Scrabble, had cups of tea and plenty of biscuits, and listened to the rain bouncing off the tent. Yes, the tent that Benjamin would be sleeping in. Zeb and Beatrix lay together on a blanket, probably discussing the madness of humans.

CAMPERVAN CAPERS

It goes without saying that I would not put any flames in the tent. I figured an electric heater was safe enough, and the cable would not be outside as it was always within the confines of the awning.

I was a little worried about the weather as it sounded to be getting wild outside. I knew the awning was waterproof, but I honestly didn't know how warm it would be without the extra inner tent lining that you can get. I gave Benjamin lots of blankets to go with his thick air bed and sleeping bag and bid him and Zeb a good night, telling him that if he was worried at all during the night, to come into the van.

Overnight, I heard the wind howling and the rain beating down on Evie and wondered how my son was. He never called on me for help at all, and I eventually fell asleep.

It was very early the next morning that a tired-looking Benjamin ventured out of the tent and into Evie. By the looks of him, he'd not had a good night's sleep, so I popped the kettle on straight away for some coffee and made us each a bowl of steaming porridge. I also warmed him one of his vegan pies in the new small oven, and he was soon smiling again.

As he recovered from his ordeal, he recalled the events of the night. He said the tent sounded like it was going to blow away; condensation ran down the inside of it because there was no lining, and it dripped on his head, making him think the tent was leaking. He said that the only thing that kept him comfortable was Zeb crawling into his sleeping bag with him.

There is a lesson to be learned there. Don't have somebody sleeping inside your drive away awning if you don't have an inner tent lining. Reflecting on this, I suppose I wouldn't have dreamed of having anyone sleep in what is really just a tent outer, especially in late November in the UK. Perhaps in summer, it would have been a different matter or if it had just been cold and not wet and windy.

Once again, my son had an adventure in Coniston with his mum that he will never forget. I did offer to buy lunch at the Bluebird Cafe as some sort of apology for his ordeal.

Despite the chilly, damp weather, Beatrix and Zeb played together in Coniston Water, chasing each other and retrieving sticks. Eventually, we managed to coax them out of the water, dry them and found ourselves a table inside the cosy, warm Bluebird Cafe overlooking the lake. I can't compliment this cafe enough for the amazing all-day breakfast we had. We needed two pots of tea to wash it all down with. Beatrix was beside herself when two plates of chopped sausages arrived and were put on the floor beside her and Zeb.

Benjamin decided that one night in the awning was enough, so by that evening, it was just Beatrix and me again. We had a fabulous time, and I thought that maybe I could write the end of Beatrix's book now. But no, the chapter would not form in my head, so I popped the kettle on and munched away on Cadbury Dairy Milk, reading a book.

As always, I got ready to take Beatrix for her last toilet trip of the night, but she refused to move from under the table. I thought she must still be tired from all the swimming during the day. I finally managed to get her out of the van to do what she needed to do before settling down for the night.

Eager to have another day at Coniston Water and possibly even have a dip myself, I was up early to take Beatrix for her morning walk, but I couldn't get her to move from under the table. Looking at her frightened eyes staring at me, I knew something was wrong. I recognised this look from when Beatrix had been ill in the summer before having her spleen removed, and a chill ran through me. I managed to help her out of the van to go to the toilet and got her comfortable again under the table.

I phoned Mr M and told him that Beatrix was ill and that I was coming home early, and I'd phone when we got to Gretna

CAMPERVAN CAPERS

Services to let him know what time we would be home so he could book us in at the vets.

Usually, when I pack up, I take my time, making sure everything is as dry and tidy as possible and in its proper place. Not that day. I just pulled the awning down and shoved it into the garage of the van. It was wet, the pegs were still covered in mud, and stuff was crammed into any space I could find. I just needed to get home. Getting Beatrix to the vet was my priority, and the awning was the least of my worries.

Stopping off at reception, I told them I was going home a couple of days early because of Beatrix, and they were very sympathetic. If I remember correctly, they credited me with the cost of a couple of nights' stay.

I had a very strange drive home. As we left the campsite, I looked up to the Old Man and noticed all the high fells were covered in snow. Winter had arrived. Both Beatrix and I love winter, and I called out to her, telling her the snow was here.

Quite honestly, I don't remember the drive home in detail. We stopped at Gretna Services, but Beatrix wouldn't get out for the toilet, and I didn't force her. I sat on the floor by her and shared a moment with her as she rested her head on my arm. I phoned Mr M, trying to talk through my tears,

"That's us at Gretna Services. We'll be home in an hour or so. Could you get us an appointment at the vet, please?"

After what seemed like the longest journey ever from Gretna, watching the fuel gauge rapidly dropping down because I wasn't sticking to 50mph to conserve diesel, after driving on what might have been fumes only, I pulled into the drive at home, and Mr M opened the side door. Whether it was because Beatrix had rested in the van or she was just relieved to be home and see her dad, she jumped down from Evie as though there was nothing wrong.

But I knew differently.

The following day, Beatrix crossed over her dog rainbow bridge, leaving behind two heartbroken human parents.

Debra Murphy

The next few days passed in a blur, and I spent time putting the awning up in the driveway and cleaning out the van. I know that you might think this would be the last thing I wanted to do. Strangely enough, it was very comforting. I could smell Beatrix in the van, and I remembered the fantastic few days she had, having one last swim in Coniston.

For all those people who have never had a dog or a pet, you'll probably wonder what all the fuss is about. Those of you who have been in this position of losing your best friend will understand why I needed to include this in my book about campervan life.

A few weeks later, I met with my good friend, Greg, and I apologised to him that I had not been able to empathise with him about the death of his dog a couple of years earlier because I'd never been in that position. I assured him that I now fully understood how he felt and if I could turn back time, I'd react differently to how I did when he turned up late to our very first business meeting, and I rolled my eyes at him.

One Last Swim in Coniston became the last chapter in *Beatrix The Time Travelling Collie*. Beatrix had sadly written the end of her book for me.

Chapter 30

Can I Sleep In Evie, Mum? - Christmas Eve, 2022

When I was trying to decide whether to buy a campervan or not, one of my reasons for spending all my money on one would be that my children and grandchildren would be able to share the joy of it. As you've just read, Benjamin had a bit of a scary night in the awning in Coniston, and I hoped it had not put him off Evie.

At home, we have quite a small house and don't have room for many guests. Chloe and her gang were staying for Christmas, so our house was already full. Benjamin was coming, too, and I was trying to figure out how to squeeze everyone in and where we would put them.

"Can I sleep in Evie," he asked over the phone, "and is it OK for me to bring Zeb?"

My ever-sensitive son was worried that it would be too difficult for us to have another dog coming to stay at our house without Beatrix being there. Of course, my dog-grandson was always welcome.

Problem solved. Although it was winter, I knew Benjamin would be snug and warm in the van with the two heaters. The only thing he wouldn't be able to do was to use the toilet as there would be no water. But Evie is only a step away from the back door of our house, so that wouldn't be a problem for him.

Debra Murphy

The week before Christmas, I went out searching the shops for little trinkets to make Evie feel festive inside. I found a little Christmas tree, some lights and a battery-operated candle. Benjamin is just as clumsy as his mum, so there would be no real candles in Evie, Christmas or no Christmas.

With the bedding freshly changed and extra blankets dug out, I added some hot chocolate, ground coffee and Christmas nibbles for Benjamin to have if he wanted some time away from the rabble of the house.

Evie was a perfect host. Benjamin stayed a couple of nights and said he was amazed at how well he slept and how warm and cosy the van felt - even having to turn the heaters off because he was so warm. He is his mother's son! He even snuck away one afternoon for a power nap. It must have been cosy indeed for him.

And that's how, one Christmas, Evie had a special guest. I would like to think that one year I could spend Christmas in my van somewhere remote, but I know that would mean me spending Christmas by myself as there is no way I would get Mr M to agree to a winter break in a campervan in the UK. And, now that I have convinced him that there must always be Yorkshire puddings on Christmas Day, I actually quite like spending Christmas with my husband.

Chapter 31

You Broke It! – 11th April 2023

Maragowan Caravan and Motorhome Club Campsite, Killin, Perthshire, Scotland

My part-time work, with rotas issued only a couple of weeks in advance, made planning our trips away in Evie difficult, and we were now nearly halfway through April. My plan when I bought the van was to have at least one adventure a month from March to November. I'd love to say that I used Evie all year round, but I've not managed a snow expedition yet.

However, once I'd finally received my April rota, there was a slot in my diary for two nights away. After a quick look on the internet, I found a space at the Maragowan Caravan and Motorhome Club Campsite in Killin. We've been to this site before, and I love the area. I was a little surprised that Mr M was keen to join me on a spring adventure, what with him being afraid of the cold. I warned him that he could come along, so long as he never mentioned he was cold, squashed, wet, couldn't get into bed, the water wasn't hot enough, or the internet connection was rubbish.

This trip in Evie was going to be strange as my last one had been to Coniston when I spent my last few days with Beatrix before she crossed her dog rainbow bridge.

Both Mr M and I were still grieving for Beatrix, and despite my declaration that we wouldn't get another dog, our house felt empty without the unconditional love she filled our lives with. It was with much soul-searching that, in February, we welcomed into our lives a new Border Collie puppy, Florence. Mr M named her, telling me this puppy would look after us and nurse our broken hearts.

For those not familiar with Florence Nightingale, she was also known as 'The Lady with the Lamp' because of her efforts in nursing the sick and wounded soldiers during the Crimean War. She would often be seen at nighttime, checking on the patients in the hospital as she walked around carrying a lamp. Florence Nightingale also had far-sighted ideas and reforms that influenced the nature of modern healthcare. Her greatest achievement was transforming nursing into a respectable profession. In 1860, she established the Nightingale Training School at St. Thomas' Hospital, the first professional training school for nurses.

A very special name indeed for our new puppy.

Florence is black and white, like Beatrix was, but is a short-haired Collie. I thought that if I had another long-haired dog, I would make too many comparisons. This new puppy is unique in her own way and will never replace Beatrix. We will love her unconditionally as we did with Beatrix, and hopefully, she will love us back. I like to think that Beatrix will look down on us and our new bundle of fun with approval. Perhaps Mr M knew how my heart was breaking getting the van ready for the trip, and that's why he wanted to come along.

Did I tell you I love my husband?

Evie had not been used since Christmas when she hosted Benjamin and Zeb, although we have taken her for a couple of short drives just to keep her engine ticking over, so the next few days were spent getting her ready for humans to live in again.

This year, with the rising cost of fuel, we had decided that Evie would have to stay cold on the drive as we could not justify paying for the electricity to keep an empty van warm over the winter. We kept her connected to the mains electricity, though, because the pest deterrent doesn't work on the 12 v supply in the van. I wasn't happy at the idea of Evie feeling cold, but I certainly didn't want to allow any beasties to take advantage of her.

The van was packed with plenty of warm clothes, home-cooked meals that we just needed to reheat, and lots of treats, including a large bar of Cadbury Dairy Milk. I let Florence jump up and explore Evie every time I opened her door, and it looked like she had already found her cosy spot under the table. Perhaps Beatrix's smell was still there, making her feel safe.

With the trip being for only two nights, we had decided that we would not take the drive away awning, or we might spend our whole holiday putting it up and taking it down. The pull-out canopy would be sufficient for this trip.

As we'd been to this site before, I knew exactly where to go and also to make sure I parked well between the two white posts on the pitch. Very quickly, I had the electricity connected and the kettle on for a well-earned cup of tea. Mr M was putting the grey waste water container under the van when I heard him groan.

"You've broken it," he shouted up to me.

Jumping down from the van, I looked as he held the lever from the waste water release valve in his hand. You get the idea now of how I seem to get the blame for everything!

Mr M, the engineer, took the pipe system apart and attempted to fix it, alas to no avail. All was not lost, though, and he removed the U-bend from the pipe, allowing the waste water to run from the tank. The waste water container now fits under the van much better, in my opinion.

When planning my adventures, in an ideal world, I would go to a different site each time, but there are advantages to revisiting places. The first time you go to a site, you spend much of the first day finding your way around the pitches, checking out the facilities, and trying to find somewhere for your dog to have a run off the lead. If you are only booked somewhere for two nights, this doesn't leave much time to explore the surrounding area.

When you return to a site for another visit, getting set up seems much easier, leaving more time to venture out and about.

With a new puppy, we needed to find somewhere safe so that she could run around off the lead without worrying about her disappearing onto a road. As with most Border Collies, Florence loves a run around to chase a ball. We found a lovely, enclosed field just beyond the site grounds that was perfect. We could see all around, and there were no roads. Mr M stood at one end of the field, and I waited at the other. Florence had an absolute whale of a time running between us, and we were very pleasantly surprised to discover that not only does Florence chase the ball, but she also likes to bring it back to you and drop it at your feet to throw it again. We had spent years throwing the ball for Beatrix to chase, only for her to catch it and then drop it for us to retrieve it for her. There I go, comparing Florence to Beatrix. It's bound to happen, I guess.

Over the couple of days that we were at the site, we discovered plenty of scenic, peaceful walks on tracks, through woods and by the river. Florence was still only having short walks, and my arthritis was playing up, so this was perfect. For those wanting to do some longer walks, you could continue on the track towards Loch Tay and perhaps do some cold water swimming. It's possible to hike up the Lawers range from Killin, too, although you don't have the advantage of starting the climbs higher at the Lawers car park. If you're a cyclist, the Sustrans Route 7 runs through Killin, heading towards Callander one way and to Kenmore and Pitlochry the other.

A trip to Killin has to include a visit to the village coffee shop. I've said before that it would be very easy to be totally

CAMPERVAN CAPERS

self-sufficient in Evie for a few days, but I like to feel I'm adding to the local economy, even if only in a small way.

Both Mr M and I are chatty by nature and seem to attract people who want to talk to us. Add in a cute Border Collie, and it feels like everyone wants to chat.

As we strolled to the village, we found ourselves chatting with a man who, it transpired, was a retired college principal. With my background in learning and development, I loved hearing his tales from his teaching days. I also admired his three-piece tweed suit, polished brown brogues and softly spoken voice, remembering my grandma telling me years ago that you can judge a gentleman by his shoes. We chatted about how education systems had changed so much over the years, and I was amazed that, now in his 90s, he was delivering online courses in accountancy. I did ask him if he would like to join us for a coffee, but he declined, saying he was in a rush to get to the dentist. Half an hour later, I reminded him about his appointment and bid him a fond farewell.

With social distancing now becoming more of a faraway memory, we were able to sit inside Shutters Cafe with Florence and not be forced to stay outside in the rain. Village cafes are perfect places for chatting as you sample lovely home-cooked food. For our lunch, we had soup, toasted sandwiches and delicious cakes, accompanied by two perfect lattes, followed by two pots of tea. I'm not 100% sure the cafe is open all year round, so just check. The walk to the village from the site is only 15 minutes, so it wouldn't be a disaster, only a disappointment if you found it closed.

As it was April, it was quite chilly at times, but in the van, we were very snug and cosy with our two electric heaters. In winter, it is especially nice to have shower facilities that are clean and warm, and this site provides exactly that. I've read reviews online that moan about the outdated and dirty shower blocks. I can honestly say that for both visits we have had here, this has certainly not been the case.

Debra Murphy

To his credit, Mr M never mentioned the cold once!

Packing up to go home, it occurred to us that with a broken waste water valve, we had a potential problem because once away from the site, with the valve still open, anything could get into the empty waste water tank as we drove home or were parked on the drive. The solution? We tightly stuffed a rag into the pipe and set off home, discussing how we would solve the problem.

With Evie safely parked in our drive and unpacked, we had a trip to the local B&Q store to get a new valve fitting. Do you know how many drain pipe fittings, bungs, stoppers and caps there are? Rows and rows with hundreds, if not thousands. Was there one to fit our broken valve? No! So, we came away empty-handed.

Looking on the internet and asking for advice in the Facebook group, it was obvious this was a common problem on the Adria van, especially with the older versions.

It was back home for a pot of tea and biscuits to ponder our dilemma further. The scrunched-up rag would stay in place until we found a solution.

Chapter 32

"I Told You It Would Rain" – 10th May 2023

Blair Castle Caravan Park,
Blair Atholl, Perthshire, Scotland

For our next adventure, I had booked four nights away at my now favourite campsite, Blair Castle Caravan Park. Four nights means three full days at the campsite with no setting up or packing away. The extra space from the drive away awning and the site's close locality to a good pub serving excellent coffee should be enough to keep Mr M happy.

A couple of days before we were due to leave, I decided to sort out Evie's garage into a logical order of the things we definitely need to be in front of those extra bits and pieces we carry around with us every trip but will probably never need – except on the journey I decide not to take them with me!

We now religiously check the tyre pressures before a trip and have a new 12-volt digital tyre inflator that works off the cigarette lighter. With the addition of a handy extension lead (Amazon), we can check all four tyres in the comfort of our drive at home. Of course, this is the 'Royal we' I am talking about here! Just a note: make sure you purchase an inflator capable of reaching the higher PSI (pressure) levels required for campervans and motorhomes.

Debra Murphy

I had previously been storing our inflator in one of three large plastic containers in the garage, so we had to unpack everything to check the tyres. And I like to think of myself as an educated person! This now lives in the little cupboard above the dining table, so it's easily accessible at all times. It also means that if the worst happens and we have a soft tyre en route, we don't need to remove all our belongings to the side of the road to be ravaged by the weather (you never get a puncture in hot sunny weather, do you). Of course, we have a Green Flag membership, so we won't be changing a tyre ourselves.

Being conscious of power use with the ever-increasing charges, we have now established that the 1550 W air fryer from home can be used quite safely in Evie without blowing all the electrics in the van and the campsite, as long as we don't have anything else plugged in at the same time. So, you shouldn't use a hairdryer while waiting for tea to cook. Of course, for me to use a hair dryer in Evie, I'd first have to buy one, being the girl who likes to shower and go. I'm not even sure I could find a hairbrush or comb without organising an extensive search party.

Four nights away means four evening meals to plan for. We have the luxury of a fridge and freezer box, small but perfectly effective, which means we can carry enough food for four or five days.

This trip's meals would include homemade lasagne, roast chicken and quiche, all served with a mixture of potatoes, vegetables or salad.

The rest of the food packed consisted of fresh summer fruits, cereals and yoghurts for breakfast, bread, cheese for some lunchtime sandwiches and a few biscuits. OK, a jar of biscuits. As it was just after Easter, we also had hot cross buns, which are lovely toasted in the air fryer to bring out the warm spices. But let's be totally honest here, I'd happily eat hot cross buns all year round. I also packed enough milk for copious mugs of tea and, of course, a large bar of Cadbury Dairy Milk.

CAMPERVAN CAPERS

We now have our drive away awning, which I love, but it is a bit like trying to find a space for a dead body when it's wrapped up. I considered storing it on the bed as we travelled. Then I worried that if we had to stop suddenly, the weight of it would force the back doors open, and it would fall out of the van, causing unknown damage to any vehicle travelling behind us.

The bench seat at the dining table was already utilised for the cool box and day's essentials. The position of our table can be adjusted to hold these in place so they don't fly over the driver's seat in an accident. So, the dead body, for the moment, is being stored in the aisle between the fridge and the bathroom until we get onsite and put it up.

Have I been married to 'Mr Doom and Gloom' too long? I wondered, I was now worrying about everything!

On departure day, I put a few clothes into the cupboards above the bed. Just enough clean pants, socks and a T-shirt for each day, with a spare set just in case. Limited space does make you plan more effectively what clothes you really need.

Flasks filled with hot tea and picnic made, and we were off. Florence seemed happy in the van and went immediately under the table. We clip her lead to the seatbelt, though, as we do in the car. I'm horrified at how many dogs I see unsecured in cars and other vehicles, especially when they can stick their heads out of car windows as the vehicle travels. I dread to think of what injuries would happen in an accident.

The bumpy road out of Kirkintilloch is a great test for my packing of the van, and if we don't get drawers or cupboards being forced open and the contents pouring out at the start of the journey, I know we are good for our trip.

I'm now much more confident driving, and I don't need to breathe in and make Mr M pull in the mirrors if anything passes us.

On our previous trips, I'd noticed that, probably because Evie is an older vehicle, travelling at anything over 50 mph and you can practically watch the fuel gauge going down. I dropped to 48 mph, and within 10 miles, my estimated remaining fuel had risen by 90 miles.

I was alarmed that Evie didn't start the first time on this trip. Not a single sound, splutter or gasp. I took the keys out and prayed before trying again; she started like a dream. Starter problems in the future? I wondered.

Heading up the A9, the views were great in between the showers. The signs on the road displayed a yellow warning for heavy rain. Would we get the awning up in dry weather?

We stopped at our now usual barrier-protected lay-by for a quick lunch and to let Florence stretch her legs. It's much nicer to arrive at the site with full tummies rather than to find us snapping at each other because somebody is hangry.

"It'll be raining before we get there," moaned Mr M, tucking into his sandwich. "We'll get soaked putting up that awning."

Checking in at reception and discussing the miserable-looking weather, the Blair Castle Caravan Park staff told me they had carried out a sun dance for us. As always, they gave us our booking sheet and reminded us to take it with us if we wanted to go into the castle grounds, as it would give us free access to the gardens, and a discount if we wanted to have a tour of inside the castle.

We found our allocated pitch - some parks specify which one you can use; others allow you to choose your own – and we quickly got the awning up and everything we needed from the garage before the rain set in.

"I told you it would rain," said Mr M, sitting at the table eating a KitKat.

It was only a short rain shower, so once this had passed, we continued setting things up and fastening all the extra guy ropes. Go us! It was now time to relax and explore.

Over the next few days, we enjoyed some lovely weather. Most days, we found ourselves sitting having a picnic lunch outside the castle grounds after a walk. The castle has a cafe

CAMPERVAN CAPERS

and restaurant, but we never use it because we have always had Beatrix or Florence with us.

From the campsite, you can take a lovely walk through the wood and along the River Tilt. Beatrix loved the water and would make a beeline for the river as soon as she was off the lead. Florence is not so keen on water, although she has now started to at least go and look at it. A word of warning: the river walk has some very steep drops in places, which are lovely to stand at and watch the deep flowing water. We always put Beatrix, and now Florence, on the lead at these points because you never know what might spook a dog and make them tumble over the edge. The same would apply to children. We have seen people jumping from rocks into the water, but it looks a bit dangerous to me, even though I enjoy cold water swimming. I believe that year, there was a fatality with a youngster doing just that.

Continuing along the riverbank, you reach a very minor road. If you follow this for a quarter of a mile and take the next left at another equally minor road, you head towards Glen Tilt. Watch out for the house selling honey. I've never had any cash on me walking past this to be able to buy any. I'll remember one day because who doesn't love proper honey on hot toast?

I've mentioned before that one of the perks of staying at the Blair Castle Campsite is that you have free access to the castle grounds. As you approach Glen Tilt car park, one of the many tracks heading off to the right has a sign stating no access except for pass holders. If you've got your pass that was given to you when you checked in at the campsite reception, you can ignore the warning and enjoy a lovely walk through the wood that brings you to the edge of Hercules Garden. We wandered through this, looking at blossoms starting to appear on the trees.

By the way, I've also taken a photo of my registration sheet to show on my phone if asked to see my pass in the castle grounds, and this has been accepted. That saves carrying around a piece of paper you might lose.

On one of our walks this trip, we again chatted with one of the gardeners; he reminded us that from August onwards, the garden is full of different types of fruit growing and that we should come back and pick some. He even told us where the sweetest cherries and the nicest pears grew. We felt as though we were getting inside information, but he probably told everyone the same secret and just wanted to make sure the fruit was picked and not left to rot. As I've said before, I'm surprised to hear that the Atholl estate doesn't do anything with the wonderful bounty they produce. I discovered that the garden was originally designed to be a pleasure to walk around and use easy-to-maintain trees and bushes. There is a wealth of information available throughout the garden and on the Atholl Estate website, offering a fascinating glimpse into the history of this area.

Leaving the walled garden, you can take plenty of different routes, including a scenic one that takes you past St Bride's Kirk at the top of the hill. You can wander around the church grounds and have a great view of the castle from there. There are lots of relics, a mausoleum and gravestones, many dating from the Battle of Killicrankie. It's a place steeped in history, and there are plenty of notices and signs providing information for you.

From the Kirk, you can stroll through Diana's Garden and wonder at the massive trees there. Again, watch out for steep drops in some places, especially if you have dogs or children with you. There is a little children's play area just before you reach the castle grounds.

The castle has toilet facilities, a cafe and a restaurant, and, very often, a takeaway coffee stall. Plenty of benches and picnic tables are dotted all around the castle, but you might need to take a picnic blanket with you in case you have to sit on the grass in the height of summer, as it gets busy with coach trips. You can usually watch the piper play outside the castle every hour, and, of course, if you don't have a dog, you could take a tour around the inside of the castle. Your voucher from the campsite gives you a discount on this, but we have never managed this yet.

The joy of having three full days in one location is that you can do more exploring. We discovered a massive field behind the Blair Atholl Village Hall, with ample space for dogs to run around, a small children's play area and a couple of benches for tired adults to sit and rest.

With a sign promising coffee and cakes, we followed the directions on a notice board for the Blair Atholl Watermill and Tearoom. Strolling along the little road to the railway station (really only a platform), we carefully walked over the level crossing. I'm always nervous walking across train lines, but this is a barrier-controlled one, so the lights flash and the barriers drop down if a train is due. Once at the crossing, you have a good view in either direction, too, so even if you are like me and have a little panic, you can reassure yourself that there is no train coming.

The tearoom is not open all year round. A sign on the roadside by the Atholl Arms Hotel tells you if it's open. It's well worth a visit. Since first discovering this place, we have enjoyed many a good coffee and cake sitting in their outside eating area. It's not dog-friendly, so if the weather is poor, it might not be so enjoyable, although a few seats are undercover.

You can also get coffee, tea, or other drinks at the Atholl Arms Hotel, and, of course, meals, and dogs can go inside, which is always good to know if the weather takes a turn for the worse and you don't want to sit in your van all day.

During this trip, we were able to fully appreciate having the drive away awning. We have now decided that if the trip is for only one or two nights, we won't bother with the awning as it's a bit of a faff getting it up, especially if you're on a solo adventure. Mind you, on a solo adventure, there is plenty of room in the van without the awning. But when you do use it, it's well worth the effort. It gives you that extra room to sit in and store all your outdoor bits and pieces. That way, later in the evening, once you have retired to relax in the van, you can do so without it being piled high with clothes and boots.

What I have realised on this trip is what a difference a day makes. It's hard to explain what I mean, but having that extra night onsite really does seem to extend your relaxation time tenfold. If I could, I would now have a rule that I only ever stayed away for a minimum of four nights, but that is not always possible. And, if I'm honest, I love being away in Evie so much that if I could only ever get away for one night, I would still enjoy it.

I do believe that I am now settling into being a campervan woman. Even Florence, the not-so-brave Collie, seems happy on our trips.

What about Mr M.?

Well, he didn't seem eager to go home this time.

Was I winning my battle to turn him into a campervan man? Time will tell.

Chapter 33

A Film Called Misery – 5th June 2023
Skelwith Fold Caravan Park, Ambleside, Cumbria, England

Writing this book, I wanted to include the highs and lows of my life. 2023 was certainly filled with both for me.

A few years ago, I had hoped that having a heart attack at the top of a mountain would be the worst thing that could happen to me. How wrong I was! My heart condition is now relatively controlled with medication, give or take a few random episodes of arrhythmia, only to be followed swiftly by the progression of my arthritis. Now it was in my feet and ankles. As you can imagine, for somebody used to walking mountains and cycling around the country, this was devastating. Why couldn't I have arthritis in my ears or my little finger?

To make things worse, for the last few months, I'd also been suffering from a frozen shoulder. I know from personal experience that there is a direct link between pain and mental health issues. Grief is one of them. Perhaps I had stored up all my grief for Beatrix, and this was now causing my aches and pains. Of course, with my sense of humour, I compared myself to the writer, played by James Caan, in the film *Misery*. He is rescued from a car accident by a former nurse, played by Kathy Bates, who then locks him in her remote home, breaking his ankles with a mallet to stop him from escaping and forcing him to re-write the end of his new novel.

During the editing process for this book, I was amazed when Mr M admitted he didn't know which film I was referring to. I quickly jumped on the internet to order the DVD for one of our cinema nights during the dark winter evenings. Sometimes, I wonder where my husband has been all his life!

During the first half of 2023, my whole body ached, and I was still grieving for my soul mate, Beatrix. Slowly but surely, I had finished writing my book, *Beatrix The Time Travelling Collie*; it had been published, my pre-sale orders had arrived, and the book launch was organised for 23rd June. It had been both heartbreaking and cathartic finally completing Beatrix's story, and I felt that seven days in the Lake District would give me time to reflect on the last few months, rest my mind, and allow me to prepare for talking about Beatrix. Where would we go? It had to be Skelwith Fold, of course.

Getting ready for our break, I had a few practice sessions getting Mr M to help me in and out of my swimming costume. I knew that if I could get into the lakes to swim, I would be pain-free for at least a few minutes with the weight off my feet and my shoulder supported by the water. I realised it would be a struggle, but it would be worth it.

That's why, on what should have been the best day ever – setting off for a week in the Lake District – I found myself at my lowest psychologically and physically. I could only walk for five minutes without the pain kicking in, and Mr M had offered to drive, knowing that I was hiding my discomfort. I felt I was letting him, Florence, and myself down.

Stopping off for a break during our drive down to Cumbria, I looked in the mirror at the services at Gretna and was disgusted with myself for the weight I'd gained and how I was hobbling. So, I did what most people do when they're depressed; I went back to the van and ate a tub full of sugary, chocolate treats.

Would I ever get to cycle or walk in the hills and fells again? I asked myself. But that thought was too hard to contemplate, so I was living on hope. That's all I had at that moment. Along with Cadbury Dairy Milk.

As usual, I had booked us into a superior, fully serviced pitch at Skelwith Fold, which should have been perfect, except we needed to put up the awning tent on the exceptionally hard-standing ground. This was the year when most of the UK actually had some summer sunshine. The Lake District had an absolute scorcher of a time, with temperatures reaching into the 30's.

Mr M told me to sit down whilst he hammered in the pegs. That's him who can hardly bend down with his dodgy knees. So, picture this: Mr M sitting on a folding stool, Florence hiding under the table in the van, and me trying to act helpful, as we realised that no matter how hard he tried, the hammer was not heavy enough to drive our new heavy-duty pegs into the solid ground. All around the campsite, I could hear other people doing the same thing. Bang, bang, bang. At least we were not alone.

The sun burned down, and there was not a breath of wind. Watching the sweat pouring down Mr M's face and his T-shirt, I hobbled my way to the reception and purchased what became our most valuable tool – an extra big, heavy mallet for £9.50. It was still hard going, but we did eventually have the awning tent secured.

I've had many visits to the Lake District, but I'm sure this week was the hottest I'd ever known it, and much of our time was spent ensuring that Florence was out of the heat of the sun, had plenty of water, and didn't run about too much.

The best way to ensure that was to be beside water, so the next day, we packed a picnic, beach tent and my swimming gear and ambled down the campsite road to the bus stop to catch a bus to Coniston. Mr M moaned that I was silly, wanting to take everything I had with us.

"Surely we could manage with just a towel," he moaned as we waited at the bus stop.

After another exhilarating bus journey to Coniston (I don't need to explain it all again to you), slowly, I managed to hobble another half a mile from the village to the lakeside of Coniston Water. Finding a place between some of the few trees, I put the tent up and got myself changed for a dip. I'd invested in some swimming socks and hard-soled beach shoes, so with these and using my walking pole to steady myself, I managed to hobble my way into the clear, cool water.

But it wasn't cold at all. It actually felt warm! Once I had the support of the water around me, I tossed the pole to the shore, and away I went. For 30 minutes or so, as I swam (using one arm only) in Coniston Water, I was completely pain-free. I felt myself really smiling for the first time in months.

With Mr M passing me my walking pole, I staggered out of the water and back to the tent, by which time I was just about dry as the air was so hot. We enjoyed our picnic and relaxed in the shade of the trees and tent.

"I bet you're glad I wanted to bring everything now," I giggled, watching Mr M's eyes drooping. I have a fantastic photo of both Mr M and Florence lying asleep in the shade of the tent.

It wasn't long until I was in the water again, having another swim, before we had to think about walking back to the village for the bus to the campsite. Of course, we then had the long walk up the site road to Evie. Whether it was the water that had helped my joints or whether it had lifted my pain threshold, I managed to get back to the van without having to crawl on my hands and knees.

There was a touch of sadness to the day as the last place Beatrix had visited was Coniston Water. Beatrix was never

CAMPERVAN CAPERS

convinced I was a good swimmer and, in previous years, had tried to rescue me when I swam in the different lakes. I like to think she looked down on me that day as I swam in Coniston Water and said, as she always did, "Go on, Mum, you can do it. I'm proud of you."

Over the week, I repeated my swimming therapy in Derwent Water at Keswick and then in Grasmere, where I was amazed that the water was so clear I could see little fish below me as I swam. Florence still hadn't found her swimming legs yet, so she just watched, wondering what on earth Mummy was doing.

I hope that as you read this book, you don't think I'm boring re-visiting sites and not always going to a different location. I've said before that the beauty of going to a place more than once is that you discover different walks, places of interest and, most importantly, local independent cafes.

On this trip, Mr M found a field within the campsite where Florence could run off the lead. It's actually signposted as a recreation area, and we'd assumed this was just a park for children. There are a few things for children to play on, and it is a vast area for dogs to run around, and, importantly for me, it has benches for humans to sit on and rest our aching bones as the dogs play together.

As always, we chatted with other campers during our stay. I'm always relieved to hear that other people have made massive mistakes with their vans and that it's not just me. One lovely couple we chatted with over the week told us about an experience with their campervan they had borrowed from their son, complaining that the bed seemed too close to the roof and it was like sleeping in a coffin. How we laughed when their son came to visit them on the site and, after he had rolled about hysterically laughing, he told them that the roof extended, and they had been sleeping in the bedroom area with it collapsed! Maybe I could collect all these memories from different people and write another book called '*I wish I'd known that*'.

During our chats, they told us of their visit to a lovely cafe at Skelwith Bridge alongside the river. When they described all the different cakes and goodies, we just had to visit.

Looking at the site map, I could see that this cafe, called Chesters By The River, was a mile away down a single-track road. That afternoon, smothered in suntan lotion, sun hats in place, water bottles filled with cold water, walking sticks and a large brolly to act as a sunshade for Florence, we set off to find this promised land of cakes.

Leaving the campsite from the top entrance (which can only be used by cars and not motorhomes or caravans), we joined a single-track road. After walking for only 15 minutes or so, we had the most amazing view of Langdale Pikes. In a layby, there was a slate bench with a map carved into a large piece of slate next to it, indicating the mountains and fells we had in the vista. Mind you, as inviting as it was, we couldn't sit on the bench because the slate had been heated by the sun and was unbearable to touch.

I stood for a while under the umbrella as a shade, dreaming of living somewhere that had such a stunning view, eyeing up a little cottage close by that was for sale. Chatting to a couple walking up the hill, they told us they had seen it advertised in the estate agents and for that one-bedroomed cottage, you needed £900,000! How do locals and youngsters ever get on the property ladder in the Lake District? I bet it was soon sold as another holiday cottage, lying empty most of the year.

Dare to dream, Debra, I told myself.

The road down to the cafe was quite steep and very narrow, and I was glad I wasn't in a car, never mind a campervan. Even cycling would be hard, having to brake all the way down the hill. We discussed how tough it would be walking back up the road but put it to the back of our minds.

Caution is needed as you reach Skelwith Bridge when you have to walk over the narrow bridge that has very tight bends at either end where you can't see the traffic and, alarmingly, the drivers can't see you, but they don't seem to think this a good enough reason to slow down.

Chesters By The River is indeed a lovely place. All homemade cakes, pastries, and bread, with a wonderful gift shop attached to it. There are ample seats outside, with most of them undercover, so no need to worry about the weather. Today, we were thankful for the canopies providing shade from the heat and glare of the sun. There are tables at the river, too, so if you didn't want to visit the cafe, you could still enjoy the location and splash in the water. We decided that as Florence was not a swimmer just yet, we would sit at the cafe in the shade.

After a scrummy date slice for me, a Danish pastry for Mr M, lovely coffees, and plenty of water for Florence, we wandered, or staggered, back up the road, which seemed much steeper going up than it did coming down. As the sun had moved and was not glaring down quite so much, we sat on the slate seat and enjoyed the vista, dreaming about living in the Lakes and giving our last bit of water to Florence.

The last full day of the holiday was probably the hottest, and we were concerned that the ground was too hot for Florence to walk on. I did what all good dog owners would do and went to the reception shop for six ice cream tubs. I put three in the freezer compartment for later and sat with Mr M and Florence as we enjoyed a day relaxing outside the van, eating ice cream, drinking cold drinks, reading, snoozing, and doing anything to avoid walking on boiling tarmac and stayed in the shade until early evening. Once we felt it safe enough, we took Florence for a walk down to the recreation area for a very short run around to stretch her now-twitching Border Collie legs.

Usually, at Skelwith Fold, you have to depart the site by noon. The day we were leaving, the red road through the site was being resurfaced, and we were advised that we could not leave until at least 1.30 pm. It wasn't a hardship for us, and we enjoyed the bonus of an extra few hours of our holiday.

Debra Murphy

Taking the awning tent down was nearly as hard as putting it up, as Mr M had done such a sterling job hammering the pegs in. Perhaps next time, they wouldn't need to be knocked in quite so far, and we might also add a claw hammer to our tool kit to help pull out the pegs from the ground.

We took our time packing up, then enjoyed an extra couple of hours, relaxing in the sunshine with cold drinks from the reception, chatting with other campers who were like us, packed up, ready to leave, but had nowhere to go. There are worse places to be delayed, I can tell you.

Once we were finally on our way, we thought Gretna Services would be busy and tried out Southwaite Services. Well, that was a one-off, and we won't be in a rush to go back there. It was a nightmare trying to find somewhere to park, and we ended up in the same area as all the many articulated lorries. Having to walk in front of and between those monsters to get to the services and toilets was very scary.

However, we did have a much more relaxed and enjoyable stop at Annandale Services, closer to home, with the added excitement of finding that they are dog-friendly so Florence could come in with us.

We finally arrived home at about 8 pm, and it was still hot, despite the warnings for heavy rain on the motorway signs all the way on our journey.

What was it like trying to sleep in the campervan during hot weather? I can report that I was very pleasantly surprised that we didn't feel any more hot and bothered than at home in high temperatures. We left the windows open but closed the skylight windows just in case of sudden rain, and I didn't like the idea of beasties crawling in and dropping down on me in bed. One night, I slept on top of the duvet in my birthday suit, but that's nothing new for me when I'm at home, so I wasn't worried about doing this in Evie. Whether this would be the same on the continent with extremely high temperatures, I'm

CAMPERVAN CAPERS

not sure. I certainly see lots of posts on the Adria Twin Camper Van Owners group talking about air conditioning units, fans, and other tips to keep cool. I can honestly say that we had comfortable nights, even with two humans and a dog, in a small campervan.

What I found reassuring about this trip was how comfortable and relaxed I was in the van. I was sore much of the time and spent lots of time lying down on the bed to rest my feet, but it was still wonderful.

Would I live in Evie if I could?
Absolutely!
Would Mr M live in the van?
Absolutely not!

Chapter 34

A Storm And A Real Mouse - July and August 2023

Blair Castle Caravan Park,
Blair Atholl, Perthshire, Scotland

Yes, I'm a creature of habit, and I was soon booking another trip to Blair Castle. During July and August this year, we had two trips, so I have combined these adventures together in this chapter.

For July's adventure, I was all set to step up to the mark and be chief of everything, including driving Evie up onto levelling blocks at the campsite.

Just before the trip, I was in my friend Greg's studio at Frielance Music & Media in Glasgow, recording the audio version of Beatrix's book and came home to find Mr M had checked all the tyre pressures, packed away the power cable and sorted his own clothes for the trip.

I'll do the tyres next time.

Filling up with diesel was to be my job, but there was already half a tank of fuel left, so I didn't need to do that either.

Anyway, off we went, as always, driving extra carefully over the first mile until I was sure I'd packed everything correctly and nothing was rattling around.

I'm always amazed that even though our car is automatic, as soon as I get in the driver's seat of Evie, manual driving seems natural. It would seem I was starting to get the hang of this campervan-driving lark. I suppose it's that muscle memory idea, which 'enables you to reproduce a particular movement without conscious thought acquired as a result of frequent repetition of that movement'. Typing is also a perfect example of a task that relies on muscle memory, which is why as I type my written words on the computer, I can do so without having to look at the keyboard.

Once at the campsite, I located our pitch and was alarmed at how tight it seemed to drive into the space between the pitches at either side, but also to the pitches across the narrow track. Slowly, with a reasonable air of confidence, I backed onto our space, using my mirrors, reversing camera and common sense. I knew that I needed to be at the edge of the pitch for the awning tent to fit, but I needed to watch for the water tap and power post halfway down the pitch edge. I have to say that I surpassed myself and only had to do a re-manoeuvre once. And that was with lots of eyes watching me from the campers around me.

Then it was time to get out the levelling blocks. I was a little nervous, to say the least, at the idea of driving up onto these plastic things, but I was determined to do it. I dug out the spirit levels. As I already thought, Evie was about as level as she could be, so there was no need for the blocks.

I'll drive her onto levelling blocks next time!

The awning tent was up in a relatively swift time, and it was not too difficult to hammer in the pegs, as some of these were into the grass. Be warned, though; some sites don't allow your awning on the grass firewall at all, even the pegs.

Mr M showed remarkable interest in the proceedings, even voicing alarm that the guy ropes were jammed. As an engineer to trade, I thought he'd understand the principle of the locking mechanism but hoped I hadn't let my thoughts be said out loud.

Tea break time. Then, because I could, I got myself settled on the bed, listening to the gentle wind and the birds singing. I even had to pull the sky window blind over a little as the sun was blinding me. As I lay there, with my eyes drooping and in that mid-life state of being awake and asleep, I listened to the gentle tapping of the raindrops on the open window. It took me a few minutes to bring myself into the conscious world again to realise it was raining and the window needed closing!

We are now accustomed to using the air fryer in the van, and it really is a game-changer. During one of our adventures, another camper was asking me how air fryers work. Other than telling him that you just plug it in, I didn't know what to say. It's true, though; you basically put food in, and it seems to magically come out cooked. Anything you can cook in a conventional oven can probably be cooked in an air fryer, although jacket potatoes are not so good for some reason. Roast potatoes, chips, salmon, steak, fish, chops, whole chicken, pasties, and even a pizza, if your tray is big enough, work well. Oh, I did have a bit of a disaster trying to make a giant cookie in the air fryer. I was all excited that I'd be able to bake biscuits on adventures and had all the ingredients weighed out and measured. I knew really when I put the mixture together this wouldn't work, but I still tried it out, only to have to throw everything away! Biscuits will be baked at home or bought from now on.

As for retaining the knowledge about how these things work, I never feel the need to fill my head with such things. It's like the science behind how aeroplanes stay in the air. After all, they don't even flap their wings!

*****

For our second trip to Blair Atholl that month, the BBC weather app showed rain and thunder with a weather warning of the risk of flooding. In the five days of this trip, we had two

CAMPERVAN CAPERS

five-minute showers the whole time we were there. I wondered how many people changed their holiday plans because of those weather warnings. All probably because of Michael Fish, the weather reporter who told everyone in October 1987 that there was not a hurricane coming. The following day, what is now known as the Great Storm of 1987, struck the UK with winds of up to 100mph, causing mass devastation across the country. Eighteen people lost their lives, and over 15 million trees were blown down, damaging buildings, roads, and railways, including six of the seven oak trees that the town Sevenoaks in Kent was named after. He might even have lost his job with the BBC over that misreporting of the weather, and now we are warned every time there is the chance of the slightest bit of bad weather. Heck, we are even warned now about good weather!

On one of the days, we took a bus trip to the House of Bruar (imagine a very posh clothing and gift store), which was only a five-minute journey on a privately owned bus. I was disappointed to find that the House of Bruar is not a dog-friendly place to visit, not even in the outside eating area. I find it hard to believe that a large retail outlet in the middle of the Highlands selling country clothing doesn't recognise that many of their customers will be outdoor people with dogs.

There are, however, plenty of benches outside, so as I relaxed in the sunshine on one of these, I had a delicious ice cream that I reluctantly shared with Florence. Of course, Florence, being such a beautiful dog, attracted lots of attention and received lots of cuddles and strokes. The House of Bruar is missing a trick not having Florence as a special attraction inside the shop.

Rain was forecast again for our last day at the site, so, as the evening before was dry, just like it had been all day, we took the awning down rather than risk it getting wet overnight and having to dry it at home.

Debra Murphy

I decided that the jigsaw-type padded cushion floor we had was a bit of a faff, having to put it together and then take it apart again to get it back into the bags. It certainly helped on the hard ground for delicate toes, but I wondered if I could get a piece of cushion flooring to fit that would then fold up in the garage rather than the bulky package the tiles created. At the moment, we had to travel with these in the bathroom, so when we packed the awning away the night before, we had nowhere to put these without taking up room in the living area of the van, which was already filled with a husband and a dog.

I took my time putting the awning tent away. It's always much easier when the weather is dry and there is no wind. After drying the underside of the ground sheet with some kitchen towel, I rolled up the tent, and just as I wrapped up the very last section, what jumped out? A mouse. Yes, a real living, breathing mouse. I gave a little yelp, the mouse gave a little squeak, and I jumped up far quicker than I thought I could and stood staring at the tent. It reminded me of one of Beatrix Potter's tales, *Samuel Whiskers - The Pie and the Patty-Tin*. In that tale, a giant mouse rolled up the naughty Tom Kitten in pastry. Thank goodness my mouse was only a tiny one, and I was the one doing the rolling!

Mr M laughed at me jumping, but I noticed he was not so quick to look under the now unrolling tent to find the mouse again. It had now turned into a scene from the film *The Green Mile*. The mouse soon scuttled from my tent across the grass to find a new home, and I unravelled all the canvas to make sure I was not hosting a whole family of mice before re-rolling it.

That last evening, with no awning to sit in, I spent a lovely couple of hours watching the sunset behind the magnificent trees. Wrapped in my crocheted shawl with a hot cup of tea in my hands, the peace and quiet was sublime. The trees were glowing with every shade of green with a clear blue-sky backdrop. The joys of long Scottish summer nights.

CAMPERVAN CAPERS

A tiny campervan pulled up onto the pitch opposite us, and I watched as a woman had her camper set up in minutes. It wasn't long before we were chatting with the woman. Vicky and her lovely dog, Shadow, then gave me a guided tour of her van. I loved how compact it was, but with a roof that raised, it didn't feel cramped. I looked at Evie's large frame and wondered if I could swap her for a smaller version like this van. I felt sure I would have no problem driving that. But that would mean having to leave Mr M behind on all my adventures, as there was definitely not enough space for two humans and a dog! I was still hoping to convert him into a campervan lover.

As I chatted with Vicky, I told her about the campervan book I was writing, and she told me about one of her learning curves. Vicky knew that her van had a leisure battery, but she didn't know how to charge it. Looking around her van, she searched for different buttons and switches and finally found one resembling a battery symbol on the dashboard. For two years, she switched this on every time she set off on an adventure. It was only when she went to the garage for something else that she discovered this was not the leisure battery switch. It was the button to turn on her fog lights! So, if you are reading this and can remember driving behind a little campervan that had its fog lights on in good weather, that was Vicky, and she apologises.

The only major drama this trip was that as I lay in bed reading whilst Mr M was brushing his teeth, I thought I could hear a drip of water. Mr M, of course, hears nothing first thing in the morning before he puts his hearing aid in. Sure enough, with my ear to the cupboard under the bathroom sink, I could hear a tiny drip. That would need to be sorted before we continued using water in the sinks or boiler because if this dripped into the van, who knows what damage it would be doing. Perhaps this was from when the shower tap was damaged before Evie became ours.

Chapter 35

Minnie Comes To Stay - July 2023

A little bit of a change for this chapter. This is an adventure in Evie, but we never left the comfort of our drive. How could that be?

This month, my four-year-old granddaughter, Minnie, came to stay for a whole week. Of course, Minnie could tell you that she was, in fact, four and a half! It was only her second time away from Mummy and Daddy, all those miles away in Yorkshire, so it was a big deal for her. She had a short visit last October when sadly she was quite poorly, and I hoped that wouldn't be her only memory of staying with her grandparents in Scotland.

Minnie was becoming a bit of an adventure girl. She was, though, still nervous about lots of things, including hand dryers and thunder, but she always wanted to go inside Evie when she came to see us. This holiday was perfect. There were no illnesses or anything to scare her.

"Can we have our tea inside Evie, please?" Minnie asked with her cute smile.

Grandad told us to go and get comfortable in the van, and he would bring our tea out. Just a reminder here that we Yorkshire folk have breakfast, dinner, tea, and supper. I don't want you to think we were just having a cup of tea.

CAMPERVAN CAPERS

Minnie was beside herself. I opened all the blinds and the side door. She tried every seat, including sitting in the driver's seat with sunglasses on. She particularly needed to test the swivelling front two seats, although I needed to help her with this as she was as light as a feather.

Grandad had told us it would be half an hour before tea, so Minnie looked in every drawer and every cupboard and wanted a full explanation of how the toilet worked.

"I don't think I want to use the toilet in here," she whispered.

I told her it was OK as I hadn't turned the water on, so she would still need to use the toilet in the house.

Minnie tested the glass covers for the sink and cooker, but we didn't practice cooking anything in the van, as Grandad had that under control in the house.

Like a grown-up, Minnie put the folding steps up and climbed onto the bed, taking off her shoes, of course. She was very keen to know which side of the bed was mine, which was Grandad's, where Beatrix used to sleep, and where Florence now slept.

When Grandad phoned to tell us tea would be ready in five minutes, Minnie found the knives and forks in the cutlery roll and put them all in place, ready for our feast. Taking Grandad back to his tearoom days, he served us two delicious plates of fish fingers, chips and beans, accompanied by glasses of Ribena. What a banquet!

With our first course finished, Minnie phoned our waiter and asked if we could have pudding. Two minutes later, our plates were cleared away and were swapped for two scrummy white chocolate desserts.

After our massive meal, we sat at the table playing dominoes and then Snap. Minnie then decided we needed to have a lie-down.

Climbing onto the bed, I lay alongside my granddaughter, answering very serious questions: What would happen if a seagull crashed into the open roof window? Who would help if Grandad cut his thumb off? How do you know what time it is in Evie? We practised phoning the emergency services, varying between needing the police, fire brigade and ambulance.

Twice during her stay, Minnie and I had our meals in Evie, with Grandad making it extra special because we could phone him and put in our order, tell him when we'd finished our meal and that we were ready for a pudding or another drink.

I spent the most wonderful hour in Evie with Minnie after one meal, lying on the bed and looking up through the skylight window. We had to have it wide open once Minnie realised we were safe from birds and bees trying to fly in. We watched the clouds floating past and tried to make out faces or animals in them. I think we even saw a unicorn cloud. Minnie was very interested in what would happen if I cut myself when I was in the van and needed an ambulance. A very serious question indeed. I wondered if Beatrix had told Minnie how Grandma needs looking after all the time.

Anyway, by the time we went back inside the boring brick-and-mortar home, Minnie knew how to phone the ambulance, what to say, what Grandma's name was and where she lived. If people think it's funny listening to me pronounce Kirkintilloch, you should listen to a four-year-old with an exceptionally broad Yorkshire accent trying to say it.

They were probably some of the best hours I had spent in Evie, and I hope that Minnie will remember that day when she is older. Hopefully, next year when she comes to stay, being a year older, she might feel confident enough to spend a couple of nights away with Grandma and Evie.

Chapter 36

Evie Service Day - 2nd August 2023

Earlier in the year, the MOT identified that the van's tyres were beginning to deteriorate, but with my low mileage, they would be OK until the service in August. It was now that time, so Evie was booked in at Struans for the service and tyre change, to investigate a noise in the driver's side front wheel and to check for a possible loose wire on the starter motor.

It's always a bit of a long day going up to Perth, but after the experience of the MOT fiasco with the local garage and the gas vent, I feel it is worth taking her to somewhere I trust. We have become loyal customers at Struans, and it's also another opportunity for me to continue to grow my confidence as a solo driver.

Evie needed diesel, and according to Mr M, that's a bit of a worry as it's dodgy getting the key to work on the fuel cap. After an early bowl of porridge and the heavy tent and other loose items in the habitation area removed, I was ready for the off. Mr M and Florence were staying at home this time.

I turned the key.

Nothing.

I took the key out, swore under my breath, put the key back in and turned it again.

Nothing.

Debra Murphy

Mr M came into the van and took over. He turned the key, and Evie started immediately. What was all that about?

Now I had a double dilemma: I didn't have enough diesel for the return trip to Perth. Should I stop on the way and risk Evie deciding not to start again for me, or would I head straight to Struans? I decided that as I had Green Flag cover, if Evie refused to start once I'd stopped to put diesel in, I could phone Green Flag, and they could then take me to Struans. I could leave Evie with them and get the train home if they needed to keep her overnight.

I pulled into the services easily (very easily, Mr M!), unlocked the fuel cap and put £50 of diesel in. I remember a time when paying that amount of money at the service station would see the fuel tank topped right up in a car. It's scary how much diesel Evie needs and how expensive it is.

Evie behaved perfectly and had stopped her non-starting nonsense, and another twenty minutes later, she was parked at Struans. I reported the non-starting again and admitted that swearing had worked. They assured me they would check this out, but intermittent faults were difficult to find.

With the complementary taxi service, I was soon in Perth, with my first stop being the local library. What a lovely, calm place. It doesn't matter which library you find yourself in; there is always an air of peace, a desk waiting for you and, at Perth, a coffee machine. So, surrounded by books and armed with a coffee, I spent the next two hours writing, checking emails and relaxing before heading off for a walk towards the river.

That week, Perth was hosting one of the cycling world championship events, and there were road closures throughout the city, reminding me just how much I longed to get back out on my bike. My frozen shoulder was getting a little better – more cold than frozen now. All being well, before the end of the year, I'd be having a winter solo trip in Evie and taking my bike with me.

CAMPERVAN CAPERS

Mr M had packed me a butty with the last of his new sourdough bread creation, and I enjoyed this in the park by the riverside. Still awaiting the phone call from Struans, I took a stroll into the city centre for a coffee and cake. I can find any excuse for cake.

Evie was ready by mid-afternoon with four lovely new tyres and fully serviced. Struans couldn't find any problem with the starter motor but recommended that her brake pads and discs be cleaned and changed at her MOT in March. She was now fit and ready for a new adventure.

Chapter 37

A Trip To The Seaside – August 2023

Ayr Craigie Gardens Caravan and Motorhome Club Site, Ayr, Scotland

With my aim to have a trip away in Evie every month, I'm always thinking about where I'll be going next. August had been a busy month, with book launches, network meetings and having Minnie staying with us for a week.

When we were deciding which campervan to buy, one of the must-haves was a bench seat with fitted seatbelts so that I could take my two grandchildren away with me. I've not managed this yet, as they are still just babies; Minnie is four, and Harley is two. Living in Halifax, they already have a long journey to get to Grandma and Grandad's house in Scotland, so further travelling might be just that step too far for them. However, during Minnie's week with us I did realise that the excitement and wonder of a campervan for a four-year-old girl is just as great when you are having your tea in it, even if it's only parked outside Grandma and Grandad's house.

Once I'd taken Minnie back home and caught up on some sleep, my mind turned to booking a trip away in Evie. I thought that I'd be brave and go further up North to try out the campsite at Camusdarach on the West Coast of Scotland near Arisaig. This campsite is situated beside one of the most magical roads you could imagine. The A830 from Fort William to Mallaig is known as 'The Road to the Isles', as it leads to the ferries crossing to the islands of Rum, Eigg and Skye. As you travel this road, some of it single track, you pass through mountains and have the most fantastic views of lochs and beaches. The main road continues past Arisaig and onto Mallaig, but I'd recommend a detour along the alternative coastal route on the B8008. This is single track, and the most amazing road I've ever travelled. It twists, dips, and rises, but from memory, I knew it was wide enough for Evie, and it had plenty of passing places. Arisaig to Mallaig on this road is about twelve miles, but I remember cycling this, and it taking such a long time as I kept having to stop and look at the ever-widening views. It seemed like every time I freewheeled down one dip and flew up the next rise, the beaches seemed to be getting whiter and the sea more turquoise. It really did look like a scene from the Mediterranean.

Of course, cycling this road is very different to driving along it in a campervan. In my mind, I thought that if I booked and paid for the campsite, I couldn't then run scared of this road as it's the only one you can use to get to the site.

Alas, the only time I could manage to have a few nights away landed right in the middle of the last bank holiday in August. This site was fully booked, and my plans were thwarted. I can assure you that I will be having an adventure in Evie at Camusdarach in the foreseeable future.

I spent the next few days looking for other sites, but even my trusty Blair Castle Caravan Park was fully booked. Heck, I was beginning to think I would have to take a leaf out of Minnie's book and spend a few nights staying in Evie outside the house!

Fortunately, I was able to book a four-night stay at the Ayr Craigie Gardens Caravan and Motorhome Club Site. This was a new site for me, so I looked at the website to check that I could get a hardstanding pitch with an electric hook-up. Being a member of the Caravan and Motorhome Club gets me a discount at their sites, which is always a good thing. I'm still at the stage where I want to have a hard-standing pitch, as I know how quickly a nice, solid grass pitch can turn into a squelchy mud bath. It's a bit more difficult hammering the pegs for the awning into the hard ground, but well worth it for my own peace of mind.

Mr M, the camping hater, has been with me on every trip this year so far, so I informed him that I had booked a trip, and he could decide whether he wanted to come along or not. I told him that it was totally fine for him to say that he wanted to stay at home as I would be taking Florence to the beach, writing more of my book and doing some crocheting (I had a blue dinosaur to finish for Harley).

It probably took Mr M a whole three minutes to decide he would let me have this trip alone. I was a little surprised at how quickly he made his mind up and didn't seem at all bothered that I'd be away for four days.

"I think I'll go to the horse racing with Danny on Friday and Monday," he said, smiling.

This month, we decided that we were going to get back to doing more home cooking and baking. Mr M had been trying to make sourdough bread using his own sourdough starter. It's a bit like watching something out of *Alien* as this strange mixture of flour, water and grapes ferments in a glass jar on the kitchen worktop, eventually providing enough raising agent for the bread without the need to use yeast. We have had some exceedingly nice loaves, but for me, sourdough is not my first choice of bread.

"Could you make me a wholemeal loaf to take away with me, please," I asked pleadingly.

And the following day, there it was, my own wholemeal loaf sitting on the cooling rack, looking splendid, waiting to go into the freezer, ready for my trip away.

CAMPERVAN CAPERS

I made some Quiche Lorraine and added a couple of pieces of these to my freezer stash. Home-made gingernuts and caramel shortbread were already in the freezer, so I was well on my way to being already packed food-wise.

Mr M is my personal shopper. I know. Spoiled. But I know and admit to it, which makes it OK in my mind.

Four nights' meals needed – quiche, chicken breast, omelette and fish and chips at the seafront was my menu.

I told you a couple of chapters back that in the awning, I've been using some foam floor squares that fit together like a jigsaw, which work quite well to keep your toes warmer in the tent and add a bit of comfort. But these are a bit of a faff having to fix them all together and then take them apart and re-pack them into their bags. They also take up quite a bit of space. Space is always tight in the van. I'd been looking at what other people use in their awnings, and I seemed to be the only one using this jigsaw system. Most appeared to have lovely-looking carpets of a fashion.

I did some research and found one that would fit my awning tent, was not too ridiculously high priced, and promised to offer warmth and comfort, while packing away into its own bag at the end of the trip. The one I chose was from Leisure Outlet. I ordered this and hoped that it would arrive before my trip to Ayr for me to try out. I did, of course, leave the foam jigsaw pieces in the van, just in case.

The carpet arrived, and it looked OK to me. It's not as thick as the foam jigsaw, but it's nice and comfy and certainly would take up much less space in the van when not in use.

One of the things you need to check when you book a campsite is what time you can arrive at the site. I did think this was a bit overkill by the site owners. However, I've now realised that it's necessary to avoid a long trail of campervans, motorhomes and caravans arriving at the campsite at the same time and causing a traffic jam on what is usually a small road leading to the site.

Debra Murphy

I could arrive after 1 pm. Google Maps told me it would take me just over an hour. So, my plan was to leave home at 11.45 am, drive at the now standard 50 mph to conserve diesel and, well, just have a stress-free journey.

The site is just outside Ayr, meaning most of my trip would be on the motorway – M8 and M77. No problem. I've driven these motorways many times, but I was taken quite by surprise how nervous I felt driving along the M80 and then the M8. Usually, I don't panic at all. I know exactly when to swap lanes for the motorways merging, when to jump lanes for the never-ending roadworks and lane closures on the M8 heading towards the Kingston Bridge, and I can keep an eye on what all the other drivers are doing by watching my mirrors. Driving Evie, that view from the mirrors is restricted, and the rearview mirror only gives limited sight. The wing mirrors are good, but not for those drivers who don't understand that if they drive so close to the van in front that they can't see the wing mirrors, then the driver of the van can't see them. Swapping lanes, I felt I was taking my life into my own hands, and I was mightily relieved once I had left the busy M8 and joined the quieter M77.

Despite the heavy rain showers that seemed to follow me from Kirkintilloch, the rest of the journey was quite pleasant. That was until I reached, according to my satnav, my destination. Only I hadn't. What was I to do? It's not like you can just pull in at the side of the road with a campervan like you can in a small Yaris car. So, I did the only thing I could. I continued along the road to the next roundabout, praying that I would not find myself on a single-track road, but then I reminded myself that my plan had been to drive on the Road to the Isles. I told myself to get a grip and, at the next roundabout, retraced my tracks. There, hidden at a small junction, was the Caravan and Motorhome site sign, with the notice underneath that the road was now closed. Eventually, I did find my way to

CAMPERVAN CAPERS

the correct road, and for the first time since Evie came into our lives, I had to queue to check in at a site. Of course, by now, I was bursting for the toilet. I was about five vehicles down the line, so I jumped out and asked the van control man in his yellow jacket if I could nip to the toilet.

"No! You will have to wait until you have checked in or use the toilet in your own van," he gruffly told me.

Not the best of welcomes, then! Of course, the beauty of Evie is that she does indeed have a toilet, so I gave the keys to Florence and told her to keep an eye on things as I did what I needed to do.

The queue quickly vanished, and whose van was holding everyone up? Yes, the Adria Twin with the Yorkshire lass using the toilet and the Border Collie holding the keys. The shame!

We were soon checked in and told we could pick any pitch as they were all hard-standing and large enough for our van and an awning. I knew the pitches on this site were hard-standing EHU, which means they have electricity, but the water is not next to the pitch. So, I chose a pitch not a million miles away from the shower blocks, water and chemical waste disposal for the toilet.

I was rather pleased with myself that I reversed Evie into the pitch slap bang between the two white posts. Go me!

With Evie parked, I checked if she was level or whether I needed to use the dreaded levelling blocks. Nope, we were as level as we needed to be, so no need for the stress of the blocks.

Next was the electricity. I always try to do this first so that the fridge can then start to cool down, ready to transfer the food from the cool box to the fridge and freezer compartment. I know that some people set off and drive with their fridges working on the 12 v or, even more scary, with the fridge working on the gas. I'd rather wait until I arrive, get the fridge working and then sort the food. If you don't open the cool box and there are plenty of ice blocks in there, it's usually OK, especially if you have some frozen food in there as well.

At every other campsite I've stayed at, connecting to the electricity has been simple. Just plug one end of your cable into the campervan socket and the other end into the power tower with your pitch number on it. You can't get the ends the wrong way around as they are like a computer, the leads only go in one way. Today, I plugged both ends of my cable in and waited for the green light to appear on the indicator board in the van.

Nothing.

I took them out again and put them back in. If it had been a computer, I'd have turned it off and on again.

Still nothing.

I asked the lady in a pitch near me if there was anything I had to do, and she advised me I had to turn the whole fitting clockwise to make the connection. She also told me that they had arrived the night before and had to spend the whole night with no EHU because they couldn't get it to work.

I shuggled it, and turned it clockwise (checking that I was not turning my incorrect left-handed way), but still nothing. I asked the person on the other side of me if he had any suggestions. He came along and gave it a good old twist.

"You just need to be firm with these things," he told me.

The green light on my panel was now shining brightly. I had electricity, and the fridge was finally working.

Usually, the next thing to do would be to connect the water and fill the tank with fresh water, but this was not a fully serviced pitch, so I didn't have water next to my van. The sensible thing would have been to find the motorhome service point and put some water in Evie there, but I never remembered in time, and once I had amazed myself with my reversing and finally connected the electricity, I wasn't going to move Evie again until I was going home. There was only Florence and me, so we didn't need a lot of water. The watering can would allow me to fill the tank up sufficiently for our needs.

From our last trip, I knew we still had a tiny leak from the pipe under the sink in the bathroom. I needed to work out how to get to the back of the sink unit, and that's still under investigation. This meant that we couldn't turn the water boiler on for hot water, as to get the water running through the boiler again, you need to turn both the bathroom tap and the kitchen tap on. For the moment, I was using the site facilities to do the washing up and using bottled water for brushing my teeth and handwashing in the bathroom.

Without any need for hot water, the only water needed is to flush the toilet. Remember the subtitle of the book, *Have You Turned the Water On?* With just me in the van (Florence doesn't use the toilet), five watering cans of fresh water took the water level up to the second mark on the water level indicator, which would probably suffice for the whole trip. Of course, this needs sorting before the colder months when standing washing up at an outside sink might not be so much fun. Mind you, the site sinks are much bigger than Evie's, with ample space and lots of hot water. So, who knows, I might still use them and just wear an extra jumper.

The next job was to put the drive away awning up. I decided that I was going to time myself and see how close I could get to the 20-minute assembly by one person stated by the manufacturers. I'm reasonably confident putting this up now, and I'm not even sure I want to put myself under time pressure. I have my way now and, without the assistance of Mr M, I can simply work my way through the task undaunted.

I now know that the trick is to have the awning laid out in roughly the position you will peg it down. Make sure you have the canvas the right way round, so the inside of the drive away tunnel is facing the ground. Then, it's just a matter of winding out the van's canopy so that it's low enough for me to reach to slide the awning beading onto the groove of the canopy. On my awning, there are two sets of beading to choose from, depending on the groove in your canopy frame. I put the legs of the canopy down to take the strain off it whilst I feed the awning onto it. Once the awning is all the way along the canopy frame, I wind the canopy back up, leaving it out about six inches to stop the awning from catching when I open and close the van's sliding door. I don't think this is supposed to happen, but it does on mine, despite being assured I have purchased the correct size, and this adaptation works for me.

With the awning attached to the canopy, I inflated the two air poles, and the awning suddenly took shape. If this is what the manufacturers deem as putting the drive away awning up in 20 minutes, then I can do this easily. It's the peg hammering that takes the time, especially on a hard-standing pitch.

Do you remember a couple of chapters ago when I was rolling up the awning and found myself wrapping a field mouse up? Well, that mouse might not have been in the awning very long, but it had certainly made the most of its time in there. As the awning took shape, I noticed holes in the bottom of the canvas in one corner. With some trepidation, I looked all around the awning. Thankfully, the mouse had only nibbled one corner at the bottom and some of the ground sheet. Nothing that can't be repaired. I did call it several names that can't be repeated here. I could only think what a disaster it would have been if I hadn't seen the mouse as I wrapped it up in the awning. No doubt the awning would have been totally destroyed and the mouse dead.

In no time at all, the awning was standing proud and all the pegs and guy ropes well and truly hammered into the ground. I proudly unwrapped my new awning carpet and placed this inside the tent. Much quicker to put down than the jigsaw sponge pieces. It was certainly comfy underfoot but not as thick as the foam pieces. Would this be sufficient in winter? Only time would tell.

Ninety minutes later, I was sitting in the awning having a well-earned drink and homemade gingernuts, admiring my handiwork and listening to the rain as it began to patter on the tent. Perfect timing.

CAMPERVAN CAPERS

Florence is now finding her own feet as our Border Collie daughter. I'm not sure if she thinks she's a human yet, but she certainly has some of Beatrix's endearing traits. One of these habits is that she likes her tea (dinner for anyone not in Yorkshire) at a certain time. 5 pm, to be precise. Then she likes to go to the park with Dad (Mr M) to play with her friends at exactly 6 pm.

Just as you do with human children, I wanted to make sure Florence would enjoy her mini-break in Evie. I opened up a tin of sardines for her, mixed these with some of her lovely, dried food and gave her some fresh water—a meal fit for a princess. Then I went to find her somewhere to play. Just outside the campsite, I found a suitable park far enough away from any roads so that Florence could spend a good half hour playing catch with her ball. It's not something I usually do, but as Mr M was not there, I took on this important role. Once Florence had noticed the hundreds of squirrels watching our game, I knew it was time to head back to the van.

Tea for me tonight was homemade Quiche Lorraine, potato wedges and baked beans. The air fryer worked its magic, and I only had to use the gas to warm the beans.

It's always exciting the first night on a new site getting to know where everything is and where are the best walks from the site. Finding a spotlessly clean (if a little dated) shower block, along with dishwashing facilities, was tonight's highlight.

Another consideration that might be of importance to you is whether the campsite has internet and if so, do you have to pay for it. Ayr Craigie Gardens might not be the most up-to-date campsite, but it does have a very reliable and free internet connection. So, emails and access to my OneDrive to save my writing are not a problem. I do wonder why not all sites can offer free internet. I'm quite paranoid about losing my writing and always save to my OneDrive, to my computer, to an external hard drive, and then I also email a copy to myself.

Debra Murphy

With both our teas finished and the washing up taken care of, we went for the final walk of the night. Back at the van, the curtains were closed, the lights on, and it was time to relax with a bit of writing, a bowl of porridge for my supper and a teeth chew for Florence because she doesn't like to brush hers.

Then it was off to bed. Oh, the joy of being able to stretch out in a double bed. Obviously, I miss Mr M when I'm away without him, but a whole bed to yourself really is a treat sometimes.

For the first time since getting Evie, I had a disturbed night with drunken people shouting at 4 am. It sounded like they were walking right past the van. We survived, though, and Florence allowed me to have a little lie-in until 6.45 am. Talking with other campers about this, they told me that although it sounds like they are on the site, the revellers had not even been in the camp.

Holidays in Evie seem to follow the same pattern for me. Get woken up by the dog, go for a morning walk, come back to the van, feed the dog, make the bed and put the plastic coverings over the bed to create an extra workspace without getting the bedding dirty or wet. Then, amble down to the shower block and return to the van refreshed and in clean clothes. Breakfast, make a picnic for lunch and a flask of tea (even if you don't know what your plans are for the day), and wash up. Then maybe it's time for another cup of tea and a biscuit while you plan what you will do that day. Bliss.

Of course, this campsite is in Ayr, and I was keen to visit the lovely Ayr Beach. Google Maps told me it was a 25-minute walk. I decided that my sore feet could manage that, and I'd be able to have a rest at the beach before having to walk back home.

What I hadn't anticipated was the unpleasant walk to the town centre. That's what happens if you don't check the location of the campsite out fully before booking. I now know that this site, lovely as it is, sits in a residential area recognised for its social deprivation. It's the first site I've stayed on where I have felt uncomfortable walking in the surrounding area. That's not me judging people, by the way. It's just an honest reflection of how I felt that day.

As I followed Google Maps, I first took a little path through a tiny, wooded area alongside the site. I was unnerved by a white car parked in the middle of the track. I've obviously read too many crime thriller books, and my mind was working in overdrive as to why the car was there, where the driver was, and whether Florence would be able to protect me like Beatrix would have done.

Once past that section, it was then through a dark underpass to get across the busy main road. Yep, my mind was wandering again. Florence didn't like it either and was walking with her ears pinned back, her stomach nearly on the ground and her tail between her legs. When your Border Collie is uncomfortable, it makes you nervous, I can tell you.

I passed quite a few people who were under the influence of alcohol or drugs, possibly both, and a pub with more inebriated people, smoking what was clearly not just tobacco, standing outside.

Finally, I reached the town centre and knew that I was once again safe. The last stretch to the beach is a pleasant walk (despite my now sore feet). Ayr Beach is amazing. It seems to stretch for miles. On a good day, you are spoiled with beautiful views of Ailsa Craig, the Isle of Arran and Pladda.

My first task was to go to the toilet before going down to the beach. The public conveniences only accepted contactless card payments, which, thankfully, I had with me. Gone are the days when you used to spend a penny! But what would I do with Florence? Being such a beautiful Border Collie, I was worried that if I tied her up outside the toilets, I would come back out to find that she had disappeared. So, I took her into the toilets with me. There were some strange looks, I can tell you. The next time you see somebody taking their dog into the toilets with them, just remember that they might not have anyone to look after the dog. You wouldn't leave your human baby outside the toilets, would you?

Toilet adventure over, I then found myself a quiet spot on the beach up against the sea wall and plonked myself down. Florence was beside herself, seeing all the open space and knowing I had her ball and thrower with me. Of course, just as anyone who knows me would expect, my rucksack had everything I needed. A blanket to sit on, a towel to dry my feet and dog, a picnic, a flask of tea, hand sanitiser, water, treats and black poo bags for Florence. I also remembered to bring my swimming shoes to wear because now, even the ridges in the sand made by the tide are sore on my feet.

Then, it was time to let Florence run wild. I threw the ball, she ran, brought it back and dropped it at my feet, over and over again. There is nothing more satisfying than watching a Border Collie running along a beach, collecting their ball, bringing it back to you and dropping it at your feet, smiling at you. Yes, Border Collies do smile.

Of course, Florence was still only a puppy, so I had to limit how long she ran for. Once I'd decided she was sufficiently tired, I popped her lead back on, and we returned to our picnic spot. Sitting propped up against the sea wall, enjoying a banana sandwich, a homemade caramel slice, a flask of hot tea, and watching the clouds skip along the sky across the Isle of Arran was just the most sublime experience. To share this moment with my new best friend, Florence, just added to the joy.

Walking back to the campsite was not quite so much fun as my feet had decided they had walked quite far enough. I think I may have been crying by the time I reached Evie. Tea was soon on the go – homemade Quiche Lorraine again tonight – and Florence was tucking into another tin of sardines. Creatures of habit, the pair of us!

CAMPERVAN CAPERS

It wasn't long before Florence was tapping on my leg to let me know it was 6 pm and time to go and play. She doesn't understand about sore feet! So, with a couple of paracetamol tablets taken and some painkilling gel rubbed into my feet, I was once again playing ball with Florence in the nearby park. The joys of being owned by a Border Collie puppy.

Before too long, we were back and enjoying a well-earned supper in the tent awning as I did some more writing. I'm not a lover of porridge pots at home, preferring the real deal of slow-cooked porridge oats, but somehow, having a porridge pot in the campervan seems like a treat.

With the washing up done and our teeth cleaned, we were ready for bed. I'm pleased to say that we had a peaceful night with no drunken singing and shouting from passing strangers.

Despite my painful feet from the day before, I decided I'd have another day at the beach. After the usual early start, breakfast, and then shower, I spent the next hour or so writing. Then, with picnic and flask made up and rucksack packed with beach essentials, we trudged our way back down the unscenic route to Ayr Beach. It's perhaps just because this beach is so beautiful that I was prepared to make this unpleasant journey again so that we could once more enjoy a beach afternoon.

I didn't have to do much ball throwing for Florence as a young family was so taken with her that they spent an hour playing with her and throwing the ball.

After another long and painful crawl back from the beach, tea was a bit late, but Florence didn't really seem to mind as she was still tired from the beach adventure. She tucked into another tin of sardines, and I set about making roast chicken for myself in the air fryer. Of course, Florence had some roast chicken for her pudding.

After just a little runaround tonight and all our usual tasks completed, I settled down to do some writing but decided that an early night was required, so I was soon tucked up in bed with my book.

Debra Murphy

The last full day of my trip soon arrived. With the usual routine played out, Florence was back under the table enjoying a snooze, and I was taking time to proof-listen to some tracks for the audio version of my book, *Beatrix The Time Travelling Collie*, sent to me by my producer. Aiming to concentrate fully on these, I was listening to them wearing my headphones. It was a blissful time. Of course, tea and biscuits were involved. You can't concentrate without them, can you?

As I was sitting there, I started to think about the rest of the day. What would I do? Could my feet cope with another walk into Ayr to take Florence to the beach for one last play? Was the awning going to dry out today so that I could put it away tonight? Rain had been forecast for the next day.

I chuckled to myself as I was once again reminded that I had now joined the ranks of the weather watchers. There was a time when I didn't care what the weather would be like. If it rained, I'd put a jacket on; if it were cold, I'd wrap up well; and if it were hot and sunny, I'd pray for winter. But now I am the owner of a drive away awning, the weather forecast for the day of departure and the day before has become very important. If rain is forecast for departure day, and the evening before is dry, then packing the awning away is planned for the day before departure day.

My plan for the day was sorted. I'd spend the morning listening to audio tracks and writing, and then, despite my still-sore feet, I'd waddle my way to the beach for Florence to have one last play. As a special treat, I'd decided that I'd get fish and chips at the seafront for a late dinner (lunch if you don't live in Yorkshire), then spend the rest of the afternoon on the beach before returning to the site and putting away what should be a dry awning.

But best-laid plans and all that. I consulted Google Maps and found a different route into Ayr centre, avoiding the less salubrious area and dark, scary underpass. Unfortunately, this

CAMPERVAN CAPERS

involved walking along the path beside the busy main road. Florence is a very timid dog when it comes to noise, so the walk was proving stressful for her. As we walked past the train station, and she could both see and hear the trains, she was almost crying, to say nothing of how much she was dragging me along behind her. It wasn't long before I thought about joining in with the crying, as my feet were so painful despite wearing the expensive rocker-toe shoes as advised by my podiatrist. This was not how I had envisaged our last day at Ayr. Undeterred, I told Florence we would get fish and chips at the seafront, let my feet rest a little, and then she could still have a play on the beach.

Right on the seafront is the Pavilion Cafe, with a big sign drawing me to it with the lure of takeaway fish and chips, with seats outside. Win-win situation. But standing in the queue, I saw another person taking their dog into the restaurant. What the heck, I thought. So, Florence and I went into the restaurant and found the last remaining table for two in a corner. I was able to sit down, and Florence could relax after her stressful walk. By the time I'd ordered my fish and chips, Florence was sleeping like a baby on the floor beside me. I sent a pathetic WhatsApp message to Mr M, telling him that my feet were making me cry and that I was going to find a taxi to take us back to the campsite. Mr M sent a laughing face back to me. He was clearly concerned about my well-being!

I tell you, those were the best fish and chips I'd had in a long time. Lashings of vinegar in the mushy peas, a sprinkling of salt on my chips, and a hot skinny latte. The restaurant was jumping, but we were comfy in the corner, and nobody bothered us. By the time I'd finished my meal, most of the tables were empty, so I didn't feel quite so guilty spending so long at my table.

By this time, Florence had woken up and was getting lots of cuddles from the staff and customers, who thought she was just the most beautiful, well-behaved, cute dog they had ever seen. It was quite some time later before we left the restaurant, after ordering more drinks and cake.

I did, of course, let Florence have a play on the beach, although I was quite alarmed at the ginormous jellyfish dotted along the beach. A woman standing next to me reliably informed me that some were harmless and that most were dead by the time they were out of the water. She was quite pleased with herself when she found a Lion's Mane jellyfish, pointing out the long tentacles that looked like a mane, hence the name.

I didn't know much about jellyfish, so I had to go and research this Lion's Mane species. Well, Mr Google says these can have tentacles up to three metres in length, which can give a very nasty sting. The tentacles should be removed with tweezers (because everyone carries those on a day trip to the beach, don't we!), and then the area rinsed with hot water. So, at Ayr Beach, I guess you're doomed, as I'm sure I never saw any hot water stations on the beach next to the jellyfish. I'd be thinking of getting some medical attention if I'd been stung by this beast.

Even more alarming was that Mr Google told me that bits from the tentacles can sting you even once they are no longer attached to the jellyfish.

And are you reading this, the seemingly knowledgeable woman on the beach? They can sting long after they have been out of the water!

Don't think you are safe if you go to other UK seaside towns; these can be found at many of our beaches in the summer months. Watch out!

My perfect beach had just been spoiled! Now I'd be a bit hesitant to go swimming in the sea along the Ayrshire coast. It seems that most years, a variety of jellyfish, some harmless and some that might sting you, find their way to the beaches here. Reading Mr Google again, I found a local news report from

CAMPERVAN CAPERS

2017 that told of an invasion of jellyfish on Ayr beach. The photos of these massive creatures looked like seals from a distance. I know that we have to recognise that jellyfish have just as much right as us to be on the beaches of our country (probably even more because they actually need to live in the sea), but it's still a scary prospect that you might stand on one or get one wrapped around your leg going for a paddle or a swim in the sea. Or am I being overdramatic?

I won't bore you with the long, painful walk back to the campsite, but you can imagine. Eventually, I was back at Evie. It wasn't raining, the awning was dry, and I didn't need to cook tea.

After enjoying a cup of tea, I set about the task of taking down the awning. This meant removing everything that seemed to have meandered its way out of Evie into the awning over the last few days. The table had to go first because this was the first thing to go in the garage. Everyone will have their own way of packing their van. I have mine. Of course, it's not quite as simple as that because the awning usually sits in the aisle by the bed when we are travelling, but with another night remaining of our holiday, there is no room for the awning inside the habitation part of the van. It has to go in the garage for the night. Everything else is packed around it, and the things that usually pack snugly in the garage had to be shoved into the cab of the van in front of the two seats. That evening, it didn't really matter as there was only me, so I just plonked stuff on the seats.

Still stuffed from my fish and chips, there was no need for tea, but Florence still needed a last play in the park with the ball. There was definitely a sense of autumn creeping in, as it was already starting to get dark by 8 pm. Florence struggled a little to see the ball, and we cut the playtime short and headed back to the comfort of the cosy but packed van for some well-earned supper.

Walking back to the van from the shower block, my eyes were drawn to the motorhome service point. This is where you can fill up your van with fresh water and, at the end of your trip, drive your van over the grate to empty your grey waste water (from your sinks, not your toilet!) and release any unused fresh water. I've only done this once before, emptying my grey waste water at the site in Coniston last year. So far, I've not been brave enough to empty the fresh water tank. Why? Because you have to take the top off the bench seat and unscrew a massive cap. Nothing too scary there. But then you have to put your hand into the tank and reach down and pull out the bung to release the water. I know it's not going to harm me, but I just can't bring myself to do it. Mr M always does this for me because he knows I'm scared of doing it. I was hoping to find some courage to do this dastardly deed myself. Can't you just feel the nightmares lined up for me that night!

Departure day. I like to just take my time getting ready to leave the campsite. Mainly because I just enjoy being away in Evie, but also because I want to make sure I have everything packed away securely so that I don't have irritating rattles as I drive home. My mind tells me that if something is rattling, it will either break or damage something it's banging against.

Looking around the campsite, it's interesting to watch the comings and goings. Who has the biggest motorhome? Who has a fancy awning? What always amazes me is the size of the televisions I can see in caravans and campervans as I walk by them. I know everyone is different. I like the quietness provided by Evie. I don't feel the need for a TV or radio – but then we don't have a TV at home either.

I was laughing to myself, watching a family who had arrived the previous evening. Mum, Dad and two teenage daughters, by the looks of things. They had a bit of a fallout about whether Dad had levelled the caravan correctly. The following morning, Dad was sitting on a chair outside the caravan, watching something on his phone, facing away from the van. One teenage daughter was sitting on another chair,

CAMPERVAN CAPERS

wrapped up in a blanket and a big hoodie, watching her mobile phone. Both were looking as miserable as sin. Clearly, a good night was had by all in that caravan.

As the morning progressed, I worked my way through all my packing-up tasks. Dog walk, breakfast, shower and washing up all finished by 9 am. Check out from the site is up to noon, so I had plenty of time.

Florence watched me carefully as I put everything back in its rightful home. We had to have another cup of tea and a biscuit because it started to rain. And I mean rain. I wasn't going to open the back doors of the van in that.

Before too long, as is the norm in Scotland, the sun was shining again and the sky blue. I quickly finished packing everything into the garage whilst it was dry.

One of the tasks that has to be done that is not enjoyed by anyone (I hope) is emptying the toilet cassette. There is no getting away from the fact that you are now emptying out in the sluice all the stuff you have expelled from your body over the last day or so. That's why we have the rule that unless an absolute emergency, the toilet in Evie is only to be used for a wee. Nothing else! But it has to be done. It's not as messy as you'd imagine, and you never need to touch anything nasty as there is a very handy yellow button on the cassette that releases the contents once you have positioned the exit point over the sluice. There is always a water pipe for you to add more water into the cassette to allow you to give a proper rinse out of everything that might be lurking. You will know how much you have to watch for. It's not like anyone else will have been using your toilet.

I always go armed with disposable cloths and plenty of antibacterial wipes to wipe any water splashes. Honestly, if you do this correctly, there should be none of the cassette contents landing anywhere near you.

Of course, with this being a solo adventure, I had no Mr M with me to do this. You learn just to get on with things. I guess if you really can't bear the idea of having to empty your own toilet cassette, then campervan life is not for you.

I had a bit of a panic because I had to leave the site by noon, but the shower block (and toilets) was closed from 10.30 am to noon for cleaning. I guess there is never a convenient time for the cleaning to be done. There will always be somebody who wants to use the facilities when they are closed. I decided that the best thing to do was to have my roast chicken sandwich and a cup of tea and watch the world go by, and then use the facilities before heading along the motorway back home. It might mean being a few minutes late leaving, but then that wouldn't be my fault, would it? I wasn't using the toilet in Evie now I'd just cleaned it all.

Eating my sandwich, I remembered that I had to empty the water tank. Looking towards the motorhome service point, I could see that the man in his motorhome, right alongside the big grate on the floor, was now sitting in his chair, relaxing, looking straight at the service point. That was too much for me. I couldn't face having to manoeuvre the van over the grate (even though it's huge) and then do the hand thing in the scary tank.

"I'll do it when we get home, and Dad's there to supervise me," I told Florence, giving her some of my roast chicken.

Eventually, the toilet blocks were once again open. After I'd made use of the facilities for one last time, we were off. I even managed, without mishap, to drive Evie right up to the exit barrier and swipe the fob to let me out of the site without having to get out of Evie. Go me!

My trusty sat-nav guided me back out of Ayr and onto the A77 towards Glasgow. I was reassured that my driving skills were improving as I felt much more relaxed on the journey home. That was until, with a sudden panic, I remembered I'd not turned the gas off in the back of Evie, but now I was on the motorway, I couldn't just pull in. I spent the

CAMPERVAN CAPERS

rest of the journey wondering if I really needed to turn the gas off and what was the worst that could happen if I didn't.

Safely home, the first thing I did was turn the gas off. Mr M was quick to inform me of exactly what could happen if I had an accident and the gas still been left on. I think I'll put a little note on the steering wheel for future journeys.

As for the water tank, I took the bench seat apart, unscrewed the big cap and looked down into the water and the stopper waiting to be pulled out. Could I do it? No! Don't ask me why this is causing me so much stress and fear. Mr M watched me for a while before pushing me to one side and telling me he'd do it for me.

Next time, I'll do it.

Chapter 38

Beaten By Storm Babet – October 2023
Tyndrum Holiday Park, Tyndrum, Scotland

I'd sulked through September as I'd let my friend borrow Evie, resulting in my only free week for travels being Evie-less. I realised that, although it's nice to be nice, I had spent all my money buying Evie to give me the freedom to take random, unplanned trips away at the drop of a hat. It made me feel a bit selfish, but I can tell you honestly that Evie will never again go on holiday without me!

October had turned into a strange month. I was desperate to get a trip away, but life kept getting in the way. Trips from September onwards were now solo adventures as Mr M felt the cold in the van too much to enjoy autumn and winter exploits. And trust me, if one of you is not enjoying your stay in a small van, neither of you is enjoying your stay!

I'd just started a part-time job, with the initial training being two weeks from 9 am to 5.30 pm. Some nights, I was lucky to see 8 pm before my bed was calling me. It would also be our 18th wedding anniversary on the 8th of October and my birthday on the 18th, and I knew Mr M would be disappointed if he couldn't celebrate with me.

I wanted to go somewhere I'd not taken Evie before. Work had settled back down to part-time hours, and I could

CAMPERVAN CAPERS

plan a short weekend break from Saturday to Monday. With only two nights away, it needed to be somewhere that didn't involve hours of driving. After an extensive search on the internet, I found a holiday park at Tyndrum, between Crianlarich and Glencoe. After investigating a little deeper, I decided this looked like an idyllic site. It was within walking distance of the Green Welly Stop, which is always a great place to visit.

On our last trip to Blair Atholl, I met a lovely woman with a small campervan, and we soon got chatting about this and that. Of course, having dogs always seems to draw like-minded people together. Before too long, we'd connected on the magical (sometimes) Facebook and arranged tea and cake meetings. Vicky was a more seasoned solo campervanner than me, and I mentioned my planned trip to Tyndrum.

"Oh, that's a lovely site. Shall I come along and join you?" she asked.

And that was it; a stranger in a small campervan with a dog named Shadow became a friend.

I soon had myself booked at the Highland Holiday Park, at Tyndrum, from Saturday 21st October until Monday 23rd. Vicky would go up on Friday until Sunday morning, meaning we could have a good catch-up, but we would both still be able to enjoy some solitude.

That week, Mr M did the checks on Evie for me. He ensured the tyre pressures were as they should be and disconnected the mains cable that we keep Evie attached to outside our house. I've said before that I wasn't entirely sure that being constantly connected to the mains electricity was necessary, but it does ensure that the electronic bug deterrent is always operational. Hopefully, that would keep away any pests who might think Evie is a nice, snug place to move into and have snacks on her wires.

Unfortunately, Storm Babet decided to visit parts of Scotland, including Tyndrum, for my planned getaway weekend.

Debra Murphy

On Friday the 20th, after reports of severe flooding and even, sadly, a death caused by the flood water, I decided that it was a stupid idea to even consider going away whilst Storm Babet was anywhere near. Vicky had the same idea, and we both changed our booking to the following weekend when the weather should be much better. The friendly man I spoke to at the campsite could not have been more helpful when I phoned to see if I could change the dates. He was only too pleased to have one less campervan to worry about on the site as, in his words,

"It's wild. Just wild here."

Storm Babet devastated parts of Scotland on a scale that had never been seen before. Roads were washed away, bridges destroyed, and towns flooded, with Brechin in Angus bearing the brunt of the floodwater. We escaped the worst in Kirkintilloch, but I did have a pretty scary drive home from work from Larbert on the day the storm hit. The motorway was awash with surface water, and I seemed to be the only driver slowing down to cope with the driving conditions! By sheer luck, I managed to creep along the road into Kirkintilloch, wondering if floodwater would reach the engine in my tiny car and leave me stranded. I drove as slowly as possible, remembering that you are advised not to make any ripples in the water. I was mightily relieved once I got home and was cuddled up to a hot cup of tea. I was equally glad I'd decided not to risk the trip to Tyndrum.

The sky became bright again once the storm eased, and I think we even had a day of sunshine. The week passed quickly, and I looked forward to my trip up north on Saturday.

I've never really watched the weather forecast, but now I check regularly for places where I'm due to take Evie. Searching for Tyndrum for the coming weekend, I was alarmed to see that a new yellow weather warning had crept in for rain across parts of Stirlingshire. But nothing was flagged for Tyndrum.

CAMPERVAN CAPERS

Over the week, I gathered the few clothes I thought I'd need, including waterproof trousers, a jacket, gloves and a hat. It might be a wet weekend, but I'd be warm and dry.

For me, planning for a break is part of the enjoyment. I love thinking about what clothes to pack, how many meals I'd need and what books, crochet or writing I'd take.

I'd arranged with Vicky that we would treat ourselves to fish and chips for tea on Saturday evening at the Real Food Cafe close to the campsite, so I only needed one other meal. Mr M had already made me some of his scrummy lasagne, so I was sorted. A couple of porridge pots, some milk, hot cross buns, bread, butter, cheese, biscuits, and Cadbury Dairy Milk, and I had all my meals planned.

Saturday, the 28th, as I was leaving from Larbert at 1 pm after work, I was up at the crack of dawn, had breakfast and packed my food into the cool box to go into Evie. I wanted to leave home early enough to take my time driving to work, get parked and have a cup of tea before starting work at 9 am. Leaving the house at 7 am, I was alarmed to realise that I'd never driven Evie in the dark before. I'd been a passenger when Mr M had driven in the dark, but I'd never been the driver.

"You'll be fine," said Mr M, pushing me out of the door. "Just see it as a learning curve."

I guess that's a sign that there is plenty more to write about in this book, as I'm not yet a proper campervan person. The book will be finished once I can do things without panicking. At this rate, it will be as long as *War and Peace*!

The journey to Larbert was uneventful, and I had no difficulty driving in the dark. Well, Evie does have headlights, after all.

Leaving after work, I thought I'd have no problem getting onto the M9, but I put the campsite into the satnav, just to be sure. A couple of roundabouts, and I'd be on the M9 and on my way. I thought! But the exit off the roundabout to join the motorway was closed. Don't panic, Debra, I told myself. The satnav will direct you. And there are diversion signs.

Have you ever tried to follow those signs? Which way does that mean? Does it mean this way? Should I take this exit off at the next roundabout? Or not!

So, I found myself driving through Stirling, trying to find the road I knew I needed. The satnav suggested I turn around at the next roundabout and re-trace my route. This roundabout was one of those little full-stop things. Again, my skills as a campervan woman were tested. Would I get Evie around the little white spot in the road in one go? With a line of traffic behind me, I decided not to try. Then I began to worry about what the road ahead would be like. Was I heading towards a narrow road? Would it be wide enough for Evie?

What should have been a relaxed 1.5-hour journey turned into a stressful event.

Eventually, I was on a familiar road. I'd cycled along this road many times on my way to Callander, and I knew it would take me to the big roundabout that would cross over the M9 to join the A84, and then I'd be on my way.

As I settled into my now familiar route, I thought about the yellow weather warning for rain. I saw nothing to suggest that this was heading my way. The sky was not too heavy, and the sun kept popping out to say hello. I trundled through Doune, feeling like a pro when I didn't panic about the bridge that was only wide enough for one vehicle. I crept through Callander at the new 20 mph speed limit, surprised at how busy the main street was, then I remembered it was the start of the school holidays.

Leaving Callander, with no other traffic behind me, I knew I could enjoy the journey, take my time, and not feel guilty about holding up other drivers.

I've driven and cycled the road from Callander alongside Loch Lubnaig many times, and I'm never disappointed by the views. That day was no exception. The autumn tints had burst into colour. Reds, golds, yellows, and browns in so many different shades lined the route. I wanted to be a passenger and be able to soak in the views more than I could as the driver.

Through Lochearnhead and up to Glen Ogle, it was the same. Mother Nature is truly amazing. Yes, I could see lots of rainwater coming down the hills and a few places where it was clear there had been a couple of landslides recently, but it wasn't raining.

Dropping down from Glen Ogle and heading towards Crianlarich, the speed limit is 50 mph. Clearly the drivers who passed me on this road obviously thought it only applied to Evie. I can never understand why people need to speed on stretches of roads that take you through the most stunning scenery. They must drive with blinkers on and not enjoy their journey. Their stress levels must be so high, constantly driving close to the vehicle in front and looking for the next overtaking spot.

I knew the road to Tyndrum but was unsure where the campsite was. I'd examined my maps thoroughly at home the previous week many times (yes, I'm obsessed with maps) and knew it was on the left-hand side just before reaching Tyndrum. Thankfully, there were several obvious signs. On the approach to village, I took a left turn to drive down into the campsite and pulled up outside the very clearly marked checking-in bay.

I had arrived.

The woman in reception gave me my site map and directions to my allocated pitch.

I'd already decided that as it was just me on this trip, I didn't need the drive away awning, so it didn't take long to get set up. I was quite proud of how I chose to reverse into the pitch as I decided that this would be the best position for the van and ensure that the bed was almost level.

No, I'm still not confident enough to drive Evie onto the levelling blocks!

Debra Murphy

I connected the electricity, turned on the power, and switched on the fridge. My pitch was a two-minute walk from the shower block and toilets, so I figured I didn't need much water in Evie, just enough to flush the toilet if I needed the loo during the night, and I didn't want to have to get dressed to head to the shower block. Although I like to wear a pair of pyjamas to relax in the evening, my sleeping PJs are my birthday suit, and I'm sure there are laws against walking around naked in public.

I was equally pleased that I could get everything out of the back of the van when it wasn't raining.

Tyndrum Holiday Park met all my expectations. The pitches were hardstanding. I had water and electricity close by. The toilet and shower blocks were immaculate. The site was not too large, so even though it was just about full, it didn't feel crowded. Best of all, it was surrounded by trees, hills and mountains. What more did I need?

Armed with my flask of tea, I set off to find Vicky and her campervan. We were soon catching up on gossip, drinking tea, eating cake, and laughing at the yellow weather warning. I felt slightly guilty that I was being kissed and cuddled by Shadow, Vicky's dog, when I didn't have Florence with me. What would Florence think when I got home and she could smell another dog on me?

It was soon teatime, and the fish and chips started to call us, so we headed for the short five-minute walk to the restaurant.

Walking through Tyndrum, I was surprised at how this one-shop stop had grown into a thriving community. There were now hotels, pubs, the holiday park we were in, holiday lodges and several eating places. And, of course, The Green Welly Stop.

I first visited the Green Welly Stop many years ago when I travelled to Fort William from Halifax to climb Ben Nevis with a couple of friends, Sally and Julie. Three young women

CAMPERVAN CAPERS

from Yorkshire; we didn't realise at the time that this was a well-known stop. I just needed a rest from driving and some cake. Researching it more whilst writing this book, I was pleasantly surprised to find that it was 'born' the same year as me.

I'm always interested in why businesses were developed and felt that if there were ever a good place to start a new venture, Tyndrum would be the perfect spot. In 1965, Betty and Les Gosden did exactly that when they took over a six-bedroom house, post office and shop, petrol pumps and a coal business.

Why, in the middle of nowhere, was Tyndrum the perfect spot for a petrol station and cafe? Well, you can't avoid Tyndrum if you're heading North. Situated at a main road junction on the A82, travellers must pass through Tyndrum en route to Oban, Fort William, and beyond. There are two train stations, Tyndrum Upper and Tyndrum Lower, and the area is surrounded by mountains. Walkers also flock through the area as the West Highland Way long-distance walk passes through it.

At the time of writing, 58 years on (that's how old I am!), the Green Welly Stop is now a famous establishment in Scotland. Everyone who has travelled that road knows it and loves it. It's no longer just a little petrol station and cafe. There is a restaurant, cafe, petrol station, gift shop and outdoor shop. Be warned, though. Their cakes and bakes are to die for!

Vicky and I planned to have brunch in the Green Welly Stop Cafe in the morning. Needs must.

I can tell you that the fish and chips at The Real Food Cafe were delicious. And there were mushy peas, but alas, no dandelion and burdock. At home in Yorkshire, my idea of the perfect fish and chip tea is fish and chips with lashings of salt and vinegar, scraps, mushy peas and a bottle of dandelion and burdock. Scraps seem to be a thing of mystery in Scotland, mushy peas a hit or a miss, and dandelion and burdock a miracle if you can get it.

Several hours later, we left the cafe feeling full and walked the long five-minute trek back to the campsite. We chatted a while longer in Vicki's cosy van, with Shadow loving the attention of a new person, before I headed across the campsite to Evie.

There is something about getting into your own van, locking the doors, and feeling the peace in your own little space.

I was soon in my PJs and made myself a cup of tea, which, of course, had to be accompanied by a couple of digestive biscuits. The electric kettle was perfect, but I turned the heater off whilst this was boiling as I was too worried about overloading the electrics in the van. I knew that I needed to keep my usage below 2 kW. It's only a few minutes, and it avoids using your gas. Mind you, I do miss the singing of the kettle on the gas stove. I wondered if I could get a singing electric kettle.

Then it was off to bed. I was now getting used to the different lights in the van, like the flashing pest control, the fridge and the power indicators. When we first got the van, I had to cover these, but now I can switch myself off to them, and they no longer disturb my night.

What I noticed when I turned the lights off was how dark it was. I love it when I'm not surrounded by street lights or on a campsite that has lots of bright lights all around the site. I found myself opening the blind on the skylight window to see if there were any stars to watch, but it was a bit cloudy for that.

That's the sort of thing that you take time to appreciate when in the campervan. I'm not sure I'd lie in bed with the curtains open at home to see the stars. It just doesn't seem the same. Perhaps being in a campervan makes you take time to appreciate the finer things in life.

I loved being by myself in the van and certainly enjoyed having the double bed to myself, but I did miss Mr M. So, I folded up my big hoodie and put it next to me where Mr M would usually sleep, just to give me the feeling that he was there. I'd never admit this to him, though. You don't have to be lonely to miss somebody, and I'd hate him to feel he had to come along on the cold winter trips just because he thought I was lonely.

Despite the weather warnings, my first night in the campervan passed without mishaps. I was woken a couple of times by bits of branches falling around the van, but nothing too alarming. That's the drawback of a campsite surrounded by trees. They protect you from the elements, but you risk having branches and leaves finding their way onto your van roof.

The following day, after breakfast, I met up with Vicky and Shadow, and we followed a path through the park, over the wooden bridge, into the woods, and through the gold mine. Yes, there is an actual gold mine. I'm not sure you can keep any gold you find, though, and I wouldn't want to encourage you to do something that would lead to imprisonment!

We continued on the path and just took a left turn at any junctions, guessing that would eventually get us back to the site. Before too long, we had to cross a large cattle grid, but there was the usual gate for you to use, especially when walking with dogs. The path then joined the well-surfaced cycle path running from Crianlarich to Tyndrum. The views were amazing: Stob Binnein, Ben More, Beinn Odhar, Ben Lui, and many more mountains. There were a couple of benches on the way, allowing us to stop, have a breather, and take in the peace and quiet. The round trip only took us an hour. You could make your walk much longer by following the many signs for the West Highland Way.

My excitement about brunch at the Green Welly Stop was dampened somewhat when I realised it was not a dog-friendly establishment, so Shadow had to stay in his van. The nosh was very good, and I ate so much that I didn't need to cook a meal in Evie later that day.

Vicky and Shadow left for home after brunch, leaving me to enjoy the rest of my short break to myself. As I returned to the campsite, I realised that this was my first campervan experience without other humans or dogs staying with me. It really was just me and Evie.

I didn't know the hills and fells around Tyndrum all that well so that afternoon, I had a short walk following the signs for the West Highland Way. This was an easy walk, and in no way could I get lost. Again, the views were fantastic, with the mountains on Rannoch Moor tantalisingly close.

With a full tummy, tea that night was a scone from the Green Welly Stop and Cadbury Dairy Milk. I spent the evening in my perfect writing retreat and then went to bed to sleep like a baby, except for the sound of branches dropping from the trees.

The following morning, as I began to organise myself to go home, I realised that the falling branches were not actually branches; they were just millions of pine needles. Evie was covered. I knew I needed to clear them off her, especially the windscreen and the vents on the bonnet. My neighbours had a large caravan and awning, and they were equally covered in pine needles.

"Happens all the time here," the man told me, setting his hose on his caravan to wash away the needles.

"Oh, that's a good idea. I wish I'd thought of that," I said enviously, knowing that I didn't have the proper nozzle in my van to wash them off Evie.

"Here's a spare attachment. Keep it," he said, handing me what, at that precise moment, felt like a chunk of gold to me.

I was soon washing away all the pine needles from Evie but knew I'd probably still find some in five years' time.

That's why, at the moment, I choose to stay at campsites rather than wild camping. There was still so much more for me to learn, and there would usually be people around ready to lend a helping hand when needed.

CAMPERVAN CAPERS

Wait for it, though, readers. That day, I solved a problem for a couple in a campervan similar to Evie. Yes. Honestly.

The couple had parked their van near the water tap and were trying to fill their fresh water tank. I saw the water coming out of the bottom of the van as quickly as they tried to fill it.

"The frost guard's been activated," I called out to them as I washed away the last of the pine needles from Evie's windscreen.

Then I realised they were in a foreign van and didn't speak much English. After lots of hand signals and me digging out my manual from Evie to show them what I meant, we were soon able to go through their manual, find the frost release button, and sort it so they could fill up with water and continue their tour of the Highlands.

Did that take me one step closer to being a proper campervan woman?

Chapter 39

A Reflective Trip To Coniston - November 2023
Coniston Park Coppice Club Campsite, Coniston, Cumbria, England

Winter was fast approaching, and I knew that I would probably only have one more trip in Evie this year. There was only one place I wanted to go to, and that was to make a return trip to Coniston Park Coppice Club Campsite. Of course, this was going to be a trip filled with emotion. It was November last year that Beatrix and I had our first trip to this campsite. Little did I know then that those would be Beatrix's last few days before she travelled the dog rainbow bridge. But what a fabulous last few days she had in the Lake District.

It might seem strange to some readers why, a year on, both Mr M and I were still consumed with grief over the death of a dog. Until Beatrix came into our lives in 2013, I wouldn't have understood it either. But we were. We're grieving together but also alone. We still chat about Beatrix every day. I talk to her most days, and I know Mr M does, too. We both had our own special relationship with Beatrix. Mr M took her to the park to play with the ball for hours and hours. I took her up the hills and mountains. For that reason, I felt that I needed to have my own private time to grieve for Beatrix. I knew that Mr M would probably do the same whilst I was away.

CAMPERVAN CAPERS

The evening before my trip, I attended a book event and got chatting with a couple of men at my table. The conversation soon became about the dogs in our lives. I shared my tale about Beatrix and one of the men told us that he had just lost his dog and that he was still grieving. The other man, who, he told us, had just recently got his first dog, was interested in the reasons I had a new puppy.

"Did you get the puppy to replace Beatrix?" he asked.

The horror on the face of the other man matched how I felt. I explained that in no way was Florence a replacement for Beatrix, but having experienced the unconditional love of a dog, I knew I needed to feel that same kind of love again. Beatrix will never be replaced or forgotten, but I wanted to give a whole new heart load of love to a new dog.

I likened it to being a mum. When I had my son, Benjamin, I thought that I could never love anything as much as I loved him. Then I had my daughter, Chloe. Did Chloe have to share my love for her with her brother? Not at all. I have a whole pot of love for each child. Then, along came the grandchildren. They each have a whole pot of my love, too.

That's what it's like when you have a dog in your life. My heart still holds the same love for Beatrix that I had when she was here, but I now have an equally full pot of love for Florence, our new puppy. (Although she may wonder if I still love her after I found her chewing a hole in our lovely bedroom carpet).

Days off were booked from my part-time job, and I went on the internet, and before I knew it, I'd booked four nights at the Coniston Park Coppice site. That would mean three whole days without any travelling. Bliss.

Planning my break, I knew that I'd be walking into Coniston Village and down to Coniston Water to revisit the place where Beatrix had her last swim and, of course, visit the cafe where they gave her the whole sausage to eat. I also wanted to take the opportunity to do some cycling in the Lakes. Something I've not done for over twenty years.

Debra Murphy

When we got Evie, she came with a bike rack attached to her back doors. At home, we have tried putting bikes onto the rack and even purchased a waterproof cover to protect the them whilst in transit, but somehow, we never seem to get around to taking the bikes. Probably because there has usually been either Beatrix or Florence with us, but this time, I would be having a solo adventure, meaning I could take the bike with me.

I don't know about other campervan owners, but I look at bikes on the back doors of vans I pass on the road and wonder just how safe they are and whether the weight of the bikes and the carrier are putting any strain on them. I was always the same when I travelled in the past with bikes on a roof rack on a car. I'd spend most of the journey wondering if they were going to fall off, and would they, or the car, be damaged.

Discussing my worries with the very tolerant Mr M, he suggested as it would be just me, why didn't I travel with the bike inside the van? Perfect idea. I could drive with the bike in Evie, then once I was set up on the site, I could lock the bike to the rack on the back doors of the van and cover it with my new, still in the packaging, waterproof bike cover. Perfect solution.

As usual, in the few days just before departure day, I packed all my clothes for the trip, including the extra cycling essentials, and not forgetting my cycling shoes and helmet. I planned how the bike would fit nicely into the aisle between the cooker and the bathroom. I'd fasten it to the seatbelts on the bench seat with some bungee cords, and it would be as snug as a bug.

Wanting to be ready to leave the house by 10 am at the latest on departure day, I tried to have everything except for the fresh food, laptop and bike in the van the day before. The bike did indeed fit nicely in the corridor, but I realised that if I needed to visit the toilet en route, I wouldn't be able to get into the bathroom because of it. With a little bit of rethinking and testing different positions, I finally decided the best option would be to lift the tabletop, put that upside down on the bench seat, and let the bike stand in the table space.

CAMPERVAN CAPERS

Departure day. Mr M, as usual, made a splendid bowl of porridge for me and some extra toast to keep me going during my journey. I did wonder if he thought I was cycling to the Lakes!

The food and final bits and pieces were soon packed snugly into Evie so they wouldn't rattle their way down the M74 and M6. My plan for the bike worked perfectly. A couple of bungee cords had it secured so that it couldn't roll or fall over during the drive. And I could squeeze past to get into the bathroom if needed.

The journey down to the Lakes is always a lovely drive, no matter what the weather. Leaving home, it was a crisp morning, but once on the motorway, a thick fog descended. It amazes me how people still like to drive fast even though they can't see what they are driving into. I can tell you that Evie didn't go over 50 mph. Mind you, that's because I imagine I can see the fuel gauge going down as I drive if I'm travelling anything much over 50 mph. These people must be either stupid or rich (or both).

However, nearing the border between Scotland and England, the mist began to clear, and it was back to sunshine once more.

I decided to stop at Gretna Services, as I know they have a section for caravans, and I also needed to top up with diesel. It was with a heavy heart that I pulled into the service station, parked Evie and wandered down to the facilities. Usually, I'd have to walk around the Travel Inn area for Beatrix to smell every blade of grass before deciding exactly which spot was the best to do her business. The times I'd moaned to her about this. How I wish I could moan again about it.

So, I consoled myself with a latte and caramel cupcake in a well-known coffee place. Of course, I couldn't sit at the table in Evie as this was now a bike!

Refreshed and re-fuelled. I continued my journey down the M74, which seamlessly turns into the M6 just over the

Scottish/English border at Gretna. Approaching Junction 40 and the turn-off for Keswick, I noticed ahead of me a long line of traffic queuing for the junction, taking up the inside lane of the motorway. I slowed down, touching my brakes so the drivers behind could see there was something ahead of me. Leaving plenty of room between Evie and the car in front of me, the traffic ground to a halt.

Glancing in my wing mirror, I saw what I can only describe as carnage waiting to happen. Clearly, not everyone plans for potential driving hazards in the same way I do. Even before I'd reached Junction 40, I was already watching out for slow-moving traffic. This junction is always busy, and the queue often tails back onto the motorway. I'm not sure exactly why this happens, but I can count on one hand the times I've been able to leave the motorway at this junction and not have a bit of a wait.

One driver had clearly not been observing the traffic but wanted to leave the motorway at junction 40. Except he had only just been able to stop before the end of the queue of traffic. But only half of his car was in the inside lane. The back end of his car was now stationary in the middle lane of the motorway. I watched as if it was in slow motion as a lorry travelling in the middle lane had to take evasive action by moving into the outside lane of the motorway (where they should never go!). Heaven knows how the lorry driver or the traffic in the outside lane of the motorway didn't collide. All because one driver didn't take enough care and attention.

Then I started to think about what would have happened if the lorry had hit the back of the car in the middle lane. That car would have been pushed into the car in front of it. The one just behind me. Had I left enough of a gap between me and the car in front for me not to get pushed into it if the car behind was forced into the back of Evie? Would she be strong enough not to fold in on herself (and me)? I was even thankful my bike was further up the van so it might be saved in the impact.

CAMPERVAN CAPERS

Thankfully, there was no crash, so I could breathe easily and continue my journey.

Leaving the M6, a tootle around the ridiculously large roundabout with a million exits, looking for the lane I needed, I was soon taking the correct exit for the A66 Keswick, not A66 Brough, which would take you towards Scotch Corner and the A1.

The A66 towards Keswick is a lovely stretch of road, and it is along this road that you get your first clear views of the Cumbrian mountains in the Lake District. Unlike in Scotland, where all the fabulous Munro mountains are scattered across the whole country, it seems like the Cumbrian mountains have all been herded together. As you drive along this road, it feels like you could almost put your arms around them all.

Once beyond Penrith, you pass the sign for Greystoke. I always think about Tarzan as I pass this. I discovered that in 1912, Edgar Rice Burroughs, who was a regular visitor to Greystoke Castle, wrote *Tarzan of the Apes*. He used Greystoke as Tarzan's ancestral home. Sadly, this castle is not open to the public, so we can't visit and imagine Tarzan being there.

There are a few large lay-bys on this road, but I would suggest missing the first couple and waiting until you reach the one where you get the most amazing view of Sharp Edge on Blencathra. This is a large lay-by well off the main carriageway, protecting you from the fast-moving traffic of the A66. These are my lay-bys of choice as they make me feel safe enough to relax, have a drink and a snack, and even a snooze, without the van getting buffeted about by the cars and lorries as they pass by on their journeys.

Today, I was rewarded with an incredible vista of Sharp Edge on the right and the Helvellyn range on my left. There were a few clouds about, but the visibility was excellent. I felt I could see the route right along Sharp Edge. Not that I'll ever be tempted to climb this mountain via this route. No. I've climbed Helvellyn and tackled Striding Edge. That was bad enough for me. The first time I crossed this ridge, I was on my hands and knees. For some reason, just to make sure I really had been scared, I made that same ascent of Helvellyn several years later with my Halifax walking buddies, Sally and Julie. That time, I had to cross the ridge almost on my stomach as I was so frightened. Never, ever again will I knowingly climb a hill or mountain that involves a narrow ridge with steep drops where there is a distinct possibility of death. Adrenaline is good. Fear is not. But I love to see this mountain and Sharp Edge and admire its elegance and beauty. Maybe it's also because I know that I'm almost in the Lake District when Blencathra comes into view.

Of course, Alfred Wainwright, the famous fell-walker, didn't approve of the A66 being constructed. He said it was like an ugly scar being drawn through the Lake District. I can see his point, but it does allow for more traffic and travellers to visit the Lakes. I know that too much traffic is not good, but many of the businesses in this stunning National Park rely on tourism to survive. That's why, even though I can be totally self-sufficient in Evie on trips, I always try to add to the economy by using local shops, cafes and tearooms. Don't think it's just because I love visiting cafes and eating cakes!

After a short break enjoying the flask of tea and tuna mayo butty Mr M had made for me, I continued my journey. Approaching Keswick, the A66 continues, but my route takes the junction for Windermere and the A591. I've taken you along this road before and told you that it's just sublime. It rolls up and down like a roller coaster, passing mountains on either side. In places, it gets a bit narrow, but there's always a good view of traffic coming towards you, so you're never really taken by surprise. And, of course, there is that strange little bit of dual carriageway.

Within thirty minutes or so of leaving the lay-by, I was passing the beautiful village of Grasmere. But sadly, I was not stopping here. This, of course, is the village that the poet

CAMPERVAN CAPERS

William Wordsworth said, *'This is the loveliest spot that man hath ever found'*.

I'll let you in on a secret here. I thought I knew my stuff about Grasmere, Wordsworth and the Sarah Nelson Gingerbread shop. I love wandering through the Daffodil Garden by St Oswald's Church in Grasmere. A few years ago, because Mr M loves Grasmere and Wordsworth's poem, *I wandered Lonely as a Cloud* so much, I bought him a large canvas print of this poem so he could think of Grasmere every time he read it. It was only this month, when I was reading *Lost in the Lakes* by Thom Chesshyre, that I discovered Wordsworth did not get his inspiration for this poem about the daffodils he and his sister, Dorothy, saw at Grasmere. No, they saw these at Glencoyne Bay on Ullswater. You live and learn every day! But Wordsworth did love Grasmere and lived there for many years.

Soon, I was driving through Ambleside, which today looked remarkably quiet for a Friday, but I still had to wait for a few pedestrians to move out of the way so that I could get Evie through the gap in the parked cars. I avoided them and was soon heading towards Coniston on the A593 and the humpback bridge on a tight bend that's only wide enough for one vehicle. Thankfully, sitting high in Evie, I got a good view over the wall of the bridge so I could see if anything was coming.

Once again, I ignored the lovely scenic road you could take via Hawkshead on the B5286, as I know how narrow this is once beyond Skelwith Fold Campsite. Even the A593 to my campsite is a bit on the narrow side, to say the least. I don't worry now about traffic behind me as I take my time, but even then, I did hear the bushes tickling the side of Evie from time to time. Almost sighing with relief, I knew I had just one more tight bend up a hill before I reached Coniston. I slowed down to creep around the bend to see if anything was coming down the road. Well, yes, there was. A lorry. A very big and fast-moving lorry! It never slowed down, and I heard the awful noise as it smashed into my driver's side wing mirror. And the driver didn't even slow down or stop to check I was OK. Maybe he was oblivious to what had just occurred. I was on a bend on a hill with a line of traffic behind me, so I had to drive on until I reached Coniston and was able to pull into the parking bays at the side of the road. Taking a deep breath, I opened the door and climbed out to inspect the damage. By some miracle, the lorry had just clipped the mirror and pushed it inwards. There were a few scrapes on it, but the wing mirror was soon back in position, and all was good. If I'd had the chance to note the company the lorry driver was from, I'd have phoned them there and then to complain about their driver.

Through Coniston and over another bridge on a bend, I had just a mile to go to the campsite. I knew to look out for the site turnoff on the left-hand side as it's not all that clearly signposted. With no further incidents, I was soon parked outside reception and checking in for my stay.

I had a lovely conversation with the man at reception about my last stay here with Beatrix, and it warmed my heart when he remembered her as the dog who played with sticks with the children.

Coniston Park Coppice Club Campsite allows you to select your own pitch from the ones still available. I picked one in the same area as my last visit but chose not to have the exact same pitch.

As with my trip to Tyndrum the previous month, I'd decided that I only needed to put enough water in to allow the toilet to flush, as I'd be close enough to the shower block for washing up. That way, I didn't need to run the water through the still-leaking tap in the bathroom.

With the electricity connected and everything out of the back of the van while it was still dry, I soon had the bike out of the van and locked to the bike carrier on the back door and covered with my now out-of-the-packaging cover. Looking at the weather forecast for the next few days, I was beginning to wonder if I would even use the bike. But, if not, at least it had been to the Lakes!

Filling up the water tank, I thought that four watering cans would be sufficient. I checked the water level gauge inside the van, and could see it had reached the second mark. That would do. I turned the water on in the sink and flushed the toilet to get the water running. There was a distinct gurgling noise below my feet. I realised too late that the frost guard must have been activated in the recent cold spell we had back up in Scotland. The precious water I had painstakingly put in the tank with my watering can was now pouring out of the bottom of the van. Now I had to unlock the bike from the back of the van so I could open the back doors, pull everything out of the garage to get to the pull-cord to reset the frost guard on the boiler, all the time, hoping that not all the water had been dumped from the tank.

This was a learning curve for me as I'd not had to reset this myself before. I was quite chuffed at being able to do this so easily. Mr M always does this by putting his hand into the cupboard at the back, but I wondered what the cord was for, so I pulled it. Hey, presto, the button was reset. Of course, when I tell Mr M how I reset it, I can guarantee that he'll say that using the cord is too dangerous and that I could damage the button by doing so. But then, why does it have a pull cord, I could argue. Let's not forget that this is the man who has made me panic about the petrol cap getting damaged by using the key as it's too fiddly. I've never had a problem with that. He says the bung in the water tank will get damaged by pulling it out to release the water at the end of the trip. You know the one, the one that's designed to be pulled out to release the water. And don't forget the lock on the toilet flap. That can easily be damaged by unlocking it. You get the picture!

Debra Murphy

A couple more watering cans of water and the water tank was filled up enough, and I wandered back up to reception to advise them which pitch I'd taken and to be given the keys to the all-important shower block and toilets.

With my memories of Beatrix, the incident with the lorry and the escaping water, I'd decided that I'd have a well-deserved drink in the local pub that night.

"I'm going to the Ship Inn tonight for a quick half of cider," I proudly told the man at reception.

"The Ship's closed for renovation until mid-December," was his reply.

Oh well, I thought. A celebratory cup of tea in Evie would be just as good.

Not wanting to leave Mr M without the air fryer at home, I had decided that the small portable oven was sufficient for my needs. Maybe we need to buy Evie her own air fryer. Once everything had been put in its rightful place in the van, I was soon in my PJs and enjoying a hot, tasty quiche, beans, the other half of my tuna mayo sandwich from lunchtime and a now lukewarm flask of tea. I really do live the high life on my trips in Evie.

Later, for supper, I spoiled myself and had a chocolate bomb in some hot milk. My daughter had given me these last Christmas and I'd been promising myself I'd use them on a trip. It seemed an extra special treat because I heated the milk up on the hob and had that special feeling of cooking by gas. I know. It's a strange thing, but I do love using the gas when camping. It doesn't feel special using the gas hob at home, but camping or in Evie, it just feels right. And can I just say, the chocolate bombs are amazing. It was like putting a large chocolate ball into my mug of hot milk and allowing it to melt. Then, just at that moment when the chocolate sides collapsed, out popped a whole load of mini marshmallows. Chocolate bombs are my new favourite thing.

CAMPERVAN CAPERS

I was cosy as toast in Evie. The blinds and curtains were closed, and the heater was on. Outside, there was no sound at all except the hooting of an owl. Just at that moment, when I was enjoying the silence and the sound of nature, I had some WhatsApp messages with my friend, Greg, who'd just finished working on the audio version of *Beatrix The Time Travelling Collie*. I told him about the silence and that Mr M thinks I'm mad doing these adventures by myself. Greg agreed, and, of course, it didn't take long for his messages to turn into things like, 'Did you hear that?'

Thanks, Greg!

Despite being cosy, comfy and not in the least bit scared, I still had quite a sleepless night. When you're in a campervan by yourself, away from the noise of traffic and other people, all noises are exaggerated. A leaf falling on the skylight window sounds like a branch, a gentle breeze like a howling gale, and the rain! Well, it rained all night. I heard every drop of rain as it bounced on the outside of Evie. I no longer worry the rain is going to come into Evie as I've realised that she's been parked outside our house in many a storm, and she stays bone dry. But rain on the outside of a van sounds like a drum being played. All night. Somehow, even though it kept me awake for much of the night, it was not an annoying noise. Cars and people making noises at night (and during the day) irritate me, but sounds of nature I find quite reassuring.

The following morning, I pottered around the van and had breakfast. Porridge pots are my new go-to breakfast in Evie as it's just a quick boil of the kettle, and there's no pan to clean. I wouldn't thank you for instant porridge at home, but I'm getting used to having these on my adventures.

Looking at the weather forecast, I decided that the bike would stay attached to Evie, and I'd take a stroll into the village at Coniston for lunch. It was too wet even for a picnic outside. And, of course, I needed to revisit the Bluebird Cafe to say my final goodbyes to Beatrix.

Debra Murphy

One of the most important snippets of information you need to learn on campsites is the cleaning times for the shower block. Showers and anything else you need to do that you don't want to do in your campervan bathroom need to be timed around the closures. At this campsite, the shower block in my section of the site is closed between 11 am and 12.30 pm.

With this in mind, I enjoyed my leisurely breakfast, did some reading, and, of course, some writing. There is very little Wi-Fi around this site, but I was amazed that I could get an almost perfect signal with my phone for WhatsApp calls and messages. Mr M likes to hear from me now and again to know that I'm still alive (and vice versa, of course). The lack of Wi-Fi was giving me a headache with my writing as I couldn't get access to my OneDrive to automatically save my work. Thankfully, I did bring my external hard drive to save it to. As I've already told you, I now like to work on my OneDrive to keep things permanently saved, but I also back this up with the external hard drive, and I even send an email to myself with the document I'm working on. The email option couldn't be used this trip, so the hard drive would have to suffice for the few days I'm here until I can connect to the Wi-Fi at home again. I'm not sure whether the lack of Wi-Fi is due to the campsite organisation or whether it's the location and there is no Wi-Fi for anyone. Some sites seem to have good connections, and others, none. If it's important to you on your trip, make sure to check it out before deciding which site to stay on, or sort out other connection options like a mobile dongle. Maybe I should take my advice here.

The danger with sitting in the campervan for any length of time is that the kettle always seems to be switched on, and you drink copious amounts of tea and eat biscuits without realising how many you've eaten. But it's certainly a treat I enjoy. It's very comforting watching the weather outside when you are dry, warm and nourished inside.

CAMPERVAN CAPERS

On this site, the shower blocks are of a high standard. They are clean and, importantly for an arachnophobe like me, appeared to be mainly spider-free. And the bonus is that the shower stayed on and didn't have those ridiculous buttons you keep having to press to keep the water flowing. I totally understand that these help to conserve water and discourage people from staying in the shower any longer than necessary. But I hate them. Another bonus is that there is a bench seat in each shower. Why all shower cubicles can't have this simple thing is beyond me. Trying to balance on one foot as I dry my legs and get my knickers and trousers on without getting them wet on the cubicle floor is a skill I don't have. I need a bench, or at the very least a little stool, to sit on. And hooks to hang your clothes. In some places, there are none, but at this site, you're spoiled with three hooks. In camping terms, these shower blocks are like a palace.

And while I'm on my high horse about facilities, it's nice to have a sink in a cubicle where you can brush your teeth without everyone having to watch you. This would not usually be an issue for me as I'd brush my teeth in the bathroom in Evie, but as we have the leaking tap problem, this is not possible at the moment.

Musing over these points as I enjoyed my undisturbed roasting hot shower, I decided that this winter, Mr M and I would investigate how to take apart the walls of the bathroom in Evie to repair the leaking tap. After all, what's the point of being married to an engineer if he can't sort this out? I wonder if that's a sign of how my life is that I'm seeing repairing a leaking tap in a campervan as quite an adventure. Would I be quite so keen to do this in the house? I don't think so. That's why we pay an extortionate amount of money to our utility company so they can come and sort any leaking pipes.

Oh, and talking of showers. I must mention my recent purchase. The humble travel towel. I bought this as part of my birthday present from Mr M. Actually, I got two as I got one half-price at a well-known outdoor store. Standard bath towels take up so much room in Evie's small bathroom and take so long to dry. When there are two of you in the van, it's even worse! So, when I saw these, I thought I'd give them a go. I didn't expect a travel towel to become my new best friend. But it has. When you're not using it, it can be rolled up into its carry bag, which is tiny, even smaller than something you'd fit your waterproof trousers into. But, when taken out and given a shake, it's a massive 120 cm x 60 cm. And this is only the medium size. The key features are reported as:

- Super-absorbent and quick drying (it really is)
- Soft (good when you've had a hard day)
- Anti-bacterial protection (stays fresh for longer)
- Compact when packed – (carry bag included)
- Size - 120 cm x 60 cm (even big enough for me!)
- Colour – green (but you can get blue)

I can't quite believe I'm dedicating so much time and words to the humble travel towel, but it's a game-changer when you're living in a tiny space with no central heating. I've found myself smiling as I'm getting dried because the towel doesn't even look to be getting wet, but my body is getting dried. It is so light, and in a matter of thirty minutes, it's dry once more and ready to be used again.

Then, it was time to venture out into the rain. Taking the road to the bottom of the campsite, I was soon at the lakeside. If there had been anybody else with me, I'm sure I'd have been tempted to have a dip in the water. Cold-water swimming alone is not to be recommended.

The walk into Coniston along this Lakeside track is an easy ramble with a good surface and is virtually flat once you've descended from the campsite.

Passing through a gate into the next field, there was a small flock of Herdwick sheep minding their own business and munching on the grass. Herdwick sheep are native to the Lake District, which is why they can cope with the cold and sometimes never-ending rain on the high hills. I'm not a shepherd or a farmer, but because my favourite author, Beatrix Potter (or Mrs Heelis as she became), was a well-known and respected Herdwick sheep breeder, I feel that these are my favourite sheep. I've spent many a day or years, wishing I had lived the life Beatrix Potter did, writing stories and becoming a farmer and a protector of the Lake District.

Just before I reached the next gate, I noticed a fabulous-looking ram with magnificent curly horns. He watched me, and I watched him. I did wonder if I should make a dash for the gate before he came to investigate me further, but I was brave enough to get a few photos of him. These were zoomed in and not close-up shots I'll let you know. I'm not daft or irresponsible enough to forget that these are wild animals, and I was walking in their garden.

Photo shoot over, I soon reached the end of the track and joined the road to take me down to the Bluebird Cafe, where I enjoyed a scrummy posh fish finger butty and pot of tea. Emotions were high remembering how Beatrix loved this cafe and its owner for giving her a sausage.

Coniston Water was at its highest level I've ever seen it. The water was almost covering the jetty. The sandy beach area where we usually spend a few hours in the summer was completely submerged. I'm not sure if this is typical for Coniston Water in winter or just because of the relentless rain the country had had these last few months.

After having a few moments looking out onto Coniston Water, remembering Beatrix, it was a short meander up the road to the village of Coniston, passing a couple of houses with for sale signs outside them. Taking photos, I messaged Mr M and asked him if I could buy one of them, but when I looked at the estate agent website, I was horrified to see that one of them was priced at £995,000. With prices like that, my dream of living in the Lakes is never going to happen. Even a win on the lottery might not be enough nowadays.

Coniston Village is very quaint and far removed from the hustle and bustle of the likes of Ambleside and Bowness. It's only twelve miles to Ambleside from Coniston, but you could be a million miles away. Of course, situated near the slate mines, the buildings are all slate. There is something magical about slate if you ask me. The village has a few gift shops, cafes, pubs, a couple of outdoor stores, slate mines, a tourist information centre, and a museum dedicated to John Ruskin, who was known for being a critic of art, architecture, and society. I've realised that I know very little about Ruskin, so I must visit this museum next time I'm in Coniston without a dog. It doesn't take long to walk around the village as it really is just a one-street village.

As it was November, I was conscious that darkness falls very quickly, especially in locations where there are few streetlights or brightly lit buildings. As much as I would have liked to spend more time and perhaps indulge in a coffee and cake at one of the other cafes, I wanted to get back to the campsite whilst it was still light. Of course, my torch and my headlight were safely back in the campervan! Will I never learn?

If you walk up Station Road after the hump-back bridge by the petrol station, you can join a lovely high-level track to walk most of the way back to the site. Don't be put off by the numerous signs telling you it's not a dedicated footpath and the graphic photographs of sheep killed by dogs. There's even a sign informing you that, for legal reasons, the path must be closed to the public on the last Sunday in November every year. But today, it was open. Walking on this, you're spoiled, even in poor weather, to a good view of Coniston Water, and, of course, you don't need to walk on the road. It's not a busy road, but there is no footpath. Reaching a gate, you do have to re-join the road for 100 yards until you reach another gate on the other side of the road. This takes you along a further track, leading directly to the campsite. This path was a bit like a river today because of all the recent rainfall.

Now, one of the important things to remember when staying on a campsite is where you put the keys for the toilets. You can guarantee that by the time you reach the site, you're bursting for the toilet, and it's easier to go to the toilet block than fumble around trying to get into your campervan. That's my experience anyhow.

Once back in Evie and my wet clothes now hanging to dry, I was in agony with my arthritic feet, but I'd walked about five miles, revisited places I'd been with Beatrix, and had a lovely lunch. There was no need to cook that night as I was still full, so it was just a fruit scone and a cup of tea.

It wasn't long before darkness fell, and I could hear the wind howling around the van. Checking the weather forecast (again), I was slightly alarmed to see that there were now thunderstorms due any time. I was pretty sure that the pitch I'd chosen for Evie was quite sheltered from the wind and certainly from any potential flooding. But sitting in the van with no other noises, the wind sounded like a force ten storm. At one point I did post on the Adria Twin Camper Van Owners Facebook group about my concerns about the wind. The response? Make sure all the windows are closed, nothing is around the van, take the van off levelling blocks if using, point the van into the wind, open the wine, and enjoy, but they did ask me to let them know in the morning how I'd gone on. It is worth joining a group for fellow campervanners as the moral support is great, and there is always someone about to answer a question or query or just to reassure you that you'll be OK and not to worry about being blown away.

Taking my last trip of the night to the shower block, I was very relieved to find that the wind outside didn't sound or feel quite so ferocious as it did when I was sitting in the van alone.

Perhaps I'm not quite as brave as I like to pretend I am.

And it was another sleepless night with the rain rattling on the van.

Another day with no prospect of cycling, so it was to be a second walk into Coniston. This time, I took the non-public footpath to the village so I could walk along the lakeside on the way back to the campsite.

There's a lovely cafe in Coniston on the road out to Ambleside called the Herdwick Cafe. I had taken Beatrix in there last year, so I thought it would be a nice place to revisit. I hadn't anticipated the emotions that would hit me as I sat in the cafe waiting for my jacket potato to be served. Tears arrived, and I was sure people were looking at me, but I soon gathered myself. A few text messages to and from Mr M helped me remember the good times with Beatrix. A scrummy piece of mint chocolate tiffin helped, too.

As I left the cafe, it was still raining. I was looking forward to a stroll along the lakeside but was still feeling very emotional remembering Beatrix. As I went through the kissing gate to the track, there was a sudden break in the clouds. The sun made a weak effort to pop through the rain, and out of nowhere appeared a bright rainbow. I like to think that it was Beatrix reminding me that she was always walking beside me. Did I cry again? Of course, I did.

Tears wiped away, I continued my ramble along the track. This was the field that the day before was full of Herdwick sheep, including the ram I'd been brave enough to take photos of. From the top of the field, I could see the very same ram making his way towards me. I stopped for a moment to see what he was going to do. I knew that a ram wouldn't want to eat me, but I wasn't so sure he didn't want to do any damage to me with his huge, impressive horns.

He strolled down to the track and stopped, looking directly at me. Was he guarding his territory and his family, or, as I like to think, did he recognise me from the day before and was simply saying,

"Hi, there. How are you today?"

I smiled at him, said, "Hi, Mr Ram," and walked around him, making sure not to get too close to him or make eye contact. It was his field, after all. I was the intruder. But I was secretly glad I had both my walking poles with me and had already decided that I could use these to keep him at arm's length if needed. Once I felt I'd put enough space between the two of us, I turned around. Mr Ram was still standing on the track, and I smiled to myself as a group of walkers stood at the other side of the kissing gate, pointing at me and the ram. Had they been waiting to see how I fared crossing the field with the ram before they attempted to go through the gate? I wondered.

The walk back to the campsite from here was a lovely stroll, and I was soon back in Evie, wondering what I'd make for tea.

Then, horror of horrors. The worst possible thing to happen in a campervan. The dreaded dodgy tummy. It came out of the blue, and I wondered if I should just use the toilet in Evie, but remembered it would be me emptying it later.

Fumbling to put on my wellies and waterproof coat, I made a dash to the toilet block, remembering to pick up the key on my way.

No details required here, but once back in Evie, I had a dilemma. Should I risk eating anything for tea or go without food until tomorrow? Ten minutes later, I had to go through the whole dashing to the toilet block rigmarole again. That answered my question. There would be no tea that night.

My more pressing issue was that I still take heart medication following the heart attack thingy a few years ago. Would I be able to keep the tablets in my system long enough for them to be digested? If not, would I have a heart episode? I gave myself a severe talking to and told myself that if I continued getting worked up, I certainly would have a heart episode. So, with what felt like a break in the tummy movements, I took my tablets and hoped for the best.

Whether it was because I felt a bit under the weather, I'm not sure, but that evening, the noise of the rain on Evie was starting to get to me. It was constant. Sometimes, a little drip, then a gush. It was like somebody playing a rubbish tune on a drum. Again and again. With nobody else in the van, no dog and no noise outside, it was too much for me to cope with, and I resorted to finding music to play on my phone. YouTube came up trumps, and I listened to some soothing music by Cat Stevens.

Telling Mr M about my exploits that night, once he'd stopped laughing about the tummy explosions, he told me that I could play the radio in Evie, and that was what the speaker was for in the bed area. Would that drain the battery? I asked him. But he didn't really know, and, not wanting to be alone in the back of beyond with a flat battery, I decided YouTube on my phone would suffice. Usually, I don't need any noise in the van, so hopefully, once I'd got over whatever was making me feel rubbish, I'd be back to enjoying the drip, drip, drip on the van roof!

Explaining my worries to Mr M about the capacity of the toilet cassette in Evie, he reassured me that if my dodgy tummy reoccurred too quickly for me to reach the toilet block, the toilet cassette in Evie did indeed have a large capacity!

Tonight, for the first time since getting my campervan, I wondered if I even liked being in a campervan.

Thankfully, for me and the other people needing to use the toilet block, there were no more episodes that evening or during the night.

Sometimes I feel like Mother Nature has a bit of a laugh at us mere humans. Still feeling under the weather in the morning, I decided that I wasn't up to doing any cycling, so I would have

CAMPERVAN CAPERS

a day pottering around. What did Mother Nature do? She got rid of the rain and brought out the sun.

Typical!

There was no longer the constant drip, drip of rain on Evie's roof, but I did realise that I could download an app on my phone to listen to the radio. So, now, if the silence or rain gets the better of me in future, I'll be able to find some music to listen to. Where would we be without an app or two? Currently, I'm tuned to a 70s station, listening to Bruce Springsteen's Born to Run. The Lakes and Bruce are my go-to things when life is tough.

That day I realised that having a campervan that I only use to get me from home to the campsite and back has its disadvantages in remote areas. I decided that a trip to the lovely village of Hawkshead would be a good day out for me. But to get to Coniston village to catch the bus, I had a thirty-minute walk (more when you're feeling rubbish). The bus to Hawkshead only runs every two hours. I would miss the first bus as I still had to get dressed but could manage to get the 11 am bus for the fifteen-minute journey. However, the bus back to Coniston also only runs every two hours, so I would have to time my stay at Hawkshead to ensure that I was back at Coniston in time to allow me to walk back to the campsite before darkness fell. I did ensure I had my headtorch in my rucksack today. Aiming for the 2.30 pm return bus back to Coniston would give me a good couple of hours at Hawkshead for a stroll and some lunch.

Of course, lunch would be dependent on how my stomach was feeling.

For those campervanners who are happy to use their vans during the day as transport, you would not have this dilemma. Using your own vehicle would only take you fifteen minutes to get to Hawkshead, and you could choose when to return. I'm prepared to deal with the travel issues and not have to worry about the little, very narrow, twisting lanes of the Lake District in my campervan, wondering if I'd packed everything away, did I remember to turn the gas off, did I close all the windows and leave a sign saying my pitch was reserved, only to have to reset up Evie on my return that evening. And I didn't have to worry about whether there would be any car parks big enough for Evie.

So, my morning was planned: shower, breakfast, a bit of writing, then a stroll along the track to Coniston. The only disaster was that I forgot to take my flip flops with me to the shower block. But I survived.

I won't bore you about the bus journey to Hawkshead as I've already written about this 505-bus service and how much in awe I am of the skilful bus drivers. That morning was no different. I was certainly thankful that I didn't have to take Evie up and down Hawkshead Hill. If you're ever coming to this area with a campervan, motorhome or caravan, think carefully about your route and check if it's suitable for your vehicle. It might be my imagination, but the drivers of large vans and lorries seem much more courteous and careful when they need to negotiate passing a bus than they do when they pass me in Evie. Especially a certain lorry driver!

Hawkshead is a picturesque village, much smaller than even the likes of Coniston, but it has so much history to it. William Wordsworth went to school there. The Hawkshead Grammar School Museum is in the centre of the village, and one of the school desks there is alleged to have carvings by William Wordsworth. So even famous poets could be graffiti artists before they became famous! Of course, this museum was closed for the winter when I was there, without a dog, so I could have taken a trip inside if it had been open!

Beatrix Potter also loved the area and her home, Hill Top, where she wrote many of her books, is in Near Sawry, which you can walk to in about 45 minutes from Hawkshead. You can drive there, but there is very little parking there.

CAMPERVAN CAPERS

History is not the only attraction at Hawkshead. It is situated in one of the most beautiful areas of the Lakes. Grizedale Forest and Tarn Hows are two of the prettiest places I've ever been to, especially if you go when you can see the magnificent colours of autumn.

I discovered that in 2023, Sarah Nelson's Grasmere Gingerbread shop opened in Hawkshead. There has only ever been one place you could buy this (other than online), and this was in the village of Grasmere. I absolutely love Sarah Nelson's Grasmere Gingerbread, but today, like the museum, the shop was closed. My dodgy tummy didn't object too much about not having to try some. Although a bit of ginger when you're out of sorts is never a bad thing. I remember when I was pregnant, and I had worse morning sickness than the Princess of Wales, I would try to nibble on gingernuts to get me through the day.

A pleasant couple of hours was spent in Hawkshead, having a walk around the hillside above the village, risking a cheese and ham butty in a lovely cafe and, of course, purchasing another Beatrix Potter collectable for my growing crowd of her characters on my Lake District unit I have at home in the front room.

After another interesting bus journey, watching the traffic coping with a large bus on the road and then a stroll back along the high track to the campsite, it was time to think about what I could pack away, ready for leaving the site in the morning.

The thing about camping, whether that be in a campervan or a tent, is it's all about being organised. Having a place for everything and making sure you know where everything is. It's also about getting packed up and ready to go home. I always start to plan that the day before I go home. What will I not use again on this trip? What can be packed into the garage of the van? Much to my disappointment, on this trip I would be sorting out which food to throw away as I'd not eaten much of the lovely food Mr M had prepared for me. I hate wasting food and like to think I've started getting it right just how much food to bring away with me, right down to how many slices of bread and the number of biscuits. Sadly, not this trip!

I packed away the mini electric oven and the various pots and pans that I'd unpacked but not used. I'd be having a porridge pot in the morning, so I only needed the kettle, a spoon and a mug for making a cup of tea.

Packing away was not too much of an issue this time, as long as I put things in places so they don't get damaged or rattle all the way back to Scotland. This will be my last trip before the winter, so over the next week at home, I'll be doing a winter clean of the van and taking all the bedding and cushions out and storing them in the house.

It's easy to think that the packing and unpacking is a bit of a faff, but you'd have to do that if you go on holiday to a cottage or a hotel – it's just a more compact space in your campervan.

Chapter 40

Storm Isha, Storm Jocelyn, And A Broken Headlamp Protector – January 2024

The start of 2024 will be remembered as the month of storms, and I was glad that Evie was parked safely on our drive away from any possible falling trees. Storm Isha hit the UK with winds of up to 99 mph and caused devastation across the country, and sadly, people lost their lives. The day after, while many people were still without power and dealing with the horror of Storm Isha, a second storm, Jocelyn, whipped in, causing more damage.

We're very fortunate because we don't live at the bottom of a hill or near rivers or streams, so we never have to worry too much about flooding. With the two storms, though, we did wonder whether the rain would ever stop and how long our windows and roof would survive the monsoon. We even contemplated buying an ark! The house opposite had tiles blown off, rubbish bins were blown across the street, and trees blown down in the local wood where we walk Florence.

But on the grand scale of things, Kirkintilloch escaped relatively unscathed.

Then, just as Storm Jocelyn was giving her final blasts, she somehow managed to whip a gust of wind that wrapped itself around Evie and hearing a loud crack, I ran out to investigate.

Debra Murphy

One of Evie's headlight protectors was lying on the ground. Don't ask me how that happened, as it still doesn't make any sense to me. But there it was, broken and lying on the ground. I asked the Adria Twin Camper Van Owners group for suggestions on where to get new ones, if I could fit them myself, and if it was difficult.

I watched a few videos on YouTube and decided that, yes, I could order replacements without having to pay an absolute fortune, and I should be able to fit them myself.

A couple of weeks later, my parcel arrived with two lovely, shiny new protectors and instructions on how to fit them. I say instructions. There were words typed on a piece of paper that made absolutely no sense to either Mr M or me. But, watching the videos again and again, we worked out how to attach the new fastenings to the protector. I did wonder why the fastenings couldn't have been already in place as surely they would be in the same place for every van they were suitable for as they were very fiddly.

However, a couple of hours later, we had the new piece of plastic in place and secured. We decided that we would only replace the broken one and would keep the other new protector as a spare in case of any other catastrophes, storms or other incidents.

Chapter 41

Worrying About The Cost Of Everything - March 2024

Winter was slowly melting away and giving way to Spring. Some days! Over the winter months, I'd looked out at Evie every day, wondering if she was OK. Was the cold getting to her? Were beasties making their home inside her? Would the electrics be OK? Would the van rust away in the bad weather? I'd also watched with disgust the dirt on the outside of her and the green mildew starting to develop. Each week, I thought I'd be able to clean her, and each week, Mother Nature said no!

I'm toying with the idea of buying a new, taller ladder specifically for washing the roof of the campervan. But they are not cheap. I think I need to wait to see what happens at Evie's MOT in April. I don't want to buy a new ladder and then, heaven forbid, discover that Evie needs work done on her that I can't afford.

When I bought Evie, I never imagined that the world would go into such a recession and everything would be going up in price. It seems that every day another bill comes in, telling us how much more we will be paying this year. Electric, gas, groceries, petrol, diesel, dog insurance, household insurance, car insurance. I'm dreading MOT day for Evie and discovering how much that has gone up. We also need to get the habitation check done, as we missed it in August last year. The insurance for Evie is not due until August, so we can breathe a bit easier until then. The car insurance renewal quote has just plonked on the door mat, an increase of £100. Florence's pet insurance is £100 more this year. Our Denplan for looking after our teeth is going up another £20 a month. Don't even get me started on the gas and electricity. The food bills are so high now that I sometimes wonder if Mr M is feeding the whole neighbourhood. Train fares and mobile phone costs are increasing at an alarming rate. I can't think of anything that is now cheaper than it was last year. The only thing not going up is wages.

There, I've had my little moan now. I think I'm just scared that this year, I might find I can't afford the upkeep of Evie.

But with the worst of the winter weather behind us, I knew I needed to give her a bit of a run to get her engine ticking over again. So, when we had a week of no snow and ice in February, we told Evie she was going out to Stirling for a run. She gave a bit of a cough and a splutter when Mr M tried to start her, but in a few minutes, she was ticking over nicely. We gave her a good blast on the motorway, leaving her in third gear and getting the engine up to 3000 revs. I've been told before that for a diesel engine, you should do this every now and again to stop the valve becoming clogged with harmful black stuff that then gets spat out of the exhaust. In our last diesel car, it actually had a light that came on telling you when this needed to be done. I don't like doing it as it sounds like you're blowing the engine up, but I always do as I'm told.

Our plan was to head out to Dobbie's Garden Centre just past Stirling. We know there's a big car park there and we could stop, have a look around Lakeland and the Cotswolds Outdoor store, then have a coffee in Dobbie's Garden Centre Cafe. I was pleasantly surprised at how well Evie drove after the winter break and that I had not lost any of my confidence driving Evie. After a short break and now full of coffee, Mr M asked me if I wanted him to drive on the way home. So, I enjoyed the journey home, relaxing, feeling the joy of being in our campervan once again and planning more adventures.

Just before we arrived back home, we had a strange experience with the reversing camera. Usually, this only comes on when you select reverse gear, but today, it kept coming on as we were driving. This was actually quite good because normally, you don't get to see what is behind you, and you just have a little bit of sight from the rear window, which shouldn't be happening. I wondered if this meant that the reverse gear was somehow being engaged or if the gear mechanism thought it had. Did the drivers behind us see the reversing lights coming on and think we were heading back to crash into them?

When we got home, the first thing I did was Google the problem. I never knew it was such a common thing. People were the same as me, saying that it was an error but a good one. I even learned that you can set your camera to be on all the time if you wish. That's something to consider. But the most important thing for me to know was that it had something to do with the wiring on the camera and not the gear mechanism of the van. That's another thing for me to discuss with Struans.

I now realise that Mr M will not be joining me on the first few trips of the year because it is just too cold for him, and, as I've said before, if one of you is miserable in the van, you're both miserable.

We knew from the last service that Evie would need her brakes sorted, and we still had the problem with the driver's front tyre losing more pressure than the other three. The garage looked at this last year, and we thought that when we had all her tyres replaced, this would solve the issue. But it was still happening.

The service and MOT department at Struans is very busy and gets booked up for sometimes months in advance. So, in February, I phoned and organised for her MOT and for them to sort the brakes and have a look at the tyre problem. Maybe the rim was damaged, or the valve was leaking. Worst-case scenario, it might need a new wheel. Then we also needed the habitation check, but I told them that the MOT, brakes and the tyre are the most important issues, and I could book her back in for her habitation check if they didn't get time that day to do everything. That was all booked for April, a week before her current MOT certificate expired. Fingers crossed.

Chapter 42

Off With A Puff Of Smoke – 23rd March 2024
Tyndrum Holiday Park, Tyndrum, Scotland

I was trying to decide where to go for my first trip of the year. Would I go to a campsite I've already been to or try somewhere different? Would I take Florence, or would it be a solo trip?

Although I love my campervan adventures, I must admit to still being a bit nervous about trying new places, especially if I'm by myself. So, I decided that if the weather was kind to me and the winter snow and ice were gone, I'd take a trip up to the Tyndrum Holiday Park, where I went last year.

I was all set to take Florence with me so she could have a run around in a new part of the country, but then the weather forecast for the days I had booked showed that the temperature was going to fall, and there may even be some sleet and snow showers. Would Florence, with her smooth, short coat, be warm enough? I wondered. She is a bit of a softy and doesn't like going out in the bad weather at home. So, I decided that she should stay at home for this trip. But then somebody tagged me onto a man on social media called Sean the Sheepman. I've been watching some of his videos, and I absolutely love them. He was talking about how we are making our Collies too soft by treating them like human children and that they will be happier and more confident if we remember they are dogs. We wouldn't be happy to be treated like dogs, after all. He was talking about using coats and boots for the dogs in winter. His Collies are outdoor dogs, so they are used to the weather, but they love it. And the snow doesn't melt on their coats, so they are retaining their heat. Also, dogs control their temperature through their feet, so if we put boots on them, they can overheat easily.

After watching some more of his videos, I decided that Florence would indeed be able to cope with the temperature in the van, so plans were quickly changed to pack all her holiday gear – towels, dog bags, harness, a couple of extra blankets for her to lie on if she wants to, food and treats for the three days.

Florence watched with interest as I packed all my stuff in Evie, but her giant ears pricked up even more than usual when I started to put her blankets in and measure out her food into bags. Don't shout at me for mocking Florence's big ears. She has the biggest ears on a Border Collie I have ever seen, and you'd agree with me if you saw photos of her. I think she knew she was going away with me, but I couldn't tell if she was excited or not.

That was sorted then, two nights away, Saturday and Sunday, to Tyndrum with Florence.

Another thing I'm ashamed to say is that with the dire wet weather we have had over the winter, I have not been inclined to try and sort out the little leak we have in the bathroom, so I've decided that I will not be filling up with water this time. The only water I need is to flush the toilet, but it will only be me, and there will be no number 2s!

I phoned the campsite and asked if they could put me next to the shower block, and they emailed back to say they had given me the same spot as last time. So, even with a sudden emergency, I would still be able to use the site facilities. The washing-up area would be almost within arm's reach, meaning I wouldn't even need water for doing the dishes. A bottle of fresh water to make cups of tea and for Florence to drink would suffice.

My plan was that I would sort the leak out myself once the weather was warmer.

I'm also very aware that the gas cylinder we were currently using must be ready for running out. We don't have a gauge, but I know that it will run out just when I'm not expecting it. We have another full bottle, but I'm not 100% sure I'll be able to remember how to change it. Mr M very kindly went hunting in the shed at home through his old tools and found me a spanner that fits the gas connection. This is now in the first aid kit right next to the gas storage area so that I don't need to pull everything out of the garage to find it. I told Mr M that I'd ask the campsite to give me a hand if it ran out. That's the beauty of staying on a site and not wild camping – there is always somebody you can call on for assistance.

My personal chef helped me plan my meals for the trip. I was determined I would not go into the wonderful fish and chip restaurant 100 yards from the campsite.

On my menu this weekend: homemade tomato and lentil soup, venison stew, porridge pots, cheese, and some chicken breasts to roast for tea on Saturday night and for a picnic on Sunday for a walk in the hills around Tyndrum. I did add in some nuts, oatcakes, and sourdough bread just in case I was starving. Oh, and an apple.

Saturday morning arrived, and there was no rush to get ready as I couldn't check in at the campsite until 2 pm. That gave me time to pack everything and still have time to have some lovely scrambled eggs on Ryvita made by the lovely Mr M.

I watch with interest, sometimes commenting, but usually just a spectator, to the Adria Twin Camper Van Owners group on Facebook. I've seen quite a few people posting about how they have damaged their electric cable and socket by driving off with the mains electric cable still attached to their van. I'm not sure how this happens because I double-check and often triple-check everything around my van. But then I'm the girl who didn't know I had to put water in the van to flush the toilet, so who am I to pass judgment? This morning, I was very aware that I still had to disconnect my EHU cable and put it in the back of the van. Usually, I would wind it onto the cable tidy, but today, as I would be reconnecting it in just over a couple of hours, I decided that I'd just gather it together and shove it into the garage. I've now remembered why we got the cable tidy last year because an unwound cable takes up far more room than one on a winder. That's the last time I'll do that! Another valuable lesson learned.

"Would you like me to reverse the van out for you?" asked Mr M. He knows me so well.

I reversed the car out and parked a couple of houses down the street, watching as Mr M fired up Evie. I was alarmed to see lots of black smoke coming out of her exhaust and then nothing! Mr M fired her up again. There was an even bigger cloud of black smoke from her exhaust, but then she was being reversed off the drive and onto the road. I swiftly drove the car back onto the drive, holding back the tears because I was sure Evie was poorly.

"I think the van just needs a good blast up the motorway," said Mr M. "You'll be fine in her."

I admit to being a bit hesitant, but then that's what we pay breakdown cover for, isn't it?

By noon, I was off. The sun was shining, and the mountains were calling me. Except I was feeling very anxious. Was it because it was the first trip of the year? I don't know. Evie felt way too big for me to drive. I was looking out of the side window to see if there was still smoke coming from her exhaust, but there was nothing. She sounded perfect. The dials were showing what I expected – enough diesel, the temperature gauge OK and the music system playing Radio 2. Life should be good.

CAMPERVAN CAPERS

But today, I wasn't enjoying the drive. I was worried that Evie was going to break down and I would be stuck somewhere in the middle of nowhere.

The trip up the M80 and onto the A9 was a pleasant journey, with the sun shining and the hills in the distance were standing out against the blue sky. Once off the motorway and on the A84 towards Callander, I decided that I should pull into one of the lay-bys, turn Evie off and then see if she started again for me without any issues. That way, if there were any problems, I could either phone the breakdown people or try to make my way back home. Of course, stopping meant that I could get up and have a bit of a stretch, walk around and tell myself to calm down.

After a short break, sitting back in the driver's seat, I prayed that Evie would play nicely and start the first time. I waited for the yellow lights on the dashboard to go out (which I know now I should do) and turned the key. Bingo. First time. Evie started like a dream. What was I worried about?

We were soon back on our way, and I was starting to enjoy the drive. Through Callander and past Loch Lubnaig, I was a good campervan driver, pulling in at appropriate places if traffic was building up behind me. I don't rush anywhere in my car, so I certainly don't rush in Evie. Passing Lochearnhead, the views, as always, were magnificent. The Munros were capped with snow and looked very scenic. There were a couple of sleety showers heading towards Crianlarich, but nothing to be concerned about.

I'd not set my satnav for this journey because I know the way. I knew there were a couple of signposts for the site, and sure enough, I saw the first one, *Tyndrum Holiday Park One Mile*. Then another, *Tyndrum Holiday Park, Take Next left*. And then we were there.

Campsites usually have an area for you to park outside reception as you check in, and this one is no different. It's clearly marked with big white letters, so even I can't miss it.

Debra Murphy

I chatted with the people in reception, and they gave me a goodie bag for Florence – some poo bags and treats. I also discussed how I expected my gas to run out and would they be able to help me change my gas cylinder if it did.

"Of course. Just let us know and we will be over. Even if outside open hours, there is always somebody to help you."

We were booked on Pitch 8, the same one as last time, so I knew exactly where I was going. I was proud of myself for taking my time, reversing Evie into the pitch and checking that she was just about level.

I pulled out the untidy EHU cable from Evie's garage, and within minutes, we were connected to mains electricity. I had everything I needed: a reasonably level van, electricity, water tap nearby and the shower/toilet block a minute's walk away. Yes, I know I still need to drive Evie onto levelling blocks at some stage, but not today!

With Florence fastened onto the long lead outside the van, I gave her some water, then sorted everything out, turning the fridge on and pulling the windscreen blinds closed. This does shut out some of the lovely sunlight, but it means that you're not having to do this later when the van is already cold and dark.

A quick phone home to let Mr M know we had arrived safely, and I put on my walking boots and headed out for an afternoon walk with my now excited Border Collie.

From my previous visit to this site last year, I could just about remember a lovely walk I had with Vicky, which I seemed to think took us around about an hour. It was still early and a clear day, so there were a few hours of daylight left.

The great thing about the location of the Tyndrum Holiday Park is that within five minutes of leaving the van, I was in the wilderness, and Florence could be off the lead. Border Collies hate being on the lead and pull constantly, making for a tedious walk for both the dog and the human. We followed the

CAMPERVAN CAPERS

track that took us down to the gold panning area, but the pot of gold for me was the magnificent views of the snow-capped mountains, Ben More and Stob Binnein. Florence was running along in front of me, but not so far away that I didn't know where she was. Of course, we now have a tracker on her, so I'd be able to locate her if she did stray too far away.

What I had forgotten was that a little further on, there was a cattle grid. I heard the noise before I saw it. Yes, Florence had tried to run straight across the cattle grid, but one or more of her legs had gone down between the metal strips. She let out a horrible cry, and I ran to reach her before she tried to run back over the cattle grid to get to me. Fortunately, there were three women just over the cattle grid who saw what had happened and ran to Florence's assistance. By some miracle, with a couple of cuddles and all her legs being gently felt to see if there were any broken bones, she was running again within five minutes.

That's a lesson to be learned there; if a dog has never seen a cattle grid (or a young child even), they may do just what young Florence did and try to run across it. I'd like to think Florence has learned her lesson, but I won't take any chances!

All was well, though, and we enjoyed the rest of the circular walk that eventually joins the cycle track from Crianlarich to Tyndrum. We were back at the van before dark, all legs and limbs intact.

I was horrified when drying Florence after our walk and rubbing under her tummy and chin, and I saw a huge gash. This was clearly an injury I had not noticed when she fell down the cattle grid. I had a little cry as I hugged her and shuddered to think how that could have been a much more serious injury. Florence was a very lucky pup that day! I left that bit of information to tell Mr M when we got home. There was no point in him worrying about Florence when there was nothing he could do.

Now, to sort out our tea. I had planned to have roast chicken tonight with some beans and rice. I'd cook two chicken breasts in the mini electric oven, one for tea and one for our picnic tomorrow. Alas, I took the chicken from our little fridge only to find that they were still frozen in the middle. It still amazes me how effective our little campervan fridge is.

Flip. What was I to do now? The venison stew and the lentil soup were still frozen. I looked at my meagre supplies, wondering if I was destined to eat the famous Tyndrum fish and chips. But, no, I could rustle something up. So, tonight's tea was a plate of toasted cheese on sourdough bread, with a side helping of baked beans and a fried egg. Can I just tell you something. It was delicious. And, to my amazement, the gas still didn't run out.

I was feeling a little chilly in the van at this point as I was worried about overloading the electrics, so I had not turned on our little portable electric heaters. But once the oven was turned off, the heaters were switched on, the curtains closed, and the lights gently glowing.

The posh cheese on toast that I had for tea reminded me just why I love being away in my campervan.

The evening passed quickly with some writing, talking to Florence, and having another cup of tea. As I worked on my writing, I folded back the duvet on the bed to allow it to warm up – well, it is the first time out this year. Florence has decided that her bed is under the table, although she does sit on the bench seat watching me type and advising me which commas to take out. I do have a few extra blankets that I put over the seat for Florence to sit on. That's the joys of having a dog in a campervan. They decide where they are comfy.

I've still not investigated whether I can play the radio in the van without draining the engine battery, but I wasn't bothered. A little later, I was tucked up in bed, reading a new

CAMPERVAN CAPERS

book and enjoying the peace and quiet. Although I have to admit I was grumbling to myself that this was spoilt a little by the rumbling of traffic on the A82. But that's the consequence of choosing a site just off a main road.

The site is generally quiet, though, and I had an undisturbed night's sleep. Florence decided that 6.30 am was a good time to get up and start exploring, so we had a nice little walk before breakfast.

I didn't need to worry about the gas situation as I was having a porridge pot, so I just needed hot water and I now use an electric kettle for that.

Of course, the previously frozen chicken breasts were now fully defrosted, so as we pottered around, I popped them into the mini oven so they would be ready for us to take one of them on our walk.

After a lovely shower, I packed our picnic and planned our walk. Heading in the opposite direction of the cattle grid, you can follow the West Highland Way for however far you choose. This is the 96-mile long-distance walk that starts in Milngavie and ends in Fort William. Of course, I wouldn't be walking to Fort William, but I decided that even without a map, I could simply follow the well-trodden West Highland Way path for about two hours, stop for our picnic, and then walk back the same way.

This was a beautiful walk with the most amazing scenery looking towards Glencoe and the mountains beyond. Alas, one thing I'd not taken into account was that there were sheep on the track in places, so for much of the walk, Florence was on the lead, which neither of us enjoyed. It's also worth noting that you are close to the main A82 in places, although you are always separated by a fence, a railway line and then another fence. But the traffic does travel along that road at ridiculous speeds, and it always seems to be loud sports cars and motorbikes, which, for a noise-sensitive Border Collie, adds to the frustration already caused by being on the lead. I would seriously consider whether your dog is going to enjoy walking the West Highland Way with you. Does it like to be on the lead? Does it like the noise of traffic?

The A82 is a stunning road to drive, taking you through the most wonderful scenery and through the heart of Glencoe out to Fort William. It is one of the roads I would love to cycle on, but as the traffic is notoriously fast, I have avoided doing so. When I rule the world, I will have a cycle path built alongside the road so that cyclists can safely enjoy the magnificent journey without incurring the wrath of drivers who seem to be in far too much of a hurry across this road to appreciate its beauty.

After another cosy night in the van, it was sadly time to pack up. The weather was absolutely glorious, and I couldn't face missing out on another walk. I quickly packed everything away and headed out for a meander. This time, I walked in the opposite direction from the campsite. There is a massive, very detailed map on the path, and this shows a short walk called the Cattle Creep Trail, just a couple of miles round trip. It was an easy enough track, but I did think I'd have to carry Florence over the stream as she didn't want to get her feet wet. It might be a different matter if the stream was in flood. The sunlight was fabulous, and all the hills around looked magnificent. I was disappointed I had to rush a little more than I wanted to, but I knew I had to be off the site by noon. This was a walk I could take my time over on another stay here.

I feel that Tyndrum Holiday Park has become my favourite campsite.

Chapter 43

Another Failed MOT - 15 April 2024

It was MOT day, so I was again going to Struans in Perth. I'd had Evie booked in for a while now to ensure that if anything needed doing, I would still have time to get this completed before the MOT expired. I also hoped the garage could finally sort out the problem with the front tyre that was losing pressure. Having the tyres replaced last year didn't solve this problem, so the wheel rim might be the issue. Apparently, this will be looked at and might need to be sanded down or replaced. Last year's service also highlighted that the brake pads and discs would need cleaning and changing. This was also going to be looked at today, so I expected it to be a costly visit.

My campervan friend, Vicky, was hoping to introduce me to Cashel Campsite on the banks of Loch Lomond that weekend, so we were both praying for a good MOT. I'd not booked my pitch yet, just in case, and I was hoping I wouldn't be disappointed by a full campsite. All being well, I'd have my pitch booked before bedtime.

This year, the relentless rain had continued with no sign of abating for any decent length of time. I'd even seen a warning that Scotland was set for yet another four days of snow before April was out. I'd been watching for a break in the weather during the week to allow me to make sure Evie's tyre pressures were good for my trip up to Perth. On Sunday morning, I woke up to something shining brightly in the sky. I discussed this strange phenomenon with Mr M, and we decided this might be something called the sun.

"Ah, I remember warm, sunny days," I reminisced over my hot porridge. "Do you think we could do the tyre pressures while it's dry?" I asked, trying to do that cute head tilt thing that Beatrix taught me.

"Already done. I did it yesterday when you were out."

Did I tell you I love my husband?

In the last chapter, I was bemoaning my sudden lack of confidence driving Evie. Would it be the same when I got back behind the wheel today? I wondered.

With the journey to Struans taking just short of an hour and with Evie booked in for 8.30 am, I was up early and aimed to be on the road by 7.15 am.

By some miracle, after listening to the wind and rain battering the house overnight, the morning was calm, and the sun was shining brightly. What I also noticed was that I didn't feel nervous at all. Mr M even commented that he could tell I was looking forward to my day out.

Evie started like a dream and was eager to be away. We had a little detour to get out of Kirkintilloch as the usual road was closed for repairs (about time!). This, of course, meant a longer journey on the M80 and longer sitting in the rush-hour traffic. It soon turned into a lovely drive, and once on the M9, the traffic eased, and the views opened up. I love this section of the motorway where, on your right, you have the magnificent Stirling Castle sitting proudly on its mound, protecting the surrounding land, and the Wallace Monument reminding any possible enemies,

'They can take our lives, but they'll never take our freedom'.

To your left are the mountains of Ben Ledi and beyond, which were covered in snow.

CAMPERVAN CAPERS

Despite the sunshine, I still had to turn the heater up in the van as it was very chilly. Then, as I worked my way up the motorway, I passed field after field full of bright yellow rapeseed crops. Trees along the way were starting to blossom and bloom. Strange weather indeed.

As I enjoyed the scenery, listening to Smooth 70s on the radio, I smiled, sighing with relief that whatever had caused my drop in confidence driving Evie last month had vanished. I felt like a seasoned campervan driver today!

With the detour out of Kirkintilloch, I didn't arrive at Struan's until 9 am. It was lovely to find that the woman taking charge of Evie spoke with a broad Yorkshire accent. We discussed where we both from. She was from Leeds and had been in Scotland for 18 years; I'm from Halifax (about 15 miles from Leeds) and have been in Scotland for 20 years. Small world indeed.

Struans is very customer experience orientated and, as I've said before, they provide a taxi for you up to the centre of Perth, and back of course. With all the details given and a run-down of what I hoped to be sorted in Evie, I jumped into the waiting taxi. I'd planned to visit the library to spend a few hours writing, but the knowledgeable taxi driver informed me that Perth Library was closed on Mondays, so I headed for the nearest cafe for tea and a morning cake. Knowing it would be a good few hours before Evie was ready, I had to plan my cafes carefully. My arthritic feet and legs were still sore from a recent hike up Ben Ledi so I wasn't up for a long wander along the lovely riverbank and gardens, but I didn't want to overstay my welcome in cafes by stretching out my cup of tea. My first stop would be an independent cafe, and I'd save Costa for later. Heading into the shopping centre, I found the lovely Cafe Central and was soon enjoying a perfect cup of breakfast tea and a blueberry muffin.

Then my mobile rang. It was Struans. I instinctively knew this was not going to be a good phone call. It was too soon for Evie to be ready for collection.

"Your van has failed its MOT with a major defect. Could you come back so we can discuss the problem and any options we have?"

You can imagine how I felt. Every possibility was spinning through my head on the taxi journey back down to Struans. Could Evie be mended? Could I afford to have her repaired? If not, would Struans buy the van back from me? That thought almost made me cry. Then, I imagined having Evie on the drive at home and just using her as my stationary writing retreat. Maybe I could sleep in the van on the drive when Minnie came to stay so we could still have adventures. Would Mr M even agree to me keeping a van on the drive that couldn't be moved?

By the time I reached the campervan hospital I could hardly talk, keeping my sobs at bay. The receptionist advised me that Evie had failed her MOT because of dangerous exhaust emissions, which on a diesel vehicle usually meant that the EGR valve needed replacing. I didn't even know what that was.

For the technical readers (who probably know more than I do anyway), the EGR valve is the *Exhaust Gas Recirculation valve*. Apparently it's one of the vital components in modern engines, found between the exhaust and intake manifolds. Its primary function is to reduce harmful nitrogen oxide emissions and, in Evie's case, the black smoke plooming out of the exhaust.

The sad-looking MOT report read, *'Dangerous defect. Do not drive until repaired. Exhaust emits excessive smoke or vapour likely to obscure the vision of other road users. Repair immediately.'*

Heck!

Graham, my now favourite service manager, assured me that this was the likely problem and that once the valve had been replaced, Evie would get a glowing report because everything else had been OK. The bad news was that it would be in the region of £500 to do this.

CAMPERVAN CAPERS

Feeling relieved that Evie's problem was not terminal, I phoned Mr M and discussed the cost. Maybe it was my sobs on the phone, or whether simply because he knows how much Evie means to me, he replied,

"Just get it done, Debra."

With that, I was soon on the way to the train station and had left Evie in the very capable hands of team Struans, with the clear instructions that once they had replaced the valve and the MOT a success, they would strip the brakes and look at the issue with the tyre pressure.

A few days later, I received the news that Evie was all good to go. The EGR valve had been replaced, the MOT passed with flying colours, the brakes stripped, and the leaking valve replaced on the tyre, which had been the cause of the slight loss of pressure.

The following day, I took the train back to the van hospital. Evie was ready to be discharged, but there was the small issue of a bill for £866!

After picking myself up off the floor, I paid the bill, planning how I would break the news to Mr M and wondering how much longer I could afford to keep Evie in my life.

Let this be a lesson to you all. Campervan life is not cheap. You have to keep money in reserve for situations like this. And I still needed to get the habitation check carried out! I told myself that as I don't smoke, drink or buy lots of clothes, Evie is the only thing I spend money on for myself, which made the expense acceptable.

You all agree with me, don't you?

That was enough spending for now, and I booked Evie to have the habitation check and get a new leisure battery in May.

I never did get my planned trip to Cashel Campsite, but at least the starter problem seemed to have disappeared.

Chapter 44

A Runaway Dog – 20th April 2024

Tyndrum Holiday Park, Tyndrum, Scotland

April had been a very traumatic time on my campervan journey. Now that Evie's EGR valve had been replaced and she could breathe more easily, I decided we both needed a few days away. With my Cashel Campsite debut trip cancelled last month, I felt that I needed to go somewhere I was familiar with and not too far away in case of any further problems with Evie. Even though I'd already been to Tyndrum Holiday Park in March this year, I was quite happy to go there again, so I looked on their website and booked a two-night stay.

As you all know by now, Evie is very special to me, so I'm always pleased when others think of her as more than a tin box.

Are you listening, Mr M?

I emailed the campsite to ask if, although it was short notice, I could book the pitch I'd been on before, right next to the shower facilities because we've not sorted the bathroom leak yet, and I also told them about the MOT trauma. Imagine my joy when I received a swift reply from Kirsty stating:

Evie definitely deserves a holiday after that, and where better to go than Tyndrum in her favourite pitch 8 spot!! That's your booking updated to pitch 8, and we will see you tomorrow.

CAMPERVAN CAPERS

Now, that's customer service with a smile.

Despite my sore feet, I wanted to take Florence away with me on this trip and walk towards Ben Lui. Towards, not up! I fear that my Munro days are behind me now. And, best of all, Mr M suggested that I had fish and chips at the Real Food Cafe on one of the nights, so I didn't need to cook. Did I need any persuading? What do you think?

I don't need to tell you about the journey, as you've travelled this road with me before. I was mightily glad to reach the campsite without any misbehaving from Evie. Parking outside reception to check in, I took Florence with me, and she was behind the counter like a flash, getting cuddles and kisses from all the staff.

Finally managing to drag her away, we got back into Evie. You've guessed it. I turned the key, and nothing.

Florence looked at me.

I took the keys out and said some rude words.

I put the key back in the ignition and turned it.

Evie fired up immediately.

"What is all that about?" I shouted and thumped my fists on the steering wheel. Then, I looked around to make sure nobody had seen or heard me.

That would definitely need looking at when I took Evie back to Struans for her habitation check, I thought.

But, we were soon on our favourite spot, connected to the electricity, and everything was where it should be for the next couple of days. As the days were getting slightly longer, I decided we'd do the walk past the cattle grid and back along the cycle track. That way, I could let Florence know that the cattle grid she fell down on our last visit was not scary and also see if she would remember to go through the gate rather than try to run across the bars. I could sense that she was a little nervous, but she walked beside me to the cattle grid, looked at me, and strolled straight to the gate this time. She had learned her lesson.

I thought the walk would be a breeze from there now that we had passed the dreaded animal trap, but no. The main A82 was very busy, and although we were well away from it on the cycle path and you couldn't actually see the traffic, Florence could hear it. All the way along the track, she was clearly unhappy, and her tail was between her back legs, indicating how anxious she was. I'm really at a loss as to how to get Florence to realise she is a Border Collie and she should enjoy being out walking. Life seems so stressful for her.

Eventually, with no stopping at the bench for a rest, we arrived back at the gold mine. Once through the large gate, Florence set off running like a bat out of hell. I called her, but I knew she wouldn't come back to me. Fortunately, I had put her tracker around her neck before we left the van. Opening the app on my phone, I was able to track her and see that she was now back at the campsite. What I didn't know was whether she would run straight through the site and out onto the A82. My heart was in my mouth. I walked as quickly as I could, and to my relief, the warden on the site was holding Florence at the end of what looked like a blue dog lead.

"She bolted into reception, jumped behind the counter and lay down next to the radiator," said the warden. "We knew she was your dog and that you'd appear soon."

After thanking him, I told him what had happened and how glad I was that I'd taken her into reception when we arrived, as she clearly saw that as a safe space.

As I chatted with the man, I told him about Florence's nervous personality and how different she is from Beatrix. Of course, I also told him about Beatrix's book. Would you believe it? He and his wife love Border Collies. I was invited into their log cabin (which I was in total envy of, sorry, Evie) for a cup of tea and a chat about dogs and books. The couple, Paul and Gwen, have been working on the campsites for many years. Wait for it, Gwen was born in Halifax! Small world indeed.

CAMPERVAN CAPERS

After their Border Collie, Traigh, had to travel his dog rainbow bridge, Gwen published a book about him, which was full of letters that 'Traigh' had sent to his human aunty throughout his life. Taking a copy of the book away with me, I found it funny that Traigh was very cheeky about his human mum in the same way that Beatrix was cheeky about her human dad. But it was clear that there was as much love shared between the humans and their dog as there was with Beatrix and Mr M and myself, despite the cheekiness. I mentioned to Gwen that one of my favourite beaches to visit is Traigh Beach near Arisaig. Another strange coincidence was that Traigh was named after that beach because Gwen loved it so much! If you can get a copy of this book, it's a lovely read, *TRAIGH* by Gwen Ineson.

Once back at the van, after lots of cuddles, I gave Florence her tea, and then we walked to the Real Food Cafe for some well-earned fish and chips. I enjoyed a long, relaxed meal there, sitting at a corner table with Florence sleeping at my feet. It's tough being an anxious dog. It's even harder being the owner of an anxious dog.

We had an enjoyable evening in the van, Florence by my feet, as I did some writing and reading. Then it was off to bed. It was still a bit cold at night, so I left the little heater on very low just to make sure the van didn't get too cold for Florence. I'm OK under my super-duper duvet, but she only has a thin coat. I put some extra blankets on the floor for her so that if she wanted to, she could snuggle into them.

The following day, after breakfast, I made a picnic and set off to follow the path towards Ben Lui. I've never been up this Munro before and thought it would be nice to see it, even though I knew I wouldn't be climbing it. From the campsite, cross over the bridge and follow the West Highland Way signs, but veer off left when the WHW route heads towards the A82 and Glencoe. You have to cross over the railway line, which is never a fun thing for me. The crossing is at Tyndrum Lower

Station, so as well as having a great view of whether there are any trains coming down the line, you can also see the overhead sign telling you when the next train is due.

Safely over the railway line, the track heads gently up through a vast forest. Florence was not happy. I didn't know what it was, but she was hiding in the bushes and shaking. Once I'd put her lead back on her, she seemed much happier, and we continued up the gradual climb, eventually reaching a large gate that led to a track that heads all the way to Ben Lui. The views were amazing. I felt like I was surrounded by mountains. Even I was glad to be out of the forest. Bending down to take Florence's lead off her, I could tell that she was no longer afraid. Border Collies can smile, you know, and Florence was smiling, and her tail was no longer between her legs.

We wandered on the track for a mile or so until I found a suitable picnic spot where I could sit on a large bolder looking across to the magnificent Ben Lui, imagining what it would be like to be at the top.

It was a lovely moment, enjoying the rest, the picnic and seeing Florence relaxed at last.

I packed up, and we headed towards the large gate that would take us back through the forest. As soon as we were through the gate, Florence's tail was between her legs, and she was lying on the ground. I realised then what it was. Florence was afraid of the dense forest with its giant trees. I didn't have a map with me, but I had enough signal to get Google Maps on my phone. I could see that there was another way to get back to the campsite by walking all the way down the track that we had just been on and coming back to the campsite from the other direction. It looked a little longer, but if it meant Florence would be happier, I was prepared to do it. We went back through the gate again and onto the track. Florence was immediately back to her happy self, knowing that we were not going through the forest. It was indeed a much longer walk back, but a happy dog makes for a happy owner.

CAMPERVAN CAPERS

Back at Evie, for the first time ever, I was glad I was only away for two nights because I felt this trip had given Florence enough to deal with already. Maybe I'll bring her back again later in the year to see if she enjoys it more now that I know to avoid the scary forest.

That night, as I lay in my bed, I wondered if I was destined to have solo trips without a husband or a dog.

Am I the only one who really enjoys being away in Evie?
Was I forcing Mr M and Florence to follow my dream?
I hoped not.
That night, I had a little weep as I fell asleep.

Chapter 45

Two New Batteries! - 16th May 2024

Today, I took Evie back to the campervan hospital for her habitation check. It's easy to think that because this is not a legal requirement that it's not necessary, but when you're living in a small, confined space where gas, water and electricity are all used, it's vital that any problems are spotted early before they become an issue or a safety hazard. You've probably spent a lot of money on your van, so you need to try all you can to help it maintain its value so that even if you keep it for a few years, you'll still be able to sell it and get back some of your investment if and when that time comes. Evie was also getting a new leisure battery.

I remembered at the last minute that I had to unpack the garage for the habitation check. It's surprising how much stuff is in there. I really do need to get a lightweight folding table. Ours is great, but it's quite heavy.

We had just had a few glorious days in Scotland with plenty of warm sunshine. Over the weekend, the whole of the UK was treated to a magnificent show of the aurora borealis. Social media was flooded with amazing photos. Obviously, some were taken with posh cameras, enhancing the fantastic colours, but I could see purples, pinks and greens with my naked eye outside our house in Kirkintilloch. It was only my

CAMPERVAN CAPERS

eye that was naked, I should stress, and I was wearing a clean pair of pyjamas! I did manage to get some photos with my phone, and I giggled when I looked around and saw other neighbours out in their PJs. I thought it was just campsites where people wandered freely outside in their nightwear.

That night, I was a bit perplexed by Mr M because he didn't seem as excited about the lights as I was and said he couldn't see anything until, after nearly 20 years of marriage, he told me he was slightly colour-blind! Now I wasn't upset any more. I felt sad that he might always miss these fabulous displays. If I ever manage to fulfil another dream of mine, which is to travel to Nome in Alaska to see the Northern Lights, maybe I need to reconsider my travelling partner!

Setting off to Perth at 7.30 am, I joined the rush hour traffic for what was a dull, misty start, with the van's headlights on. Despite this, everywhere looked green and lush. The rapeseed was still blooming, and even with the windows closed, I could smell it. At one point, a huge field of this crop turned the low-lying mist yellow. It wasn't bright yellow, just a bit like the water when you've washed your paintbrush after working in watercolours.

I'm not sure why I made that comparison because I don't even draw, never mind paint with watercolours. That's a skill I don't possess.

I was enjoying the drive, listening to Heart '70s on the radio and an array of music from Bruce Springsteen, Eric Clapton, Diana Ross and Barry White. What a playlist that made.

Arriving at Struans, the sun was breaking through the clouds, and it was lovely to be greeted by Graham, saying,

"Hello, Debra, let's get your van booked in."

That's why I drive that long journey when Evie needs anything doing to her.

Leaving Evie in their capable hands, I took the courtesy taxi to Perth Library, where I spent a couple of hours writing surrounded by books. My tummy began to disturb the peace and quiet of the library, so with the sun now beating down, I had a short walk to the city centre and once again found myself in the Cafe Central, where I enjoyed a scrummy plate of macaroni cheese, chips, garlic bread and a large pot of tea.

After receiving the phone call to tell me Evie was ready, I sat in the sunshine, waiting for my return taxi. It was Perth races that day, and my entertainment was watching all the posh outfits and fascinators as people staggered their way towards waiting coaches. I mean, what is the point of a fascinator? I was sure there would be some of the revellers who might not remember even going to the races as they were already very intoxicated.

But I had more important things to think about. With Evie once again sorted, I'd be able to go away in the morning to Blair Atholl. Mr M had told me I was being optimistic booking the pitch before I'd got Evie back.

Talking to the mechanic at Struans, he told me that he was worried about Evie's main battery as when he tried to start her, he had to jump-start her, even with her new leisure battery. We discussed how this had been an ongoing problem but I told him I'd never needed to jump-start her, just turn the key a couple of times and pray. The mechanic advised me to have a new battery fitted because the old one was not keeping its charge, and that was probably the cause.

Rather than have me drive all the way home and then have to drive back, they sorted out the delivery of a battery and told me to sit and do some more writing and have a cup of coffee.

A couple of hours later than expected, Evie was full of power, and I was able to drive home confidently, knowing that her starting problems were over and everything was tickety-boo with the habitation and gas system.

Blair Atholl, here we come, I thought.

Out of curiosity, once home and on the drive, I turned the engine off, waited a few minutes, and then turned the key again.

CAMPERVAN CAPERS

Nothing!
I couldn't believe it. I tried once more, and Evie fired up with no problem. So, the issue was still there. I would speak to Struans when we got back from Blair Atholl.

Chapter 46

A New Campervan Fear Unleashed – 17 May 2024

Blair Castle Caravan Park, Blair Atholl, Perthshire, Scotland

After the palaver of the batteries, I could now enjoy a few days away. Evie was repacked, and even the drive away awning was in the garage rather than filling the kitchen aisle. I had made the executive decision that as I'd managed the last trip without filling the van with fresh water or needing the grey waste water container, it could stay at home, freeing up the space for the awning in the garage.

I had a fretful night wondering if Evie would start. When did being a campervan woman become so stressful?

Everything was finally packed, and I spoke nicely to Evie and told her we were going on a lovely holiday. She behaved herself and started the first time for Mr M.

"You need to let the glow plugs warm up first. That's why it doesn't start for you," announced Mr M.

I said nothing but knew that this intermittent fault would need further investigation if it continued.

The drive up to Blair Atholl was stunning. The world really had woken up. There is one stretch as you approach Birnam and Dunkeld where the road opens out, and you see thousands upon

CAMPERVAN CAPERS

thousands of trees, all lined up on the hillside in a multitude of greens. We both said together how amazing it looked.

"How many greens can you count?" I asked Mr M.

We were slightly disappointed that we were not in our usual spot in the campsite, but were allocated an equally good pitch, maybe not as quiet as our normal area, but it was hardstanding and had water and electricity.

The weather forecast had been for rain in the afternoon, so I wanted to get the drive away awning erected before it started. The only rain that afternoon was the sweat pouring from me as I manoeuvred the tent from the inside to ensure it was pegged out correctly.

By this time, Mr M was sitting basking in the sunshine. Florence was asleep under the table, and I needed a cold drink.

I love watching the comings and goings in the different campsites and looking at the range of tents, campervans, motorhomes and caravans. I'm always amazed that even those with massive motorhomes still need to add extra awning tents. How much space do you need when you're on holiday? I wondered if some people stayed on site permanently.

Sitting with my cold Diet Coke, I was astounded at the number of people cutting the grass around their caravans. One person even had a large electric lawnmower.

Just let the grass grow!

Our neighbours that night were a lovely couple from Shetland on a seven-week tour. They had an Adria motorhome that was nearly twice the size of Evie and were trying to convince me that if I could drive my campervan, I could drive a larger motorhome. I was not convinced. It was interesting discussing the different layouts and how the larger vans are not always the comfiest. Their large double bed is raised, and they need a ladder to get up onto it, but it does then give them two lounges when the bed is folded away. It seems that no matter what van you have, there are always things you like and things you would change if you could.

Debra Murphy

It was such a lovely sunny day that we decided to treat ourselves to fish and chips from Food at the Park, which was just a five-minute walk from the campsite. They were very expensive but absolutely delicious and freshly cooked. If you wanted to, you could sit inside the bar area to eat and watch a large-screen TV. We sat at one of the many picnic tables outside, enjoying the evening sunshine and peace.

The following morning, I was up at 6 am taking Florence for a walk. It's always good to see her running around off the lead, and she is much more confident in herself when she is free. She also knows her way around the surrounding lanes and fields at this site. I always watch out for other dog owners to see if they have their dog on a lead and put Florence back on hers as she thinks that all humans and dogs want to play with her.

With our pitch being further away from the shower blocks than usual, I had to trudge across the field to carry the dishes to wash them. Was Mr M smiling as he had told me it might be a mistake to leave the grey waste water container at home?

"Isn't it time you fixed the leak in the bathroom for me?" I responded to his grin.

For this trip, Mr M's knees were so bad that he couldn't manage the long walk along the riverbank, back around Hercules Garden, and down to the castle, so I took Florence on the walk and arranged to meet him at the castle for a picnic. He could take his time hobbling up there and carry the food and flasks for us.

After a lovely wander, Florence and I were pleased to see that Mr M had already arrived and was sitting on a picnic bench with our lunch. It's a lovely place to while away the hours, but make sure you get a table where you are in the shade of the trees during the mid-day sunshine.

This year, the castle was once again looking stunning, especially in the sunshine. It had all been repainted white, and the scaffolding removed. The piper still comes to play every hour, on the hour, entertaining the tourists, but Florence is not interested in this. When Beatrix came here, she would bark at the piper, and we had to move away so we wouldn't spoil the show. Who knows. Maybe Beatrix was simply singing along to the pipes?

After a delightful few hours, we were back at Evie, and I enjoyed one of the absolute joys of campervan life – having an afternoon snooze on the bed with both back doors and all the windows open.

I'm not sure what woke me up. Was it the dirge-style music from the people opposite or the noticeable drop in temperature and disappearance of the sun, mixed with a gentle breeze turning into a light wind?

The weather forecast had warned of thunderstorms between 6 and 7 pm. Nevertheless, whatever the time, the storm was about to hit us. And boy, did it hit us. Thunder, lightning and torrential rain. It started with a gentle rumble in the distance and tension in the air. All migraine sufferers will understand how my head felt. I remember that at school, my fellow pupils often judged the weather based on whether I had a headache. We didn't know what a migraine was all those years ago.

Then, like listening to a band marching down the road, you could hear and feel the thunderclaps. I love a good storm, but Mr M warned,

"This awning is going to leak. You won't get much more use from this now. Another waste of money."

Florence hid under the table, ignoring her food, even with added fish for a holiday treat.

There was one almighty crash of thunder, and a lightning bolt lit up the sky. I have a bit of a heart problem, and I could feel a little flutter in my chest. I must mention this to my cardiologist. Maybe my condition is weather-related.

I swear I felt Evie bounce up and down with fright. Was I safe in the van or the awning tent?.

Nevertheless, as I watched nature's show, I still managed to cook salmon, rice and steamed vegetables for our tea.

"This rice needed more water," said Mr M, wolfing down his meal.

And people wonder why I usually let him do the cooking!

As the torrential rain fell, looking around at our neighbours, tents were zipped, windows and doors closed, pod doors slammed shut, and satellite dishes lay on the ground upside down.

And we all waited.

The trees at this site lean permanently, showing how the wind usually blows. Sure enough, the storm was passing in the same direction.

The sky was black above us, but we could already see the bright sky behind the storm clouds. Thirty minutes later, the rain had stopped, the birds were flying again, and the sun was peeping out. Doors opened, people re-emerged from their vans, barbecues were back out, and laughter could be heard.

Five minutes later, Mother Nature had the last laugh when, from apparently sunny skies, the heavens opened once more for a last downpour.

"Let's have a cup of tea and a caramel slice while we wait for this to finish before we take Florence out," I suggested. Neither Mr M nor Florence objected.

Waiting for the rain to abate, I scrolled on Facebook on the Adria Twin Camper Van Owners page to see if anyone else was having the storm. But the conversation I saw that filled me with horror was somebody asking if everyone had a fire extinguisher in their van. They were worried that the back door catch to open from inside had been deactivated in theirs.

The replies were that this should not have been deactivated and it was faulty and dangerous. I had a discussion with Mr M about this, who assured me that ours worked when he had checked it.

CAMPERVAN CAPERS

"How long ago was that?" I asked him.

"When we got her," he replied, now frowning.

Now a new campervanning fear had been unleashed – being trapped in a burning van. Putting my half-eaten caramel slice down, I had to go and check if I could open the back doors from the inside. Phew, ours worked, no problem.

"I'd throw you out of the roof window and save you," said Mr M, grabbing a second caramel slice.

After a few days at the lovely Blair Atholl site, enjoying the sunshine and the storm was history, I swear that Mr M had forgotten that he doesn't like campervan life.

We had a short stop on the way home, and yes, you've guessed, Evie didn't start the first time, even for Mr M. Taking charge of the situation, I phoned the campervan hospital and discussed Evie's ongoing illness.

"I think you probably need a new starter motor. Can you bring the van in and leave it with us for a few days so we can check things out?" said Graham, the service manager.

By the way, the awning didn't leak!

Chapter 47

A Book Fair In Sutherland And
A New Starter Motor For Evie - 24th May 2024

By pure coincidence, I'd already planned a trip to the Highlands as I'd been booked as one of the guest authors at the Cromarty Book Fair. I calculated it would be possible for me to take Evie to the campervan hospital on Thursday morning, then pick up my planned train to Inverness at Perth station. I could enjoy the event and stay a few nights with my good friend, Ruth, in Sutherland. Then, providing Evie had been restored to good health, I'd get my booked train from the Highlands, get off at Perth, and then drive Evie home from there.

Struans once again exceeded their customer care service and told me that would be a perfect plan and that they would pay for taxis to and from the train station for me.

Thursday morning, bright and early, my adventure began. Of course, Evie started the first time in the drive, and I have to confess to using a couple of naughty words to her. But everything went to plan, and I was soon relaxing into my short holiday. A book fair, time with good friends, a drive around Sutherland, and fish and chips at Helmsdale. Perfect.

Late Friday afternoon, Struans phoned to tell me they had done lots of tests, found the fault, and replaced the starter motor so Evie would be ready for me to collect on Monday afternoon.

CAMPERVAN CAPERS

I can't tell you how relieved I was that I could now thoroughly enjoy my time away, do my author talk, sell lots of books and see some of the most stunning scenery in Scotland. I'd tell Mr M about the cost of this latest treatment for Evie once I'd told him how many books I'd sold at the fair!

So if you passed a woman driving a campervan down the A9 grinning from ear to ear, that was me in Evie, knowing she would be in my life for the foreseeable future.

With Evie restored to her former glory and resting on the drive at home, I decided she needed a bit of cheering up and ordered some more stick-on coloured tiles to make her feel special, which arrived the following day. An hour or so later, the doors for the cupboards above the table and the large storage space over the cab area looked rather trendy, with multi-coloured tiles applied randomly and in no order. Very nice, I told myself.

I'm now very confident that I'll never park next to another Adria Twin and find the interior to look exactly like Evie's.

Chapter 48

A 'U-turn' In Evie? Are You Having A Laugh!
6th June 2024

Berwick Seaview Caravan and Motorhome Club Campsite,
Spittal, Berwick-Upon-Tweed, England

It was time to find a new campsite, and I fancied a trip to the seaside. Looking on the Caravan and Motorhome Club site, I searched for ones along the east coast of Scotland, but as usual, I'd left things too late to book, and site after site was full. Moving further and further down the map, I finally found one just outside Berwick upon Tweed at a little place called Spittal, not too far over the Scottish/English border. They had availability for three nights on a hardstanding, electric hook-up pitch. Perfect, I thought.

This was to be a solo adventure for me as Mr M had already endured a trip this year, and we were booked to go to the Lake District for a week later this month, so I wasn't pushing my luck. I was taking Florence, of course.

Google Maps told me it would take me just over two hours to get there, so it wasn't a major journey, and it was all down the A1 except for the last couple of miles.

My pitch was booked for three nights, but with just Florence and myself, I didn't need to take the drive away

CAMPERVAN CAPERS

awning, and that was taken out of Evie and left in the house, along with the grey water waste carrier. It will be no surprise to hear that I'd still not sorted the leak in the bathroom, so I would not be able to turn the water on in the van. It wouldn't be a major problem, although I would have to walk down to the facilities onsite to do the washing up as the club sites don't have fresh water taps next to the pitches. And there would be only myself responsible for whatever went into the toilet, which would not be very much, I can assure you.

I did notice that Mr M was very eager to get my food rations sorted for me and wave me on my way. Had he been worried I might ask him to go with me?

It was time to test the new starter motor. Would Evie start the first time? Of course she did.

With the sun shining, I set off along the M80, heading towards the M9 and then the A1. It was the 80th anniversary of the D-Day landings, and Radio Two was hosting a very emotional programme throughout my journey. There were interviews, chats, songs and memories from those who had survived, and about the many who perished. I swayed between being upset and angry that wars seem to continue despite the First World War supposed to have been the war to end all wars. Lest we forget, indeed.

Driving east was a bit of a novelty for me, as I tend to go north to the Highlands or south to the Lakes and Yorkshire. The east of Scotland is definitely not wild and remote like the Highlands; rather, it's lush, green and gentle. Tootling along, I admired the Pentland Hills, Hillend Dry Ski Slope and Arthur's Seat, pleasant hills but by no means mountains.

Joining the A1 beyond Edinburgh, I could almost feel the pull of the coast and the sea. There was time for a lunch stop before I could check in at the site, and with plenty of lay-bys on this tourist route, I was spoiled for choice. I waited until I found one where I felt I'd be well away from the main carriageway, pulled in and enjoyed my picnic made for me by Mr M.

Debra Murphy

With the new starter motor working like a dream, I realised then how stressed I'd been about Evie and her non-starting over the last few months. Stopping and starting was now no longer an issue, but I resisted the temptation to turn her on and off more than necessary. I was now back to loving my campervan.

I don't know about you, but even when I can't see the sea, I can sense it. At this point, I knew I was very close to the coast but couldn't see it yet. I felt that buzz in the bottom of my stomach, knowing I was heading towards it. It's a bit like when going to Blackpool as a child, which I hated because of the amusements and my lack of ability to go on any rides without feeling sick; we would look out for Blackpool Tower and the first person to see it got the biggest ice cream. I'm sure I was always the first to spot it, as I knew exactly where to look, but I'm not convinced my ice cream was any bigger than anyone else's.

Passing Berwick upon Tweed, just a couple of miles over the border, I turned off the A1 to follow the A1167 to Spittal. My satnav took me right into the village and told me I was two minutes away from my destination. Spittal is a small village with a promenade, but I could see no campervan site. Then,

"Make a U-turn," my satnav told me.

I had a little panic. A U-turn. In Evie. In this little village!

Pulling to the side of the road, I took some deep breaths. You can do this, Debra, I told myself. You've got wing mirrors and a reversing camera. It's a little village with no traffic. Go for it.

Well, readers, you would have been proud of me. I took myself back all those years ago to my driving lessons and did everything I was taught. In three swift and confident moves, I did my first-ever three-point turn of Evie on the road. I gave myself a pat on the back and wiped the sweat from my brow.

Back on the main road, I could see there was a little road heading up the hill, and the satnav wanted me to go there. Gingerly, I drove up this road with my satnav telling me I had

CAMPERVAN CAPERS

reached my destination. What! Then, out of the corner of my eye, I caught sight of the Club logo on a sign up another very tight left-hand track. Here goes. And there it was, hidden from view, Seaview Caravan and Motorhome Club Campsite. Of course, for those whose satnav brought you from the opposite direction, you would have seen this sign and not had the ridiculously tight left-hand turn. I'm just glad I wasn't driving anything larger than Evie or, heaven forbid, towing a caravan.

As I pulled into the arrivals space, there was one of the club staff members waiting to welcome me. He checked my identity, checked my membership was valid and checked how many people I had in my van. Obviously noting my surprise at these checks, he advised me that so many people were booking non-members onto sites, so they had to check everyone's membership each time now. Now I have another app to find on my phone because physical membership cards are no longer being sent out. I'm sure there will come a time when we can stop relying on apps for everything. I, for one, get frustrated trying to remember a password for this, a password for that and changing passwords because I can't remember my password. It's far easier to pull a membership card out of your pocket for verification. Call me old-fashioned, but I bet you agree.

At all club sites, you're left to your own devices to find your chosen spot, but again, I was reminded to make sure I parked within the two white posts on my pitch.

This site is not huge, and I found myself a lovely spot that I thought would be both sheltered and give a wonderful view to the sea.

I'd read reviews on this site, and a couple of them had mentioned how tight the pitches were. They were right. Initially, I drove onto my pitch, but as it was so short, really only just long enough for Evie, I decided I didn't like the idea of my bed being right next to any passing traffic, even though it would be only travelling at 8 mph. Driving the van back out,

Debra Murphy

I manoeuvred it to reverse back onto the pitch. I'm a master at this, after all, with my earlier three-point turn.

With the engine off, I climbed down, had a stretch of my legs and let Florence out, fastening her lead peg into the grass next to my pitch. Then I realised that I had parked so close to the bushes and wall that I couldn't get into the garage of Evie to get everything I needed. So, yes, I had to get back in and drive forward to give me space. Today, I was the entertainment for the campsite.

I was slightly worried about the prospect of seeing spiders in the bushes out of my bedroom window now I was so close to them that I closed the blind on this immediately. If I couldn't see spiders, I'd be safe. I know! I'm supposed to be an adventure girl, but I am afraid of spiders. There. I've admitted it.

My first problem was that no matter what I did, I couldn't get the electricity to work. I connected both ends of my cable, disconnected, and plugged them back in, but there was nothing. I knew it couldn't be the cable as it had been working before I set off from home that morning.

Hearing chattering from my neighbours' van, I shouted a friendly hello and asked them if there was anything special I needed to do. They said they had the same problem but couldn't remember what they had done to get it to work. They were very helpful and tried everything, including putting my cable into their supply. This showed that my cable was working, so it had to be the pitch connection.

I strolled down to the reception and told them my issue. Rolling his eyes, the man took out his folder with photographs showing where I should plug in, which button I needed to press, and which lever should be up or down. I refrained from suggesting that maybe it would be better to have these photos on the pitches so we wouldn't need to bother him.

But soon, I was set up, the electricity on, the fridge working, and I had the remainder of my flask of tea and a couple of biscuits, and Florence had a bone.

CAMPERVAN CAPERS

From my van, I could see the sea from both sides, so whether I was sitting at the table or cooking, I could take in the views. I think this has to be one of the best pitches I've had to date for views.

The sun was shining, but there were some dark-looking clouds floating about, and it was very breezy.

"Time for a walk on the beach," I told Florence.

I already knew how to get to the village and the promenade after my earlier tour around Spittal in Evie, and ten minutes later, we were walking along a beautiful sandy beach. But Florence's ball was still in the van. She looked at me and looked at some other dogs and their balls, and she went and stole one. Mortified, I made her return it and wandered to the promenade cafe in the hope they might have some beach toys. Thankfully, I was able to purchase a couple of tennis balls, but I also noticed with excitement the huge currant teacakes they had in the cake display. I'd be back for one of those tomorrow, I told myself.

The UK has the most fantastic coastline. This section, with its vast sandy beaches and view towards Berwick upon Tweed, is very peaceful and charming. I spent a good hour with Florence chasing the ball. I was concerned that she was trying to drink the seawater but laughed at her refusal to go into the water to retrieve her ball. Beatrix would have been in there like a shot. It just shows that two dogs of the same breed can be so totally different in character, even though they have similar traits.

Back at Evie, we had our tea and relaxed watching the glorious sunset. I did wonder if this was going to be the trip when the gas finally ran out and if I would manage to change it if I had to. I hoped not because that would, of course, mean having to move the van forward to get into the garage where the gas cylinders are stored. And we all know the spiders would be waiting for me.

Then I realised just how far away we were from the facilities. It's surprising how heavy a bowl of dirty dishes can seem after you've carried them for five minutes. I was determined that when I got home, I would get the leak fixed in the van so that I could once again have water for washing up at our sink.

It was a very quiet night, and I slept soundly.

Berwick upon Tweed is one of those places I've passed many a time, either on the train or when driving, but I've never visited. According to the maps, it was a thirty-minute or so walk to the town centre from the campsite. My arthritis in my feet and ankles was playing up a little bit, so I decided I'd have a stroll to the town centre, admire the views, and treat myself to morning coffee. I made the mistake of following Google Maps and forgot to tell it I was walking and not driving. This took me along the busy route following the road, eventually arriving at the town centre a good 45 minutes later. Florence is very nervous around traffic and pulls on the lead, and this, together with my arthritis, made for an unpleasant walk.

Once there, I have to say that, sadly, it didn't get any better. Many of the cafes were closed that day, along with a lot of other shops, and everywhere looked very rundown.

I did find a few of the paintings along the Lowry Trail, which were lovely to see. The artist, L S Lowry, is famous for his matchstick men paintings around factories and back-to-back terraced houses in Manchester and the North West.

Writing up this chapter back at home, I was distracted as I had the song by Brian and Michael, '*He Painted Matchstalk Men and Matchstalk Cats and Dogs*' playing on my computer. Mr M joined in with his guitar, and we had a real old sing-song. I was even more surprised to find out this was on Top of the Pops in 1978, written as a tribute to Lowry, who died in 1976. There's me thinking it was about ten years ago!

Lowry spent many holidays in Berwick upon Tweed and created more than thirty paintings and sketches of the area.

CAMPERVAN CAPERS

You can now follow the Lowry trail and visit the places he painted or sketched. The whole trail takes about three hours, but my sore feet only allowed me to see a few of them. If you're in the area, look it up, as it looks fantastic. My favourite was Dewar's Lane, reminding me of the very tight lanes in York, but Lowry's sketch was amazingly accurate of the actual lane.

I'd like to tell you that I found a cosy, quaint little tearoom for Florence and me, but sadly, no. Dog-friendly cafes were very hard to find. Actually, any open cafe was well hidden. In the end, I settled for one that did an all-day breakfast, and I could take Florence in. The experience was not great, but the food was OK. I gave Florence a sausage and enjoyed a lovely pot of tea. I was glad I would be walking back to the campsite, though, as my clothes had now taken on every cooking smell from the cafe. Not a pleasant perfume.

My return route back to the campsite was much better. I crossed the bridge and got some fantastic photos of the estuary. I did think I had seen some seals, but I wasn't 100% sure. In this area, it is possible to see seals and dolphins, and you can get boat trips out to Holy Island. Seasick on a rowing boat, I didn't partake in this tourist trip.

Following the coastal path and then Dock Lane, I was able to walk back to Spittal, avoiding any main roads, much to Florence's delight.

With my feet crying out for mercy, once back at Evie, I lavished them with painkilling gel, opened the roof windows and lay on top of the bed.

It was then that I realised just how windy it had become, and I could feel the van seriously rocking. The roof windows were quickly closed, and I opened the side windows instead. My neighbours had left, and now there was nothing acting as a windbreak for Evie. Could campervans blow over? I wondered. Looking on the internet, I was relieved to learn that, as campervans are very bottom-heavy, they might rock and roll but would probably not blow over unless the weather was very extreme. BBC Weather told me that the wind was changing between moderate and fresh. I now know that the order of winds in terms of strength is light, moderate, fresh, strong, gale and hurricane. Thankfully, in the next hour, the wind would return to moderate and ease to be light by the morning.

Despite the wind, the gentle rocking of the van sent both Florence and me to sleep. By the time we'd woken up, my feet were feeling a little better, and we had new neighbours with a large van, which was now acting as a windbreak.

The site itself is very close to the railway line that runs between Scotland and England, with regular fast-moving trains. Florence is absolutely terrified of trains, and we still can't take her on rail journeys because of this. I was worried that this would be a problem for her, but it worked in exactly the opposite way. The first train she heard had her cowering and shaking under the table. Then, with each train, she became slightly less anxious, and it didn't take long before she would stop what she was doing, but she no longer dived for cover.

The layout of the site means that if you wanted to, you could spend the whole of your visit without talking to anyone. Somebody once said to me that people talk to me because I'm friendly and approachable, but, on this visit, I found I was happy in my own company and able to enjoy the peace, wonderful seaside views and sunsets.

The following day, with some good weather forecast, we set off to walk part of the Northumberland Coastal Path. I didn't have a map, but I took a picnic and a flask of tea and fresh water for Florence. On a route like this, it is easy to walk as far as you want and then turn back without the risk of getting lost. I planned to walk for two hours, have a lunch break, and then walk back.

The section I followed was on the Sustrans Cycle Route 1, and if I'd been cycling, it would have been a mere 14.5 miles to

CAMPERVAN CAPERS

Holy Island and 27 miles to Seahouses. In the opposite direction, it was 4 miles to the Scottish Border and 94 miles to Edinburgh. Be aware if you are going to cycle on this section, it's OK for walking, but you'd struggle on a road bike with narrow tyres.

As we walked, we met and chatted with some lovely people. I guess folk I meet on routes like this are most likely to be like-minded souls. Florence is a stunning Border Collie and, like Beatrix was, is very well-behaved and attracts attention. She was given lots of hugs and cuddles. I settled for chatting.

After an hour's walking, I could feel my feet begin to ache. It was time to stop at the next accessible bit to a beach. Five minutes later, I arrived at Cocklawburn Beach, which had vast, wide-open sandy beaches, views of Holy Island and Bamburgh Castle, and hardly any people. This was my perfect lunch spot.

I'd remembered to take Florence's ball and thrower this time, so after sharing our lunch, she enjoyed a good run around and then settled down next to me for a nap.

Packing everything up and, of course, leaving nothing but footprints, we were just leaving the beach when a family came down the track carrying a canoe and lots of bags. They were smoking something that I was sure was not just tobacco. I wondered momentarily if sitting and breathing in their fumes might help my sore feet.

As usually happens, I had walked too far, and by the time I was approaching the promenade at Spittal, I was nearly on my knees. Cake. That's what I needed. Stopping at a resting point, I looked around. The views were great, and it was very peaceful, but I felt as though I was missing something. I just couldn't put my mind to it. What was it? I phoned Mr M. Maybe it was him. But no, even after speaking with him, there was still something missing.

At the giant currant teacake cafe, I popped in and bought one of these delights for later, then sat outside with a coffee and a scrummy mint slice. The wind was howling, and even though it was sunny, I was cold, tired and sore and needed to put on my jacket and my waterproof coat. Warm and cosy, I could have sat there for hours, but I was demented by the noise of the millions of people who had appeared from nowhere and the relentless tune from the amusements next door. Does anybody really need this sort of entertainment? I wondered.

Back at the van, once again, I had a lovely evening watching the sunset, reading and eating my giant toasted currant teacake.

The following day, it didn't take long to pack up, but I made a rookie mistake of not checking for anything under the van. I had to drive Evie forward a little to get into the garage and put everything back in there.

Crunch.

I knew immediately what it was. I had put one of the fold-up chairs under the van when we arrived but never used it and had forgotten it was there.

I got out, and Evie's back wheel was now resting on this. Back in the van, I reversed enough to retrieve this, conscious that I would once again be the site entertainment.

By some stroke of luck, the chair was undamaged, so it was back in the van to drive forward to reopen the back doors.

Finally, everything was packed away, and we were off. We had a little stop on the way home at a ginormous lay-by, having a good break and reading.

Driving back and approaching the outskirts of Edinburgh, my heart was warmed seeing the hills and mountains in the distance. That's when I realised what was missing from Berwick upon Tweed. Mountains.

The gas didn't run out this trip. Would it run out on our next trip to Skelwith Fold? At least I'd have Mr M with me if it did.

With my sore feet, I decided that I needed to make another improvement to Evie. The toilet is quite high in the

CAMPERVAN CAPERS

van, and I am on my tiptoes when sitting on it. There must be something I can do to raise the floor.

But for now, I had to hope that Mr M would help me unpack Evie when I got home.

Chapter 49

Raising The Bathroom Floor – 20 June 2024

Once my feet had recovered enough to allow my creative mind to start working again, I began thinking of ways I could raise the toilet floor in Evie. I'd seen other people using wooden bathroom mats, you know, the ones made from slats of pine. They did indeed look very pretty and sturdy, but I thought they would feel hard and cold on our delicate bare feet if we had to use the toilet in the middle of the night. I wasn't going to be using the shower in Evie unless a dire emergency arose so I could have something softer, I decided. Then it came to me. I still had the jigsaw foam matting that I'd bought for the ground in the awning tent, which had now been replaced with a proper cushioned rug. These would be perfect, I thought.

Digging out a packet of foam tiles from the garden hut, I set about making one of the squares into a rough shape for the van's bathroom floor. The matting was very easy to mark with a felt-tip pen, and cutting it with scissors was no trouble at all. One cushion square was not quite long enough, so I had to cut up two of them to fit. But as they were interlocking squares, they linked together perfectly. Then, it was testing time.

"Guess what I've made," I shouted to Mr M.

With a sigh, he put down his laptop and followed me outside to investigate my latest creation. Sitting on the toilet,

CAMPERVAN CAPERS

but not actually using it, of course, he pondered for a moment, then said,

"Good idea, Debra, but the toilet is still too high."

That was easily solved, and very soon I had cut up a whole pack of the foam pieces, stacking them on top of each other and, hey presto, the toilet was no longer too high in Evie. Even better, because they are foam matting and not fixed down, they could be washed after each adventure and the floor cleaned underneath them. Now, we have a soft, warm floor for our tootsies. Sorted!

Chapter 50

The Gas Finally Ran Out – 24th June 2024

Skelwith Fold Caravan Park, Ambleside, Cumbria, England

I had finally calmed down after the recent traumas with Evie and began to plan more adventures. There was no longer a sense of doom about the longevity of having Evie in my life. The new starter motor was working a treat, and I didn't have to hold my breath when turning the ignition key. The front tyre with the replaced valve was now holding its pressure, and tyre checks were simply a matter of ensuring they were OK rather than having to blow it up to the desired PSI.

The cold, frosty winter weather in Scotland had finally given way to a glimmer of summer, and I'd been a regular visitor to the BBC Weather app checking the weather for Ambleside for the last week in June. Yes, it was that time again for us to have a full week in Evie at what might be my favourite campsite, Skelwith Fold Caravan Park, just outside Ambleside in the Lake District. And we were once again in the premier pitch section, too. Imagine my delight when I discovered that not only was I to get a discount because of my Advantage Club membership, but the site was also giving you an extra discount if you booked a holiday there before the end of June. What a deal we got for that trip!

CAMPERVAN CAPERS

It's always worth investigating loyalty schemes at campsites if you know you will stay there on more than one occasion. By joining Skelwith Fold's Advantage Club, we have made massive savings on our pitches there, but you also get discounts at nearby shops and restaurants.

I'm not sure I've admitted this to you, but I had realised that the collapsible washing-up bowl I bought when we first got Evie is not actually a washing-up bowl. It is, in fact, a draining bowl. When we were able to use the taps in Evie, we would wash up in the sink and use the collapsible thing to drain our stuff in. Perfect. That's what a draining bowl is for. But then, when I needed to wash up and I didn't have water in the van, I needed a washing-up bowl and not a draining bowl. So, with a week's holiday planned for two humans and a dog, we had a little trip to Go Outdoors. Of course, we found ourselves walking out of the store with much more than a washing-up bowl, including another rechargeable light and some Kendal Mint Cake (which I guess is a bit like taking coal to Newcastle!). Of course, Mr M tried to tell me that he knew it was a draining bowl all the time, but I think he's fibbing!

Now, I've already told you that summer had arrived, so food preparation had to be planned. How much could we carry in the cool box? Would everything fit in the fridge when we got set up onsite? That kind of thing. But that's all part of the fun of a holiday for me. And, of course, we needed our tub of travelling sweets. There is nothing quite like having a sugar rush because you've eaten too many sweets on a journey.

As usual, we'd planned our first stop to be at Gretna Services, where we knew we could park in the caravan section. Alas, when we got there, there were police cars and vans all over, and the caravan park was blocked off. I had to drive into the main car park and find a large enough spot away from all the other cars. I ended up parking by the hotel and right opposite the commotion with the police. It looked like they had stopped a lorry for some reason, and they were taking photos and measuring it. The driver was out of the lorry and not looking at all happy. I couldn't imagine that all those police cars and vans were for that one lorry, so maybe they had been pulling in vehicles to check them.

Even though I knew Evie was probably in the best health she'd been in a long time, I felt uncomfortable being around all this going on and didn't enjoy the stop. I was the girl at school who would walk right around the corridors in the opposite direction just so that I didn't have to pass the head teacher in case she thought I was doing something wrong. Now you understand my anxiety at being around so many police checking vehicles. I felt that my worried look might just make them investigate Evie just for the fun of it.

We had a quick visit to the toilet, let Florence do what she needed to do on the grass and kept our picnic lunch for later. Needless to say, we were both hungry, and it seemed a long journey before we reached the lay-by I had stopped at previously looking across to Blencathra and Sharp Edge. I felt much more relaxed at this stop, and we had a lovely late lunch.

Arriving at Skelwith Fold Caravan Park and driving up the long red road to the reception felt like going home to me, and once we checked in, we chose the same pitch we had been on in earlier visits.

Setting up the drive away awning, because it was now very hot, was hard work. But it was worth it knowing we were all prepared for when the weather was due to break later in the week.

I have to admit that I was now beginning to worry about Mr M's tolerance of campervan life. It seemed to be dwindling with each trip and was perhaps now only as great as his tolerance of tent camping. Would this be his last long trip away with us? I wondered.

I hoped not.

I tried my best to ignore his mini tantrums about the ground being too hard for the pegs, the sun being too bright, the water tasting funny and him asking why I forgot to pack the boil-in-the-bag rice. But if he had asked me one more time where something was, I was ready to kill him. I mean, it's not like he had to look all through a mansion, is it? Evie has four cupboards and a fridge!

The more times we come to Skelwith Fold, the more we discover. This year, I was able to do a little more hobbling so I could take Florence for a walk around the wooded walks on the site and Slew Tarn. Unlike Beatrix, Florence is not an adventure girl and would not dream of getting into the water, so I didn't need to worry about her like I did with Beatrix.

In all the years I've been visiting the Lake District I've always been disappointed not to see any red deer. Strolling through the wood that first night, smiling as Florence jumped about, sniffing and exploring, the biggest red deer with enormous antlers popped up from nowhere. What did Florence, the Border Collie who is afraid of her own shadow, do? She chased it. She actually chased it. It was like David and Goliath. I know that if my dog had been 100% trained correctly, she would have ignored the deer and returned to my side with the slightest calling from me. Alas, no. She was oblivious to my commands and disappeared deep into the woods, chasing this beautiful stag. I did wonder what the stag thought. Was it humouring her and letting her have her chase? Because there was no way that massive creature would have been scared of the tiny black and white bundle of fluff trying to catch it. A couple of minutes later, Florence flew quickly out of the wood and flopped at my feet. I wasn't quite sure what her expression was. Excitement? Pride? Fear? Shock? Whatever it was, she never went chasing deer again during the holiday.

In the packing at home, I had remembered to dig out some books we had both read to leave in the library at Skelwith Fold. Of course, this meant I felt it was OK for me to pick a new book for myself from the bulging shelves in there. A fair exchange, I thought.

Debra Murphy

This year, it was Mr M's knees that were the major cause of concern. Although my arthritic feet were still troublesome, Mr M was in agony. It made us both wonder if Skelwith Fold was a site that would eventually be one we had to avoid because of its location. It's great being in the middle of nowhere, and the buses, albeit sometimes slow or cancelled, are generally good. But the walk up and down the red road to the site once you get off the bus is a long slog when you're in pain for whatever reason.

After breakfast, we decided to go to Grasmere. Mr M declared that he would be able to walk down to the bus stop if he took his time but would consider getting a taxi on the way back if needed. I even managed to get him to use one of my walking poles. He must have been in pain!

Taking our time and enjoying the stroll, we were delayed somewhat as we watched in amazement as two large static caravans were being driven out of the campsite on the back of two lorries, with a backup van following them. We wondered how on earth they were going to get over the humpback bridge towards Ambleside, and I was almost tempted to leave Mr M and Florence to catch the bus themselves and walk up to the bridge to watch the spectacle.

Once on the bus, we enjoyed the short trip before changing buses at Ambleside for the open-top 599 to Grasmere. Mr M sat downstairs, and I took Florence up to the top deck. I don't think she likes the buses as much as Beatrix did, but at least she didn't need to be helped up the steps.

Be warned. Grasmere, in the height of summer, is busy, especially in glorious weather. We couldn't find a spot in the village green to sit for our picnic, but just down the road past Sam Read's book shop, the Co-op and the chemist, there's a large park with plenty of space for dogs to run around and lots of benches. Leaving Mr M there to relax in the sunshine, I took Florence around the walk that takes you through the wood and onto the road leading to Allan Bank, Wordsworth's old house.

CAMPERVAN CAPERS

Of course, it was then time for tea and cakes, but I was disappointed that my favourite tearoom, Baldry's, was full. Just across the road is Heidi's Cafe, and we were able to get a table inside out of the sunshine for Florence. I'm not sure why it's called Heidi's Cafe, but I'd like to think that it's named after my favourite book, Heidi, written by Johanna Spyri. I have always wanted to be Heidi, and I have even tried to grow long hair so I could have plaits once, but it never got below shoulder length! And I've already told you that I don't bother with brushes and hair dryers, so I just looked a mess!

I was so glad that we had managed to get a seat inside the cafe because just as we sat down, two RAF military fighter jets flew right over Grasmere, making such a din and giving Florence a fright. I dread to think how she would have reacted if we'd been outside. These jets fly regularly over the Lake District, as it's good practice for the pilots. I've heard some people complain about them and say they spoil the peace and quiet. There was even a call for these low-flying exercises to be banned, but as the RAF say, low-flying is a skill pilots need, and they can't practice over towns and cities. Personally, I'm on the side of the pilots who are practising so that they can keep us safe and protect us if they are ever required to.

Then, it was time to head back to the campsite. For the first time ever, we had a nightmare day with the buses. The first bus from Grasmere to Ambleside was delayed by over half an hour, which meant we missed the bus to Coniston. The next bus to Coniston was cancelled, and, being only one every hour, we had a long, long wait in the heat of the sun. Mr M liked that, but I sat across the road by the library and estate agents in the shade with Florence, looking at properties in the Lakes that I would never be able to afford to buy. I asked Mr M if he wanted to get a taxi to save him from walking up the red road from the bus stop (and maybe to save my aching feet and hips, too), but he was adamant that he was walking.

So, we waited and waited and waited. Eventually, one came, and we had the fifteen-minute bus journey!

It was a long walk up to Evie, but actually remarkably enjoyable as we just took our time and enjoyed the pleasant scenery and warmth of the summer sun. OK, it was muggy, but I had water, and so did Florence. Mr M was tough and said he didn't need any.

Once we'd had a rest and Mr M was showered, we got everything ready to cook tea. That night was very posh for us. We had cod wrapped in pancetta with roast potatoes and some vegetables. Very healthy! But just as we got everything started, the gas finally ran out. At least it was at the start of cooking and not halfway through. We then had a discussion about whether I could remember how to change the gas cylinder.

"You need to do this in case I'm not here to do it for you," said Mr M.

Was he trying to tell me something? I wondered.

Thankfully, after the last episode, we now had a proper spanner and stored it safely in the first aid kit bag in the garage, so it was easily located. Well, gas running out is an emergency!

I remembered to unlock when locking and lock when unlocking. Yes, gas fittings work the opposite way to standard. I unfastened and removed the empty bottle, removed the full one and carefully put that one on the floor. I then put the empty bottle into the back of the storage area and secured it, connected the full one, secured it, and closed the storage door.

Yes, I was sweating. I'm not sure whether it was just the heat of the sunshine or the knowledge that I was handling real gas canisters and that if I didn't connect it correctly, I might blow up Evie.

"Will you remember how to do this in future?" asked Mr M.

"Of course," I replied, wiping my brow.

I can tell you, that night, my tea tasted all the nicer, knowing that I had learned another thing in my quest to be a competent campervan woman.

CAMPERVAN CAPERS

I was surprised to find that despite the heat of the sun, with the sides of the awning tent open, it was very pleasant sitting in there because it gave good shade from direct sun. Later on, once it had cooled a little, with the sides down but the curtains tied back, it was a perfect hideaway from the midges that descended as the sun was setting.

What surprised me again even more was how comfortable we were in the van at night, even though it had been so hot during the day. I had imagined we would feel roasting, but it was very pleasant. The windows were left open, though, with the midge screens across, of course.

This year, my son, Benjamin, was joining us for a few days. Skelwith Fold doesn't allow tents on their site, so he had booked himself at the campsite in Chapel Stile, just five miles from us. Before he arrived, Ben messaged me to say he had just bought himself a new teepee tent and wondered if I could help him put it up. Reckoning on this just taking an hour or so, Mr M said he'd stay with Evie and take Florence for a little walk, and then we could all go to Chesters By the River for afternoon coffee and cakes. Of course, as Mr M pointed out, with Ben and his car, we wouldn't have to do any walking up and down that fierce hill.

This was the first time Florence and Ben's dog, Zeb, had met, so when he arrived, they had a bit of a play around together, getting to know each other. They're both very social, gentle dogs, so we knew there would be no problem. Then, we left Mr M and Florence to chill and wait for us to return.

Giving Ben directions, we were soon at Chapel Stile and stopped at the well-stocked grocery store for Ben to purchase some methylated spirit for his camping stove. I was a little surprised he was still using this and wondered if he would be able to buy any. I stayed outside with Zeb, and it was no surprise to me when he came out of the store sometime later holding a new gas camping stove and canister as he had been warned of the dangers of using methylated spirits and told that the shop no longer stocked it.

By this time, there was a bit of a gale building up, and despite the good weather, there was a weather warning out for wind and rain in the Langdale Valley, with Chapel Stile being in the centre of it. But Ben found a suitable space on the farm campsite. On sites like this, there are no actual pitches; you find yourself a spot and hope for the best.

Years ago, when I camped here, there was not even a real road into the site; you just took your chances on the track and hoped the farmer had maintained it enough for you not to lose the bottom of your car. In those days, there were no facilities as such, just a couple of toilets and a tap to get fresh water from. I was amazed to see that a new shower block and toilet facilities had now been built. Comparing this to my previous visits here years ago, this campsite was now like a luxury hotel!

The beauty of this site is not its facilities. It's the location. From your tent, wherever you have decided to pitch, you can see the magnificent Langdale Pikes at the end of the Langdale Valley. Of course, today, the wind was howling down this like a tornado.

This was going to be interesting, I thought.

Ben pulled out his new tent from his car, and we set about putting this up. It took a little while to work out how it should go, but with only one pole in the centre of the structure, the rest of the work was fastening all the millions of guy ropes. I mentioned how windy it was and whether this one-pole tent could cope with the wind. Ben reliably informed me that this style of tent was designed to withstand wind blowing from any direction and that it was completely waterproof.

With the wind now a gale, it took some considerable time, effort, sighs, grunts, and groans to erect the thing. But we eventually managed, although I had my doubts that it would still be there when Ben returned later that night, and I doubted even more that it would keep him and Zeb dry.

CAMPERVAN CAPERS

It was a very surreal moment for me, putting up a tent with my nearly 40-year-old son on the same site where I had introduced him to camping as a baby. This was also where, as a baby, he taught me that he could survive without me sterilising every teaspoon, cup or plate he used because, in fact, sheep poo was far tastier than baby porridge.

With the tent looking decidedly insecure, we left, hoping for the best, and returned to Mr M and Florence to head out again in Ben's car to Chesters By the River, where we had a pleasant hour or so enjoying coffees and cakes in the lovely surroundings.

We were slightly disappointed to see that the cafe was now using compostable cups and plates for everything, even if you were not taking your goods away. I'm not convinced that using all that disposable stuff is more environmentally friendly than using crockery that can be washed and used time and time again. It certainly spoils the experience, if you ask me. But the drinks and cakes were just as delicious as on our visit last year.

Overnight, I heard the wind blowing and the rain pattering on Evie and wondered how Ben was coping in his new tent.

We were just making breakfast when Ben's car pulled up, and a tired-looking son and bedraggled dog climbed out. So, readers, let this be a lesson. Teepee-style tents are no good in wind and rain in summer. I wouldn't even contemplate using one in winter.

Over some strong coffee and toast, Ben recalled his eventful night, which resulted in him and Zeb sleeping in the car and the tent going in the bin at the campsite. Of course, the wind and rain had now stopped, and the sun shone. Typical. Yet again, Ben had an adventure from the Lakes with his mum to remember!

Taking advantage of Ben and his car, I offered him a scrummy tea later on in exchange for a drive to Grasmere to swim in the lake there, which would mean Mr M's knees and my feet could have a bit of a rest. After a glorious swim, we headed into Ambleside for afternoon coffee at Zefirellis Cafe. You might remember this being the place where I took Benjamin and Chloe and bribed them with hot chocolate after we had to be rescued from the top of the Old Man of Coniston all those years ago.

Well, it wasn't to be a repeat performance today because it seemed that every man and his dog had decided to go to Zefirellis that afternoon, and there was no room for us. Disappointed, we tried the cafe across the road, The Copper Pot. What a revelation this was. I've seen this cafe many times, but have never bothered with it because I have always wanted to go to Zefirellis. This cafe was also busy, but we got a table and had some excellent food and drinks in our new discovery. Enjoying the relaxed atmosphere, we even decided to have tea (dinner for non-Yorkshire folk) there rather than at Evie's. We will be back there, I can tell you.

Obviously, Benjamin had nowhere to sleep that night, so he had decided that once we were safely back at Evie, he would have another coffee with us before driving to Halifax. That evening, Evie once again had Benjamin sleeping in her as he caught up on an hour's sleep before the drive home.

As you would imagine, once Benjamin had left for home, summer returned, and we had a glorious few days for the rest of our holiday, including a bus trip to the village of Hawkshead, where we had a lovely lunch in a cafe in the square, had a wander around the community orchard, and watched Florence run around a path as though she was racing. Sometimes, she can be adventurous.

I'm beginning to realise that she likes the open spaces, hills, and mountains, so long as there are no human-made noises like fighter jets, trains, cars, motorbikes and guns. She is, on reflection, very much like her human mum and Beatrix. Maybe Beatrix was frightened by all these things, but was just able to mask her fears more than Florence. But at only two years old, there is perhaps still time for Florence to learn to cope with our mad world.

But all good things have to come to an end, and our week at Skelwith Fold was all too quickly over. Until next year, of course.

The drive home to Scotland was much less stressful than the drive down with all the police activity, but we decided to give Gretna Services a miss because we now knew that Annandale Services was dog-friendly. The beauty of this stop is that there is a great place for dogs to run around, there are plenty of benches outside if you don't want to go into the cafe area, and there is a massive section of the car park with extra-large spaces for caravans and motorhomes that is usually empty. Except for that day! Just like every man and his dog had beaten us to tables at Zefirellis, it seemed every man and his dog had beaten us to Annandale Services. The car park was heaving, and I had to navigate Evie into a smaller slot than I was happy doing. I managed it like a seasoned campervanner, under Mr M's guidance, of course, and we were soon relaxing over coffees and cakes in the services, looking out onto Annandale Water. A lovely end to our holiday.

Had Mr M enjoyed his week in Evie?

Absolutely.

Is he starting to love campervan life?

No. But he said that he can cope with a week in summer to keep his wife happy.

Chapter 51

The Day I Met Hugh – 22nd July 2024
Yellowcraig Club Campsite, Dirleton, East Lothian, Scotland

I was determined that before I had finished this book, I would have an adventure with my granddaughter further afield than on the drive at our house. At the end of July, Minnie was coming to stay for three weeks, so this would be my chance. Where could we go that wouldn't involve too much driving? She was still only five years old and had a big drive up from Halifax to Scotland and back down again, so she didn't need mammoth campervan journeys too. I also wanted to find a campsite that would be within walking distance of a sandy beach. All five-year-olds love the seaside, don't they?

The Caravan and Motorhome Club have introduced an offer, so you only pay a £5 deposit for your booking, and the remainder is payable on the day of your arrival. Knowing the sites would fill up quickly over the school summer holidays, I found what looked like a good site, Yellowcraig, near North Berwick, only an hour and a half away from our home. I booked a two-night stay for Florence and me in July and another two-night stay in August. My plan was that if I tried this site by myself and thought it wouldn't be suitable for Minnie, I could

CAMPERVAN CAPERS

then cancel the second booking, and I'd get my £5 deposit back. I felt very pleased with myself.

My joy soon came crashing down when through the post arrived the DVLA tax demand for both the car and Evie, due 1st August. The car was bad enough at £180, but the van was frightening at £345. All this just before the insurance and service would also be due next month. Campervan life is a very expensive hobby.

Putting all that to one side, I was looking forward to my couple of nights away to do some more writing. Evie has become a regular writing retreat for me.

Mr M sorted my meals and went to the supermarket for some extra bits and pieces. He always seems so much more willing to do this when he's not joining me for the adventure. Should I be worried about this? I wondered.

As I left home, there was still over a quarter of a tank of diesel, but I decided to top her up a little so that when I ventured out with Minnie, I wouldn't need to stop for fuel. I'm becoming a dab hand at this now, so I don't know why I still worry about visiting a petrol station.

Once again, I ventured to the East Coast of Scotland, but not as far south as my last adventure to Seaview. This trip was just to North Berwick, not Berwick upon Tweed, two places that I often get mixed up in my mind but which are very different, with one in Scotland and the other in England.

I was a little apprehensive once I'd left the A1 towards Longniddry and then Dirleton, but the route turned out to be fairly straightforward. My only drama was going around a roundabout and the freezer box wedged on the bench seat falling down onto the floor, allowing its contents to spew across the aisle. As I glanced back, I imagined my bottles of milk, eggs, bolognese and lentil soup all leaking out of their containers and pouring across the floor, under the cupboards and fridge. Yes, I was nearly crying over the thought of spilt milk. I pulled in, took a deep breath and went to investigate the damage. Fortunately, nothing had broken, and I was able to pack everything back into the cool box, wedging it properly in between the seat and the table with extra cushions, and was soon on my way merry again. No harm done.

Once through the pretty village of Dirleton, the route takes you the final mile on a single-track road, but with lots of passing places, it was not a scary time.

There was already a sign at the entrance saying the site was full, so I was glad I'd pre-booked. I picked one of the last remaining pitches close to the shower blocks, which just happened to be right next to the children's playground. On the club sites, you pick your own pitch from the available ones, get yourself set up, and then inform the warden which one you've taken. Chatting in reception later, I asked them if I could pre-book the same pitch for my next visit with Minnie as it would be perfect so close to the facilities and playground. Although this was not a definite, she did put notes on my booking requesting this, saying that this was the least popular pitch because it was right next to the park, but it made it perfect for me. Fingers crossed.

For those of you needing campsites with good Wi-Fi, be warned that this site's internet is virtually non-existent except for a hot spot by reception. Again, this was another perfect thing for me as I wanted to get some serious writing done and not be distracted by the ability to scroll through endless reels on social media! Yes, it's a bad habit I've developed, and I know that I waste so much time doing this.

As I'd not stopped on my journey to the site, I still had my picnic and flask of tea to enjoy. Reading the notes on my booking sheet, it was only a five-minute walk to the beach, so it would be the perfect spot for lunch.

Now there are beaches, and then there is Yellowcraig, with its golden, sandy beach stretching as far as the eye can see and fantastic views out to the Isle of Fidra. This is reported to

CAMPERVAN CAPERS

be the uninhabited island that inspired Robert Louis Stevenson's *Treasure Island* during his trips there with his father and uncle when they were designing its lighthouse. The Stevenson family are responsible for designing many of Scotland's lighthouses, with Robert's grandfather being known as the 'father of Scottish lighthouses'. I knew that the Stevenson family was well-known for lighthouses, but I didn't know about the connection with *Treasure Island*.

I spent a very pleasant couple of hours sitting on my picnic rug, enjoying my late lunch, reading, and playing ball with Florence, admiring the view out to the other islands Lamb, Craigleith and the distant famous Bass Rock. I was saddened to realise that Florence was still not the water-loving dog that Beatrix was, but she did love running on the sand.

Back at the campsite, the sunshine had disappeared, and the drizzle started. As it was just me and a little dog, I'd decided not to bother with the drive away awning but pulled out the van's side canopy to stop the inside of Evie from getting wet with the big sliding door open. It was incredibly warm in the van, and I think this was the first time I'd really felt it too stiflingly hot and clammy inside with the door closed.

Eating my tea of homemade soup with some thickly sliced bread and butter, I felt very peaceful. I don't quite know how to explain it. I was in what Mr M would call a tin box, and the rain was pattering more than spitting and dripping from the canopy. It was the school holidays, and the children should have been plastered in suntan lotion and demanding ice creams, but they were riding about the site on their bikes wearing waterproof jackets. Summer '24 had not had the memo that it was long overdue in the UK. I have a comfortable house, lovely crockery to eat from, a husband who cooks scrummy meals and does the washing up. So why do I feel at my most peaceful in Evie in the rain?

With Florence needing a last walk, I headed out with my brolly and was pleased to find there was a dog walking field just behind reception. This is a large area with a path all the way around it where dogs can run free. It's great to have this facility on site because Florence, and probably many other dogs, will not happily do her business if she is on the lead. Another plus about this field was that I picked up a mobile signal as I walked around it, so I could phone Mr M and let him know that all was well.

Later that evening, as the mist descended, along with the midges, the temperature dropped a little. I couldn't get the weather forecast but didn't want to risk leaving the canopy out in case of a sudden gust of wind, so I wound it back in, knowing I could dry it out another day. That night, as I lay in my bed, I could feel the gusty wind buffeting the van and hear the rain pelting down. I was mightily glad I'd done that, or I would have been out in my birthday suit trying to stop the canopy blowing about. The following morning, everyone on the site was talking about the wind that seemed to come from nowhere and gasping at the awnings and canopies that had been damaged overnight.

The facilities on the site were up to the usual standard and immaculately clean. It's only a small site, but it has plenty of showers and toilets. It was nice to find that the showers didn't have the silly button for the water that you need to keep pressing every few seconds. It's the little things that make a difference. I know why they use the push button things and that they probably save lots of water and avoid showers being left on, but still, it's nice not to have them.

I planned a walk into North Berwick later in the morning, which was, according to the information I'd been given, a three-mile saunter along the John Muir Trail. The wind and rain had now vanished, and the sun was edging its way back out.

Sitting in the van trying to write, I was distracted by the noise from machinery being used by the site workers. One was cutting the hedge, one was strimming the grass, and the other using a blower to gather everything up. All using noisy equipment. All at the same time. Just as I thought it couldn't get any worse, a mini tractor pulled up alongside my van. Down hobbled another orange-jacket-clad worker brandishing a large spade, who then started to bash with all his might at the lumps of soil dug up by rabbits or moles overnight.

That was the last straw. My ears were bursting with the racket as I didn't have the lovely big ear defenders they were all wearing, so I packed up my stuff and set off to North Berwick. I know that work needs to be done on the sites, but please, not all at the same time right next to me on my writer's retreat! And actually, I'm not convinced the grass needs cutting anyway. If I'm not mistaken, it will only ever grow to be between two and six inches. It's like if you don't dust at home, the dust doesn't take over your house, does it?

The walk to North Berwick was very straightforward and well-signposted. To begin with, it was very pleasant through the fields and across the tops of the sand dunes, but then, because of the golf course, it diverted along a track that had absolutely no views and then for the last mile down a road. It's a minor road, admittedly, and I don't think I saw any cars, but I was slightly disappointed as I had not expected to be doing any road walking.

A trek of three miles never used to be a problem for me. Now, with my arthritis, this is a major challenge, especially as I would then have to walk the three miles back. Taking my time, I was relieved when I arrived at the quaint town of North Berwick and found myself a bench to sit on, looking out to Bass Rock. Taking my boots and socks off, I was shocked to see my phone show I'd walked four and a half miles! That was going to be a long, long walk home, but I had my picnic, a flask of tea and the sun was just about shining. I did wonder if it was possible to stroll back along the beach, but perhaps I'd need to find out about the tides, or my trek might end up a swim.

Sitting there telling myself that such a long walk warranted a visit to a cafe for coffee and cake before heading back to Evie, an old man sat himself down beside me. Without looking at me, he asked,

"Are you a local?"

I told him no and that I lived in Kirkintilloch. Answering him, I noticed that he looked to be surrounded by grief and sadness. My heart went out to him. Putting my socks and boots back on so he didn't have to look at my hideous toes, I continued chatting with him. It turns out he lived in Bishopbriggs, which was only a stone's throw away from me. He said his daughter had booked him on a bus trip from Glasgow and that he had two hours to kill before going back. I assumed from that he was a widower and his daughter was trying to encourage him to get out and about. As a stranger, I was able to ask him about his wife without feeling uncomfortable. He told me he was called Hugh and that he'd been married for nearly fifty years until his wife had died from COVID four years ago. This lonely man was obviously very much still encompassed by grief and beside himself with what to do.

"I'm going for a coffee and cake. Would you care to join me?" I asked.

A little glimmer of a smile appeared, and he said that would be lovely.

Finding ourselves a nice little cafe, we spent the next hour or so chatting over tea and scones. I found out that Hugh's wife had been a head teacher, and he was incredibly proud of her. I learned about his life and listened as he shared his feelings of grief with me. Eventually, he asked me what I did.

"I know a couple who have a publishing company in Bishopbriggs called Indie Authors World," he exclaimed.

I couldn't believe it. There I was in a place I'd never been to before, chatting with a total stranger who lived near me,

CAMPERVAN CAPERS

talking about the publishing company that had helped me publish my first book! Strange world indeed. I like to think that this man felt better for chatting with me, and I was grateful that I'd had the courage to ask a stranger to share coffee and cake with me.

Leaving the cafe, Hugh gave me a little hug and thanked me for my company. I watched as he walked away, and I hoped that he didn't notice the tear I shed.

Then it was a long, slow walk for me back to the campsite, but I did stop off at a shop and purchase a large bar of Cadbury Dairy Milk for later.

I had a bit of a heart-stopping moment when Florence decided she might actually be an adventure girl and squeezed herself through the fence and onto the golf course. Thankfully, the golfers saw her and waited before hitting any more balls. I swear she ran back to me, laughing, giggling and gasping,

"Did you see how fast I ran over to those people, Mummy? They were really pleased to see me."

She was back on the lead before I could tell her what I thought, and by the time I arrived back at Evie, I was almost on my knees, wondering if I was wearing somebody else's boots as mine were hurting my feet so much.

I gobbled down some paracetamol, popped my chocolate bar into the fridge, fed Florence and had a well-deserved hour lying on my bed reading. Looking out of the skylight window, I noticed how much dirt was growing on the outside and began planning ways to clean it when I got home. Now disturbed by this sight, I managed to find enough energy to get myself up and prepare an evening meal of homemade bolognese, potatoes and vegetables, with some extra grated cheese for good measure and to disguise the green, healthy stuff on my plate. The windows could wait.

That evening, Evie became my writer's retreat once more as I enjoyed several mugs of tea and my now chilled chocolate bar, writing up more of my adventures.

Packing up the following day, I was disappointed to be leaving such a lovely area, and I was very tempted to head down to the beach, but we had to vacate our pitch by noon. The dog walking field was great, though, and gave Florence a chance to have a good run around before the drive back.

Once home, with the sun shining and very little wind, I wound out the side canopy, and by the time I'd unpacked and cleaned Evie, this was completely dry for me to put away for next time.

With some acrobatic movements, standing on the bed and reaching through the open roof window I did manage to scrub most of the dirt off the bedroom skylight. I did the same with the dining room one, standing on the folding step and the bench seat. They are not perfectly clean, but much better.

Asking on the Facebook group how others managed this, there were lots of funny answers. Alarmingly, one person said he takes his off to clean them, but I thought that a bit extreme and ran the risk of breaking the flimsy catches. The best idea was from one woman who said she parks close to her house, reaches out of her upstairs windows and cleans the roof and windows of her van that way. Alas, I can't get Evie close enough to any of our upstairs windows to do this, or I'd be trying that one.

Back to the drawing board, I guess.

Writing this book, chapters have been scribbled in notebooks, on scraps of paper or typed directly onto the laptop, and not always in the order that they happened. This adventure I wrote about in a notebook straight away and typed it up at home the same week.

As I'd finished reading it to Mr M, who raised his eyebrow at my confession about the large bar of chocolate, a Facebook message came through on my phone. You'll never guess who it was from. Yes, Hugh's daughter. He'd told her about our chat, and she sent me a photo of him holding a copy of my book, *The Magical Tearoom on the Hill*, which she had ordered for him.

CAMPERVAN CAPERS

She thanked me for taking the time to chat with her father, and I told her it was my pleasure.

Next time you see anybody looking like they need somebody to talk to, just do it. Take the time. Share coffee and a cake. You might be the person that gets them through that day.

Chapter 52

Grandma And Minnie - 5th August 2024

Yellowcraig Club Campsite, Dirleton, East Lothian, Scotland

This summer, I was delighted that I would be having my five-year-old granddaughter, Minnie, staying with us for three weeks. This was a massive thing for a little girl to be away from her home in Yorkshire for such a long time, not just a few doors away but nearly 300 miles away in Scotland.

Before she arrived, I planned lots of different activities, such as swimming, going to different parks, visiting the cinema, and even taking a trip to Glasgow to meet the real Peppa Pig in John Lewis. Not just a cartoon, but the actual real Peppa Pig. Even I was excited! But the main adventure would be a few days away in Evie, which would provide one of the last chapters in this book. As you may have read in Chapter 51, I had already made a bit of a recce trip to Yellowcraig campsite and decided that this would be a perfect place for a grandma and her granddaughter to enjoy some quality time together.

One of my main concerns about taking Minnie (who is Minnie by both name and nature) was where she would sit while I was driving. If she had been a little older and taller, she'd have been able to sit in the front seat and chat away with me,

CAMPERVAN CAPERS

but she still needed a child's car seat. I was worried about putting the child seat in the front of the van because of the airbag. Research had informed me that it was OK to put a child seat on the front passenger seat but that the seat should be pushed back as far as possible to keep the child away from the airbag in the event of an accident. I wondered if that was defeating the purpose of the airbag and decided that she would sit on the bench seat behind me because we had factory-fitted three-point seatbelts. This had been one of my requirements when deciding which van to buy at the start of my campervan journey. I wanted to know that everyone who travelled in Evie would be safe and secure.

Before this campervan adventure, I tackled my spider phobia and dug out the child car seat from the garden shed. Unwrapping the umpteen black bags I had secured around the seat, I was pleasantly surprised at how well it had survived the winter. A wipe down with a bit of soap and water, and it was good as new. I then had to try to work out how to put the child seat into the back of our car. I would be driving down to Gretna Services to meet Minnie and her family, as this is roughly halfway between Kirkintilloch and Halifax. We'd be able to enjoy lunch together at the services before waving goodbye to Mummy, Daddy and her brother Harley and heading back up to Scotland. Fiddling around with the car seat for what seemed like hours, I finally had it fitted in a way that would hold it in place until I reached Gretna, where Minnie's daddy would be able to sort it for me. How did I ever manage these contraptions when my children were younger?

Once back home in Scotland and the child car seat fitted securely and correctly, I took photos of how the seat belt slotted through the fittings, ready for transferring it into the van.

When I'm planning an adventure away in Evie, I like to spend a few days packing the van and making sure I have everything I need. This could probably be done in an hour, but for me, part of any adventure is the preparation. I love the excitement of stepping inside Evie and arranging my clothes and anything else I'm taking with me. Would it be the same in the campervan with a little child? I wondered.

As soon as Minnie was at our house, we had to have a drink and snack in Evie. She absolutely loves being in the van on our drive. Would she enjoy it just as much on a campsite? That night, we had tea in Evie, with Mr M once again acting as our waiter, spoiling us with a pudding of ice cream topped with Maltesers and a Flake.

We spent most of the following morning organising Evie for our trip. Minnie had to look inside every drawer and cupboard to decide which ones were for her stuff. The excitement of putting your wellies into a box in a campervan next to Grandma's walking boots was perhaps one of the highlights for her. Minnie was a little disappointed that we wouldn't be putting the awning tent up on this visit, but when she saw that the space in the garage, once I removed the packed awning, gave ample room for her scooter and bucket and spade, she was happy again.

Then it was the food. We planned down to the last biscuit and chocolate bar what we needed as I already knew there were no shops in or around the campsite. The joy on her face as she looked in the cupboards and freezer at our house and helped me make a list for the supermarket was lovely to see. I had a good feeling about Minnie and the campervan.

The night before we set off, I transferred the kiddie seat from the car to Evie, thinking this would be an easy task, only to find that the seatbelt in the van was the opposite way around to the car. Eventually, with some video calls to Daddy and the addition of a couple of bungee cords (just to be sure), the seat was ready for Minnie.

The morning of departure, Minnie could hardly contain herself. She helped me carry out the fresh food and decided at

CAMPERVAN CAPERS

the last minute that her baby needed to come on the trip with her. She was delighted to find that sitting in the child car seat, she could see between the two front seats of the van for a clear view out of the windscreen. Being able to look out of the large side windows and the roof was an added bonus.

As we left home, waving goodbye to Mr M and Florence, I was surprised at how relaxed I felt. I had wondered if I'd be extra nervous driving with my granddaughter in Evie with me, but no, it was like our joint excitement left no space for nerves.

For the next two hours, I read out every signpost, told Minnie whether we were going left or right at a junction, or which exit we were taking at a roundabout. I couldn't even guess how many times she asked how many miles we had to go, how long it would take to get there, and when would we see the sea. Although I don't think she actually muttered those dreaded words, 'Are we there yet?'

Eventually, we arrived at the campsite. Pulling in at reception, Minnie was a little nervous about me leaving her in the van as I went to check in, but I told her it was her job to keep an eye on things for me. I'd decided that was better than having to take her out of the child car seat and then get her back in again! Once I was back in the van, she was amazed at the automatic barrier going up and said,

"Wow, Grandma, that's like magic." She didn't see me waving the token I'd just collected, of course!

On my last trip, I'd asked if I could reserve the pitch closest to the toilet facilities and the play park. I didn't quite get that pitch, but I was happy to see they had been able to reserve one that was just two pitches down. Perfect.

As anyone who has ever been anywhere with children, the first important job was to visit the toilets. As at the last visit there, the toilet blocks on this site were immaculate. Minnie was very impressed at how many toilets there were. Yes, we had to look at every one of them before she could decide which one to use. Then we had the dilemma of whether we would use the scary hand drier or use paper towels. Minnie decided the dryer was not too noisy, and as she was now a big girl, she could use it. I took the opportunity to show Minnie the showers so that they were familiar to her before we had to use them that night. I was pleased to see that she liked the look of the facilities and planned what she would need for a trip to the shower, what she would put on the bench, under the bench and what she would hang on the various hooks.

Then it was time to get Evie set up. Minnie was so intrigued with everything. She watched and helped me as I connected the electrics and got the fridge working. The child seat was packed away in the garage of the van and the swivel seats turned round. Florence's blankets made very handy covers for the seats so that I didn't need to worry about anything getting spilt on them. I know from experience how much mess a little child can make eating a biscuit! I didn't want to spend the holiday telling Minnie to be careful. I didn't need to worry, though, because she loved taking her shoes off as soon as she got into the van and was quick to wipe around if anything was dropped or spilt.

Of course, the playground near Evie soon called for Minnie, and I was able to finish the sorting whilst she enjoyed playing on the swings and climbing frame with other children.

Grandad had made us a little picnic before we set off, so I gathered all our stuff, including a bucket and spade, beach tent and picnic blanket, ready for a trip to the beach. Minnie decided that she needed to put her swimming costume on before leaving the van and thought it a great adventure having to go into the tiny bathroom in Evie and close the door so she could get changed without anyone seeing her.

Surprisingly, for the poor summer we had been having in Scotland, the weather was lovely, and I even had to put suntan lotion on the pair of us before we set off. Minnie declared that we needed ice lollies from reception to give us the energy to walk to the beach. Who was I to argue?

It was only a ten-minute walk to the beach, and watching Minnie's face when she saw the vast expanse of sand and the sea waiting for us was heartwarming. A child's excitement is a joy to watch.

Minnie helped me put up the beach tent until she could contain herself no longer and went running down to the sea (wearing her swimming life vest, of course). We spent the next few hours in and out of the water, digging sandcastles and enjoying our picnic. I assured Minnie that Grandma would put her swimming costume on the next day so we could go further into the sea.

Then, out of nowhere, came the rain. We had already started to pack up, breaking a tent pole in the process, but we were soon drenched. I was not bothered, though. We only had a short walk back to the van, and we were having fun. Minnie was amazed on the way back when the biggest, brightest rainbow appeared, which, of course, we had to take lots of photos of. After all, Minnie is a very special rainbow baby.

Back at the van, the rain clouds were starting to blow away, and I pulled out the van's side canopy. For a five-year-old, this was nearly as exciting as the awning tent. I fastened up my clothesline between the van and the pitch fence and soon had all our sandy, wet gear hanging up to dry in the breeze, including the beach tent with a now split pole. With a bit of black insulation tape, it was soon as good as new.

We then gathered all our shower stuff and headed for the toilet blocks. There is no better way to get rid of sand between your little toes than a nice, warm shower. Once again, I was grateful that the showers here didn't have the press buttons to work them. Minnie loved that the shower cubicles were plenty big enough for the both of us to share and that she could stay in the warm shower herself as I got dried and dressed next to her.

I've never had to think about how child-friendly the shower blocks on the site were, but I could now see that these are absolutely brilliant. Another bonus was having the free-to-use hairdryers. With short hair, these are not something I need to use, but with Minnie and her long hair, they were a godsend.

Back at the van, Minnie was quick to discard her stuff and go to play in the park once more, leaving me to tidy up and prepare tea. At Minnie's request, it was sausage rolls with spaghetti hoops, followed by lemon cake. Once again, who was I to argue?

The benefit of pitching right next to the park was that I could see Minnie as she played while I was in the van. It also meant that I could say,

"Once you've eaten all your tea, you can go back to the park." I'd never seen her gobble a meal so quickly!

If you remember, I still had the problem in the van where I could not use the water because of a leak in the bathroom. Minnie was very interested in the toilet and understood the rules about what you could and could not use Evie's toilet for! Maybe this would have been an issue if our pitch had been further away from the toilet block, but I would have dealt with that eventuality if I had to.

Throughout the evening, we had several trips to the toilet block, including a final visit to do teeth brushing. Of course, we were the amusement of the toilet block when Minnie declared that I had to wait outside her cubical whilst she had a poo. Not only that, but we also had to sing a song so she could take her time. In case you were wondering, our song was, '*Where have all the flowers gone*', which is the song I have sung to Minnie since she was a little baby. As we were washing our hands and using the now not-so-scary hand drier, a woman came out of a toilet cubical and told me that was the best entertainment she'd had for years!

My plan was that Minnie would be so tired there would be no fear of her not sleeping at night. Right enough, by 8 pm,

CAMPERVAN CAPERS

she was in her PJs. We had supper and story time, and then she asked to go to bed. It took a whole five minutes for her to fall asleep in the big double bed once she had tried all the lights and sorted her pillows.

For the rest of the evening, I enjoyed reading, having a peaceful cup of tea and watching my granddaughter sleep like an angel.

Waking up in the morning, Minnie helped me to get the breakfast ready before dashing out to play in the park. I put together another picnic, re-packed the now mended and dry beach tent, and we were soon heading out for the day. An hour playing on a newly built playground on the way to the beach, then a glorious day at the seaside in the sunshine. If you want a beautiful seaside resort with no noisy amusements, then Yellowcraig is for you.

Needless to say, after the same routine of shower, tea, park and supper, Minnie once again slept like an angel. After breakfast, Minnie very kindly said that I could pack up Evie, and she would play at the park so she could say goodbye to her friends. She did, however, insist that she watched me empty the toilet cassette at the chemical waste station. She was amazed at this task, and I think it was at that point she realised why we had the rule about what goes down the toilet in Evie! Her eyes were like saucers.

With everything packed up and the child car seat back in position, we set off for home. Once again, I spent two hours reading out all the road signs, telling Minnie which way we were going and how long it would take us to get back.

Arriving home, the excitement for Minnie didn't stop. She absolutely loved helping to unpack the van, especially because she had to stand on the bed to gather all the clothes from the cupboards. We then had to clean the inside of Evie, sweeping all the piles of sand out of her. I'm sure there was as much sand on our driveway as there was on Yellowcraig Beach.

Taking all the carpets out of the van, Minnie found it hilarious to hoover them on our driveway. I think she would have hoovered the drive if I'd let her.

Did I enjoy having an adventure in Evie, the campervan, with my granddaughter? Absolutely. We are already planning next year's trip, and Minnie has said we need to stay at Yellowcraig again for 100 days so that we can put the awning tent up, too. Would it have been the same story if it had rained all the holiday? But then, if the forecast had been poor, I would probably have taken the awning tent and more things to entertain a five-year-old girl.

It's taken me four years, but I finally had the chapter I wanted for my book – A Grandma and Granddaughter Adventure in my campervan.

Hopefully, Evie will be in my life long enough for me to have adventures with my grandson, Harley, but he is not ready for holidays away from Mummy and Daddy just yet.

Chapter 53

Autumn Tints And Snow-Covered Mountains - 12 October 2024
Oban Camping and Caravan Site, Oban, Scotland

Well, dear reader, we are fast approaching the end of my book. But before we finish, I'd like to take you on one last adventure.

As you know, when Evie came into our family, I joined the Caravan and Motorhome Club, and I've used a number of its sites and always had great times. I've also visited some independent campsites and had equally good experiences, but there are still so many places I want to try.

Looking for an adventure for October, I wanted to take Evie further north than Tyndrum but not so far away that I wouldn't be able to return home if the weather deteriorated. You never really know what Mother Nature will throw at you in Scotland once we have had our two days of summer.

I found out that the company that owns the stunning Tyndrum Holiday Park also has sites at Fort William and Oban. Checking these out, I was disappointed to find the one at Fort William was fully booked for the days I was able to get away, and the Oban site didn't have hardstanding pitches. I'm still a bit of a scaredy cat at the idea of parking the van on the grass. There is a Caravan and Motorhome Club site just past

Oban, but I was even more alarmed to learn that their pitches were situated on the beach. Definitely not for me. Then during my internet search, I found a little site run by the Camping and Caravan Club, 13 miles outside Oban. Even better, this site has the Sustrans Cycle Route 78 running right beside it.

Yes, on this trip, I would leave both Mr M and Florence behind and take my bike. If you remember, back in November 2023, my bike travelled down to the Lake District in Evie but was never used because the weather was so bad. With a slow acceptance that Florence is not, and probably never will be, an adventure girl, and the pain when I'm walking from my arthritic feet is now beyond a joke, I was determined to regain my fitness on my bike. After all, I was a cyclist before a hiker. Walking the fells and mountains was something I did with Beatrix as she loved the outdoors. Florence is scared of her own shadow, trees, leaves, streams, clouds, and anything else that moves, so I'd decided she could stay at home and keep her dad company, and I would do some cycling on the newly improved Caledonian Cycle Route.

Over breakfast one morning, I slipped into the conversation with Mr M that I had booked to stay just past Oban for four nights. Taking a momentary pause from eating his yoghurt and fruit, he looked at me, raised his eyebrows a little, and said,

"OK, but do you know how far away Oban is?"

Being a girl who can spend hours poring over maps, I refrained from answering him and smiled sweetly.

"And I thought I'd leave Florence here and take my bike," I added.

We had a bit of a laugh about the extremes I would go to for a shower because our shower at home was being replaced, with problem after problem, and was now somewhere in a black hole. Of course, if Mr M had cared to join me in Evie, he would also have had access to a shower for four days. Choices!

CAMPERVAN CAPERS

As I'd not been to a Camping and Caravan Club site before, I didn't know the standard of their sites or how well-stocked their shop would be, so I took some time to read the numerous reviews on Trip Advisor. Generally, they were very positive but mentioned that the site was in the middle of nowhere, so you needed to be self-sufficient. I also read that the site is only small and within a walled garden, which reassured me that I wouldn't need to worry about being blown away in any gales.

On the morning of departure, the heavens had opened, and the rain was pouring down. Hurricane Milton had just ripped its way across parts of America, and the internet was reporting that Scotland's temperatures would plummet and we would have some early snow because of this. Once BBC's weather app had corrected itself after reporting hurricane-force winds in Scotland, it showed that the weather in Oban would be OK, a bit showery, but certainly no hurricanes or snow.

"It's a horrible day to drive all that way on that winding road," said Mr M. "Are you sure you know what you're doing?"

"Don't put a dampener on my adventure," I snapped, putting the last of my things into the van.

Just like when I took my bike to the Lake District, I'd decided that it would again travel inside the van and not on the bike rack on the back doors. I know that's what it's designed for, but over the years, I've seen the damage done to bikes and cars when using bike racks. I now put the bike on its side, chain side up, on the bed that is covered with the oilcloth. I then secure it with four bungee cords to the cupboards on either side of the bed. It's the perfect place for it and means that the aisle is free for me to get into the bathroom en route if I need to.

With the postcode keyed into the satnav, I set off, stopping to top up with diesel on the way. Yes, Mr M, I filled up with diesel without any problem. The key didn't snap, the petrol cap didn't break, and I put diesel in and not petrol, all by myself!

It wasn't long before the clouds had broken, and the sun kept popping out. Driving alongside Loch Lubnaig, through Lochearnhead and over Glen Ogle, the autumn tints colours were awesome. Yellows, golds, reds, and browns. Autumn and winter might be too cold and dark for many people, but I feel like I come alive during these seasons.

The most amazing sight was as I descended from Glen Ogle. The mountains in the Ben Lawers range were completely covered in snow. As I continued towards Crianlarich, all the mountains down this road were equally snow-covered. It was very surreal to enjoy nature's display of autumn colours at the same time as seeing winter snow. I'm convinced that Mother Nature gives us the glorious autumn tints colours to make us forget that the leaves are dying and winter is approaching. Then she sends us snow so we can have crisp, white Christmas scenes. She doesn't usually give us these two treats together, and I wondered what she had in store for us this winter! So, the internet reports were correct in their warnings. There was, however, no snow on the lower ground, and, as Oban is at sea level, I guessed I'd be OK.

At the risk of upsetting Mr M here, I must include a little discussion we had when he was listening to me reading this chapter to him during the editing stages of my book. He is always very good at checking facts and figures and making sure that any information I give my readers is correct. But sometimes!

"Are you sure that Oban is at sea level," he asked.

Oh, how I laughed.

"Erm, the clue is that Oban has a harbour, a bay and a beach," I gasped, with tears of laughter streaming down my face.

He did laugh eventually at himself.

Moving swiftly on, the drive to Oban follows the same route that I've described in previous chapters when travelling to the Tyndrum Holiday Park but takes a left at the junction just past the Green Welly Stop to follow the A85. I've only travelled this road twice in my life, once on our honeymoon 19 years ago and once in the back of an ambulance (but that's a whole different story), so I didn't know this section at all. It was A-roads all the way to the site, so I knew it would be wide enough for Evie.

By the way, A-roads are what we think of as major roads linking towns and cities. Although they can be single or dual carriageways, you can be certain that they will be wide enough for the average vehicle. Apparently, road engineers take into account the maximum width of a vehicle being 2.55 metres and the maximum length being 18.75 metres and design roads accordingly. As Evie is only 2.03 metres wide and 6.32 metres long, it should be possible to drive her on any A-road without any difficulty. In theory!

Joining the A85, the weather deteriorated a little, and the rain started. I was even convinced at one point that it was falling as sleet. I could sense that I was driving through some beautiful scenery, passing Ben Cruachan, or the Hollow Mountain, and the Cruachan Power Station on the stunning Loch Awe, but I was concentrating on the unknown road rather than admiring the views. It was a little daunting driving along this route with the threat of snow in my mind, and seeing the very tall snow poles on either side of the road did nothing to alleviate my nerves. Clearly this road does get snow, and deep snow at that! Perhaps I'd enjoy the drive more on the way home as I'd be more familiar with it.

At Connel, I then followed the A828 towards Fort William, which crosses the Connel Bridge. This, I was not impressed with. It was single track, very high over some fast-flowing water, and it felt only just wide enough for Evie. I heard myself give a huge sigh of relief when I got to the other side.

Although the A828 is a bit wiggly and winding, other than the bridge, it's not a bad road to drive. My satnav was counting down the miles to my destination, and yes, I missed the turning on the right at Barcaldine. Of course, my trusty satnav came to the rescue and informed me I could make a detour at the next roundabout 1.5 miles further along the road. If you're thinking of going to this site, be sure to watch out for the sign because I very nearly missed it on the way back, too!

Safe and sound, I arrived at Oban Camping and Caravan Site. Parking up and heading into reception, my surreal day continued when the manager of the site started to talk to me in a broad Yorkshire accent. Yes, he was born in Halifax! No, I didn't know him. We had a lovely chat about all the different places we'd both lived in and reminisced about the beauty that is Calderdale. I also took the opportunity to ask him about the difference between the Caravan and Motorhome Club and the Camping and Caravan Club.

"We always let tents in. That's the real difference."

I was pleasantly surprised that he didn't feel the need to tell me how poor the Caravan and Motorhome Club was compared to the Camping and Caravan Club. They just cater for different campers. Researching, it would seem they are both very reputable and well-known clubs, and it would be wrong for me to tell you which would be the best for you. Look at each of them on their websites before you decide. You might even want to join both or may not bother joining either of them. It's not compulsory to be a member to stay at either of the club's sites, but you do get a member discount.

After being given the options of available pitches, I picked one in the middle of the site. Usually, I would go for one along the edge of the site to get protection from the elements, but as this is a small place within a walled garden, I figured each one would be protected. All the pitches looked to be quite level, and I only saw a couple of people using levelling blocks. Evie would be fine without hers, I thought to myself.

My first job was to decide where I would lock my bike. I didn't want to secure it to the back door, or I wouldn't be able

CAMPERVAN CAPERS

to get into the garage for anything I'd forgotten to take out. In the middle of the site, just next to my pitch, was a small, fenced area for the fresh water taps. Perfect. I extracted the bike from its secure fastenings in the van and locked it to the fence, protecting it from the elements with my bike cover.

Between the rain showers, I soon had the electric cable connected, the fridge working, and everything sorted. It's certainly a case of a place for everything and everything in its place in the van. As rain was forecast for the last day of my holiday, I had decided that I would leave my makeshift shower curtain screen fastened up inside the back doors. This would keep everything dry, but I also thought it might work as a primitive insulation layer if it were to be as cold as the weather app reported. Maybe I should investigate getting some thick, waterproof material to hang there rather than a simple shower curtain. Or maybe both!

Talking about insulation, I would still like to make some sort of warm curtain to hang up over the big side sliding door, which seems to be the cold area in the van.

As I'd not stopped for my lunch on the way to the site, I was now starving. I rang Mr M to let him know all was well and enjoyed a leisurely picnic lunch and my flask of hot tea, courtesy, of course, of Mr M, sitting at the table in Evie, reading a new book. If anyone is interested, the book was *The Barra Boy* by Iain Kelly, and I would highly recommend it.

Then, it was time to explore. The site might be in the middle of nowhere, but it is a most beautiful nowhere land. Heading out of the walled garden following a sign for the beach, within ten minutes, I was walking along a pebbly beach, admiring the views across Loch Creran to snow-capped mountains and a very bright, vivid rainbow.

Of course, the highlight of my day would be using the onsite facilities. A hot, clean, working shower was something I'd been dreaming about since booking this adventure. And this site did not disappoint. With only 75 pitches, I had expected the facilities to be reduced. But no. The shower block has umpteen showers, cubicles, hand basins and toilets, all immaculately clean. After weeks of no shower at home, did I spend longer in the shower than I would normally? Of course I did.

Did I phone Mr M and boast about my hot shower? Absolutely!

After tea, Evie once again became my writing retreat, crocheting room, and reading snug. Before settling down for the night I ventured out to the washing-up area, which on this site is inside, well-lit and spider-free.

For the first time this year, I was a little cold in the van, so I had to put the electric heater on but turned it off before going to bed. Overnight, the drop in the outside temperature woke me up, and I admit to feeling a little chilly in bed. Maybe I should have put on more than my birthday suit, but I snuggled up to my soft, fleecy hoodie and went back to sleep.

By morning, the temperature had still not risen, and if anything, it felt colder. Peeping out of the back window, I could see there was frost everywhere, so I climbed out of bed, turned on the heater and tucked myself back up under the duvet for another hour's reading.

My plan for the day was to follow the cycle route 78 to Oban, so I indulged myself in some hot porridge and a toasted bagel. Needs must. The route would be about 26 miles for a return trip, according to the signs, so I knew I'd be OK. Imagine my delight when I found out that on the way, I would have to cycle past the Ben Lora Cafe and Bookshop at Benderloch.

I've cycled on many of the Sustrans routes, and this one does not fail to deliver. Meandering up and down gentle rises, the track keeps you away from the road, although you are cycling alongside it at times. My only complaint would be that when cycling through the woods and forests, there was no real view of the coastline that the road users have. But it is certainly

100% better than fighting with fast-moving motor vehicles. Mind you, this time of year adds a little excitement to your ride as you cycle through the piles of fallen leaves, and you have to take care not to brake too quickly to avoid any nasty skidding.

Once out of the woods, the scenery was breathtaking. The loch, with its backdrop of mountains, is a view I will never tire of. One of the joys of cycling is that you can admire the views as you move, unlike when driving a motor vehicle. And on a cycle path, you can stop at any time you choose.

It didn't seem to take me very long at all to reach Benderloch and the cafe and bookshop I'd been looking forward to visiting. For a little cafe in a tiny village, it was a busy place. Despite having made myself a picnic lunch and flask of tea before I set off from Evie, I indulged in a delicious bacon sandwich and pot of tea and looked through the books for sale. Somehow, I refrained from buying any as I would have to carry them in my pannier all the way to Oban and back. Chatting with the owner, it turned out that this was their last day of the season before closing for winter. Perhaps that's why it was so busy, as people wanted to enjoy one last treat of the year. If you're planning a visit, be sure to check whether they are open or not.

I passed a couple of campsites on my way, and they had the most fantastic views out towards Loch Linne and the small island of Lismore, with mountains in the distance. I did notice that, yes, the pitches were very close to the beach, but they were not actually on the sand. Maybe I could be tempted to stay there after all.

A few miles further, I arrived at Connel Bridge. The one I'd scared myself driving across in Evie. I was relieved to discover that there is a cycle lane on the bridge, totally separated from the single-track road that motor vehicles use. I was still not happy crossing the bridge and didn't take any persuading to follow the warning sign, 'cyclists dismount'. There was no way

I was cycling across. I did stop and take a few photos, and I enjoyed seeing a little island covered in seals. Drivers in their vehicles would certainly not get the view cyclists have when crossing this impressive structure.

Just over the bridge, the cycle route signs indicated I needed to follow a single track road, with just six miles to Oban. Easy peasy, I thought. I'm sure Sustrans made that distance up because it was the longest six miles I've ever cycled. And over some massive hills, a couple that I had to walk up! The views! Oh my. This road was sublime. Then it was all downhill for the last mile or so into Oban, which would mean all uphill on the way back. I was certainly glad I'd stopped at the cafe earlier and had that bacon sandwich.

Oban is a nice little seaside town with a lovely harbour and is a seafood lover's paradise. I, however, cycled past all the vendors selling oysters and the like and found a bench to enjoy my lunch, looking out to the Isle of Kerrera and watching the Isle of Lewis ferry departing. Crocheting another square for my new coat, I debated with myself whether I should cycle along the main road back to Connel to avoid that little road with the hideous hills. Then I told myself I would never get fit by avoiding hills, so I packed everything back up into my pannier, keeping some tea and snacks for the way home.

Apart from the steep hill out of Oban, the road back to Connel was nowhere near as hard as coming the other way. Maybe it was helped because the views across the snow-capped mountains took away some of the pain. If I am not mistaken, I could even see the twin peaks of Ben More and Stob Binnein beyond Tyndrum.

Once again, I walked over Connel Bridge before cycling the last eight miles back to the campsite. I was surprised at how easy it was, and I seemed to free-wheel much of the way. There was a tempting-looking bench only a couple of miles from the site, which I took advantage of for a well-earned rest and finished my flask of tea and some Cadbury Dairy Milk.

CAMPERVAN CAPERS

Back at Evie, I had just locked up the bike and put the cover on it when it started to rain. How about that for timing!

I was shattered but pleased I'd managed a cycle of 26 miles. Not a long distance in cycling terms, but I was on my way back to fitness. I just hoped my cycling muscles would return soon so I didn't have to walk up the big hills!

The best bit of the day had to be another shower. Yes, it was another long shower. Did I boast again to Mr M about it? Of course I did.

I must admit to enjoying my few days away without anyone or a dog to think about. I could take my time, have drinks and food when I wanted to, and didn't have to plan walks for Florence. And the van certainly seemed much bigger! Even though I was away for four nights, I really didn't regret my decision to leave the drive away awning at home.

Tea tonight was lasagne cooked in the air-fryer. Delicious. Then, a very pleasant evening of reading, crocheting, writing, and debating what to wear for bed after last night's coldness. I thought about leaving the heater on low but decided against it, and after visiting the dish-washing facilities to do my washing up, I went to bed in my pyjamas.

I woke up after a few hours, feeling roasting. There was clearly no frost tonight, and I stripped off to my birthday suit and then snuggled back down for some more sleep.

The following morning was once again fine, dry, and sunny. My plan was to cycle in the other direction on Route 78. Fort William was 36 miles away, which was a little too far for my current fitness, as this would be a round trip of 72 miles. Perhaps next time. So, I studied my map and tried to identify somewhere I could aim for, but this is an area I've not been to, so I didn't know any of the place names. I decided that as it was a route I could not get lost on, I would follow the signs until I was 20 miles away from Fort William. That would be far enough.

After enjoying another leisurely breakfast of porridge and toasted bagel, and making a picnic lunch and flask of tea, I was off.

Debra Murphy

There is something quite delightful about cycling along a route you've never been on before. You don't know what's ahead of you, so you don't worry about any hills that you may need to tackle. This section of Route 78 is truly a dream cycle. It follows the coastline much of the time, allowing fantastic views out to Loch Laich and the mountains in the distance. A favourite view of mine was looking out to Castle Stalker. This is the castle that was used in Monty Python and The Holy Grail when they called it Castle of Aaarrrrggh.

Then, out of the blue, the route has been transformed by somebody having the foresight to take this track through the Highland Titles Nature Reserve and Salachan Glen just before you reach Duror. It is like an alpine pass! Of course, I had to walk it. I told myself I'd manage to cycle it on a future visit to this part of the country. I felt a little better having to walk when I saw the signs warning cyclists of steep gradients. But what goes up must come down, and I enjoyed a well-earned descent back down to sea level.

After the speedy downhill section, the route followed the road again, and the signs indicated I was 21 miles away from Fort William. That was far enough, I decided. There was a sign for Cuil Bay, one mile off Route 78, down a single-track road, so I headed that way to find a lunch spot. Sometimes, you hope for the best when you take a route you don't know, but today, I found a comfy bench to sit on for my lunch at the bay, looking across to a little island, Eilean Balnagowan. There I sat with my picnic lunch and flask of tea, enjoying the peace and views. I felt as though I had the whole bay to myself, only sharing it with the birds and perhaps a seal or two. There are quite a few parking spaces at the bay if you venture there, and you could probably get a campervan down, too, but you'd have to check whether you could stay there overnight.

With a chilly wind blowing off the water, it was soon time to go back, yes, up the alpine pass. Although I had to walk again,

CAMPERVAN CAPERS

the route in this direction was not quite as severe as the other way. It was pretty steep going down, though, and I was sure that would I have no brake blocks left.

I'd saved some of my lunch to have a stop on the way back to the campsite, but with the route much easier this way and with the views and sunshine, I was soon back at Evie without having a stop.

With the bike once again locked up, I enjoyed the rest of my lunch sitting in the van, reading my book. I even had the side door open because the sun was shining in, and it felt positively warm. What was Mother Nature up to? I wondered.

Then, my treat of the day was another hot shower, before a tea of fresh pasta pockets filled with cheese and tomato that were definitely not the highlight of the day.

As darkness fell, I noticed just how quiet this site was. I know there were not very many other campers, but it is a lovely, secluded place. The walled garden certainly does give you a feeling that you are protected from the elements. I watched the stars appear and wondered if I might see the Northern Lights because there is no light pollution here at all. And there is no traffic noise either. I know for sure I'll be back to this site again next year. Perhaps I'll get my son to join me as he would be able to bring his tent, and we could do some cycling together.

The following day, I followed the same routine: breakfast, picnic making and planning a cycle route. The last couple of days had included some big hills, which my still weak legs struggled with. So, I thought I'd have an easy day and follow Route 78 to Connel Bridge, find somewhere to have my lunch, and then cycle back.

I was able to fully appreciate this route towards Benderloch because I knew where I was going and that there were no nasty surprises for me. Approaching the village, I noticed a sign, 'Benderloch Loop 2 miles'. I'm a sucker for an unknown road when cycling, and knowing this would only add an extra two miles to my trip, the temptation was too much for me. I smiled to myself, thinking what Mr M would say if he knew I was going along a road I didn't know. When he was still able to, he would happily cycle the same road every day because he liked to know where he was going and what the route was like. Yes, we really are like chalk and cheese.

Let me tell you, this turned out to be two glorious miles of cycling. There were a couple of rises, only enough to make me get out of the saddle, but the feeling of freedom was amazing. It's a bit narrow at times, with passing places, so you might struggle if you're driving a large campervan. I certainly wouldn't think of towing a caravan on this road. Along the route was another sign for the Isle of Eriska Hotel, but I ignored this. Looking at the internet later, I wish I'd taken this further detour as there's a bridge to take you over to the isle. Now, that would have been a great place for lunch. Maybe next time.

In no time at all, I was through the hamlet of Tralee and back on Route 78, following the coast to Connel. Yes, I walked across the bridge again. Today, the Falls of Lora looked very rough under the bridge, and the wind howled, so I was very pleased to feel enclosed in the metal frame along this short bridge. At times like this, people might question whether I am really an adventure girl.

Researching a little as I wrote this chapter, I discovered that this was originally a rail bridge. Then, for a while, cars and trains could use it, but not at the same time. In 1966, with the closure of the train line, the bridge was converted fully for just motor vehicles.

Once I had crossed the bridge, I found a convenient bench looking across to the Isle of Eriska. If anyone is a seafood lover, there is the Oyster Hotel right on the T-junction. I enjoyed my tuna mayonnaise sandwich, though. That's as far as my taste in fish stretches.

CAMPERVAN CAPERS

Then it was an enjoyable return cycle to Benderloch taking the little diversion again, which was just as delightful going back. A couple of miles away from the campsite, I stopped at the Racer Cafe and Argyle Pottery. Well, it was still early, and I was on holiday. This is well worth a stop, and I enjoyed a lovely piece of cake and a pot of steaming tea before cycling back to Evie.

One of the things about being on holiday, whether you are camping, in a cottage or in a hotel, there is always the dreaded packing up to be done. Although I'd been very lucky with the weather over my few days away, I knew that heavy rain was forecast for the last night and the day of departure, so I needed to get as much done before the downpours started.

As there was plenty of room in the van being just myself, I got everything I needed from the garage – cool box, electric cable winder and cover for the bed, and put them in front of the driver and passenger seats. That way, I could do most of the packing up without needing to open the back doors.

Tea that night was a simple bowl of Mr M's homemade soup. I was still stuffed from the huge cake I'd had at the cafe.

Of course, I then had to have another shower and did plan that I would have a final one in the morning as it would be the last shower for who knows how long.

I made sure the bike was completely covered and secured to the fence with the lock and extra bungee cords to make sure it was safe and well in the expected wind and rain.

Relaxing in the van, I watched with amazement as a little red car arrived and parked on one of the pitches. It was like a comedy scene. Three people got out of this tiny vehicle, then a dog. They then proceeded to erect a roof tent on top of this poor little car. I wanted to see how all three humans and a dog would fit into this, but once they had finished setting up, they picked up a large bag and wandered away. I wondered where they were going because there was nothing around the campsite.

What did they know that I didn't? Maybe I'll ask them tomorrow. I wondered how safe these roof tents are and whether any damage is caused due to them being pitched on top of the vehicles.

Then, I realised, with horror, that I was starting to sound like Mr Health and Safety!

The evening passed very peacefully despite the gentle rocking of the van. I thought I would be in for a disturbed night. Overnight, I woke a couple of times and checked out of the back window on my bike, which looked to be still secured and covered, so all was well, and I was able to fall back asleep.

At this site, the toilet facilities are cleaned between 10.30 am and noon, so I was up early to have my last shower. After breakfast, I started packing up. It was, as forecast, teeming down, so I put on my waterproof trousers and wellies for the first time during my stay. I didn't want to get wet and then have to drive home in soggy clothes.

Imagine my delight when, as I was contemplating venturing outside to wind up the electric cable, the rain suddenly stopped. Just like that. I was out of the van in a flash. The cable was wound up, the fridge emptied, and any remaining food (of which there was not a lot) was put back into the cool box, then packed away in the garage. I couldn't pack the bike into the van until the last minute, but I was pretty chuffed by how dry I'd stayed.

The least pleasant job was emptying the toilet cassette, not because it was the toilet but because the chemical waste area was a haven for spiders, and you all know how much of an arachnophobe I am. Let's just say, I didn't hang around with that task, and I think I might have been nearly crying at one point.

The weather Gods stayed with me for the rest of my packing up. After carefully removing the wet cover, I was able to get a dry bike back in and secure it in the van. Excess water shaken off the cover, I squashed it into its packet to dry off once back at home.

CAMPERVAN CAPERS

Then it was time to leave. I felt incredibly blessed with the few days I'd had at this site. I'd enjoyed lovely weather, beautiful scenery and had three cycling days. The joy of being able to exercise and not have my arthritic feet and ankles screaming at me is not to be underestimated.

I had hoped that the journey back towards Tyndrum would be more enjoyable than on the way out. But it wasn't. This road is a death trap, with motorists feeling the need to race and speed along the numerous long, straight sections that are mixed in with the winding, bendy, narrow bits. I stuck to a speed I was comfortable with and pulled in whenever possible to let the racers go past me. I had the last laugh, though, when along this road, there were some roadworks and yes, which was the car I pulled up behind? The one who had dangerously overtaken me a couple of miles earlier. The tale of the hare and the tortoise springs to mind.

Once I'd reached Tyndrum, I was back on familiar roads and felt much better. Not long after Crianlarich, I pulled into a large lay-by for my lunch. As I was enjoying my last piece of homemade flapjack, a large lorry pulled up about three inches from Evie's back doors. I don't know what it was, but I felt very uncomfortable with it parking so close to me. I'd just had four nights by myself in the middle of nowhere and felt perfectly safe, but this took me out of my comfort zone, so I quickly packed up my stuff and drove away.

Once home, the weather Gods were still on my side, and, with the help of Mr M, I soon had Evie unpacked, the bike locked away in the hut, and I was enjoying a cup of tea and a slice of chocolate loaf freshly made by Mr M.

Life is tough.

Evie still needs to be cleaned, but that can be done another day. It would be my birthday on Friday that week and I was hoping to get a birthday present of taller ladders so I could reach the roof of the van to clean it. Mr M was worried about what everyone would say if they found out that he had bought his wife a pair of ladders for her birthday, but I told him that would be the perfect present for me.

More worryingly, I have noticed a few little spots of rust appearing on the wheel arches of the van. Talking to my seafaring nephew, Daniel, he told me he'd be home from sea in December and would be happy to come and help me check this out, clean the underneath of the van and re-seal it.

I was so excited. New ladders and painting Evie to look forward to. Does life get any better?

Chapter 54

The Final Chapter – June 2025

It's hard to believe that it's been four years since my lifelong dream of owning a campervan came true. I began writing this book as Evie the campervan came into our lives, writing copious ideas in a notebook I bought specifically for that purpose. As I said in the book's introduction, I wanted to take my readers along with me on my journey to hopefully becoming a seasoned campervanner. The notes, some detailed, some just a couple of words, or a photo to remind me of something important, were often done in real-time. So every step to finding my campervan, every adventure and learning curve along the way have been documented, hopefully for both your interest and amusement.

Initially, I wanted to end the book with a chapter on having an adventure in Evie with my granddaughter, Minnie. But then I decided I also wanted to put in a chapter about me going to a new campsite and taking my bike with me to cycle along the Caledonian Cycle Route. There was always going to be something else I wanted to put in the book, so I had to make my decision of when to stop. There is a saying about books that they can never be too long, only too boring, never too short, only too brief. I hope that I managed to get this right and that you are not bored with it, but if you have reached this point, unless you skipped to the last chapter, I might just have done that. If you think it's too short, let me know. Maybe I can do a follow-up book, Life as a Seasoned Campervanner.

Here are some of my reflections on the past four years.

Once I'd decided that I could spend an absolute fortune on a campervan to follow my dream, I told myself that I'd have an adventure every month to justify the cost. I'm pleased to say that, except for October 22 and September 2023, I have indeed had at least one adventure every month.

Does campervan life meet my expectations, then?

Absolutely. But I now view campervan life without the rose-tinted glasses I wore before I bought Evie, when I thought that a van would open up a world of camping here, there and everywhere, without any restrictions, and with the benefit of being in a huge campervan and not a flimsy tent.

The first thing I had to get used to was driving the campervan. Evie is not massive compared to many of the motorhomes you see on the road, but for me, she feels like a huge vehicle. It's a very comfy drive and, when I'm travelling on wide roads and motorways that I know, I do enjoy it. But driving on narrow roads or unknown routes, I still panic. Honestly, if Mr M drove every trip, I'd probably be very happy about that. I feel I've come a long way on my campervan journey and can now take Evie to places I've never been to, but to say I love driving her would be an exaggeration.

Travelling on a ferry is something that I've not managed yet. I've never even driven my car onto a ferry, but I have been a passenger and know what it feels like. What if I couldn't manoeuvre Evie into the exact spot the men in yellow jackets tell you to? What if everyone was watching me, knowing how nervous I was? What if I were seasick (highly likely) and couldn't then drive Evie off the ferry? Never say never, because I would love to take Evie around the islands of Scotland, especially Skye, where Mr M and I were married 20 years ago.

CAMPERVAN CAPERS

The joy of adventures in my own campervan is absolutely fantastic. I love everything about it. The planning, the packing, the setting up, cooking and washing up all feel totally different in the van rather than at home. OK, so there is the toilet cassette issue, but if you can't deal with things like that, you wouldn't be contemplating campervan life yourself. It's certainly not one of the most enjoyable tasks. It just has to be done. If you set yourself the rule that there is only liquid allowed in the toilet, then you'll make the task slightly easier for yourself.

This brings us to wild camping. I've not managed this yet, and have chosen to stay on campsites every trip. If I'm honest with myself, I have realised that I'm not quite as brave as I thought I was. Wild camping with no access to facilities and the security blanket of being on a site is not yet in my planned campervan life journey. I like knowing that if anything goes wrong, especially when I'm by myself, there'll be somebody on the site who'll be able to help me. Other campers, along with the site staff, are a great source of help and support.

Would I like to try a wild camping trip with Mr M to support me? I believe I would, but I don't think Mr M would even contemplate it.

Let's take a look at some of the things I've learned.

Owning a campervan makes you want to buy lots of things you don't really need. For example, you can manage perfectly well without levelling blocks. I've never driven Evie up onto them, but Mr M has. Did being on levelling blocks make the stay on the site more enjoyable? Probably not. I think so long as you are not parked on a slope, and if you are, you position the van so that your feet will be lower than your head when you're sleeping, you can cope with not being perfectly level. Being level, though, does help the water to drain from the sinks more efficiently. The levellers didn't cost an absolute fortune, but they do take up room in the van and never get used.

Although you could guarantee that if I left them at home, the pitch I had to stay on would be on a massive slope. Fortunately, most of the campsites I've stayed at or looked at online have pitches that all look reasonably level. That might not be the case if you were wild camping, though.

Of course, not needing the levelling blocks also means that the spirit levels I so proudly bought are also superfluous to requirements. That's one of the most important lessons I have learned: don't rush to buy extra kit, as you probably will not really need it.

You will remember that for the last year or so, we've had a leak in the bathroom sink, so we've been unable to use the water system in Evie. Has this spoiled our enjoyment? For me, not at all. For Mr M, possibly. He hates having to use the toilet blocks and showers on the campsites and having to walk to the dishwashing facilities.

The lack of water has a hidden benefit in that we do not need to use the grey waste water carrier, and this now takes up room in the shed at home rather than inside Evie. Mind you, one of Mr M's dog-walking pals has just been to our house and fixed the leak for us, so once we have cleaned out the water tank with some sterilising solution, maybe we will have running water in Evie for our summer holidays this year.

What this leak and lack of running water in Evie told me was that it is entirely possible to manage in a van with just a bottle of drinking water, so long as you are somewhere you have access to fresh water and toilets. Going back to our essential features of our dream campervan, maybe running water, sink, a toilet and a shower were not absolutely vital.

There are things that are well worth all the money you have to spend on them. I thought you might like to know that for my birthday in October last year, I did indeed receive the not-so-romantic but perfect present from Mr M of a pair of extra-long step ladders so that I can clean the top of Evie. It's

CAMPERVAN CAPERS

still a bit daunting reaching right over the roof, but at least I can clean the skylight windows now.

I've also discovered a new cleaning product which gets rid of all the dirt, grime and, importantly, that green mould stuff that grows in the grooves by the windows, doors, and mirrors – MB14 Caravan & Motorhome Exterior & Interior Wash & Wax. Really, you can use it anywhere on the van, and it leaves the outside with a waxed look. It's expensive but well worth every penny.

One of the biggest realisations is how expensive having a campervan can be. Of course, you could wild camp and not have to pay for campsites or electricity. You have to decide for yourself whether you are prepared to pay for luxuries like toilet facilities, shower blocks and electricity. Personally, I believe that to be able to stay in wonderful locations with often breathtaking views, the cost of the campsite is way less than you would expect to pay in a hotel or to hire other accommodation. If hotel-style luxuries are your thing, then a campervan probably isn't.

I know that I am in a very privileged position because I was able to buy my campervan with my inheritance, but the initial cost of your van is only the start of the money you will need to inject into it. There are MOTs, services, tyres, diesel and all the extra kit you decide you need to make your van your own.

We took a long time to decide that we would buy an expensive drive away awning, but it has been well worth the cost because of the difference it makes on trips when Mr M comes along. It's that luxury of extra space and not feeling as though all your belongings, people and dogs are on top of each other. But as I sit in Evie at Maragowan Campsite in Killin writing this final chapter, I am alone. Mr M and Florence are at home. I have my bike with me, but no drive away awning. Do I feel enclosed in the van? Not really. My clothes are in the cupboards; there is only one coat, one pair of boots, and one rucksack in the van. Oh, now I feel a bit lonely. Only kidding!

Debra Murphy

Over the last four years, I've made little adaptations and improvements to Evie to make her ours, such as seat covers, stick-on tiles and using oilcloth to cover the bed to give us another worktop during the day. All these changes have been improvements in my eyes. Others might think I have spoiled her look, but all the adaptations I have made can easily be removed to put her back to her original state if I need to sell her. Although I'm sure any campervan person would love to have handmade curtains with a campervan design on them. I think the best and cheapest improvement I made was to use a shower curtain to hang down over the back doors to protect the bed when you have to have the doors open to get things in and out of the garage and turn the gas on and off. This cost me £3.99 from B&M, but I'm sure you could find something even cheaper, or you could go the other way and buy an expensive custom-made rear door curtain.

What do I love about Evie, then?

Well, apart from driving on wiggly, winding roads and the scares she has given me with her MOTs, absolutely everything. I feel very much at home in her, and general life stresses simply fade into the background on a trip away. I love making a cup of tea and sitting with Mr M as we munch our way through a packet of biscuits, watching the sunset, reading, writing, or simply enjoying the silence.

One of the special things for me is that moment when you're reading in bed, and you decide it's time to sleep. Turning the bedroom lights off and feeling the darkness and silence surround you cannot be beaten. Of course, that's until Mr M or Florence start to snore. Mind you, I'm sure that Mr M thinks exactly the same thing about me. I have no doubts that I can snore, maybe not to Mr M's level, but to a pretty good standard.

I love being able to walk or cycle in beautiful countryside away from the familiar haunts of Kirkintilloch. Indeed, on my trip writing this chapter, I cycled along the Sustrans Route 7

CAMPERVAN CAPERS

from Killin to Kenmore and back, a round trip of 34 miles. It was a tough road with many steep hills, but to be in beautiful surroundings was sublime. I was even able to look from a distance at the Ben Lawers range of Munros and imagine where the rescue helicopter landed to pick me up from the summit when I had my heart attack.

A surreal moment indeed.

Life is very different in a campervan for me. My routines change, and I do things I would never do at home. Take this latest trip. I know that the plan was for me to have four days away to write the last chapter of this book, but I relaxed more than I have ever done. Maybe it's because I knew the book was nearly finished. I had a long, tough cycle on the second day, which used up all my energy, and more. I slept fitfully overnight because I was overtired, but eventually fell into a deep sleep and didn't wake up until 9.30 am. I can't remember the last time I woke up so late at home. That day, I worked on the book, wandered to Killin for something to eat at a cafe, before wandering back to Evie, and I lay on the bed reading for a couple of hours. I then worked late into the evening writing, remembering at 9 pm that I'd not had any tea, so I toasted a couple of crumpets. The following morning, it was 9.30 am again before I woke up.

Naturally, I shower after a cycle or long walk, but I no longer feel the need to shower every day on a trip. At home, I wouldn't dream of leaving the house without having a shower.

Despite Mr M's attempt at feeding me and providing healthy food, both at home and on trips, there are times I don't eat a proper meal. Unless you can call a toasted currant teacake and a bar of Cadbury Dairy Milk a two-course meal. I drink copious cups of tea. Well, actually, I do that at home, but there, I at least wash the cup before I make another one. I can already see Mr M spitting his tea out, reading that bit, because more often than not, Mr M makes my cups of tea at home. Yes, I'm spoiled, but I know it, so that makes it OK.

Debra Murphy

Sometimes, I go to bed without doing the washing up, which I would never do at home. I wear the same T-shirt for more than one day and don't mind if my clothes are creased.

Basically, I'm a camper at heart, and being in a campervan for me is just an upmarket, solid tent.

It will come as no surprise to you to hear that Mr M, being a creature of comfort, struggles with the change of routine when we go away. He likes to get up at a certain time, have his meals, including supper, at the same time every day, and go to sleep at the same time. It takes him out of his comfort zone to be away from home, especially when the trip means going across the border into another country!

Campervan life isn't as spontaneous as I thought it would be. For me, though, I enjoy the planning and thinking about what we need for a trip. Setting up on the pitches used to take forever because we didn't know what we were doing and very often had to do things two or three times to get things working or in the right place. We are much quicker at this now. Putting everything away at the end of a trip has to be organised too. You need to find a place for everything and put everything in its place. That way, nothing gets broken, you don't forget anything, and you don't have rattles and creaks on your journey to or from home.

Once we're on a site, we don't move the van until it's time to go home. This can mean that you're isolated from shops if the site is in the middle of nowhere. So long as you know this, you can plan and make sure that you have enough food for your trip. There would be no fun in an adventure where you ran out of milk to make cups of tea to enjoy with your biscuits or Cadbury Dairy Milk, would there? There are many people on the campsites I see who do go out for the day in their campervans and motorhomes, so it is possible, but something we don't choose to do.

Of course, everyone has their own reasons for wanting a campervan. Some like to go away as a group, enjoy large

CAMPERVAN CAPERS

barbecues and long drinking sessions. But for me, I like to be away from the hustle and bustle of life, noisy shopping centres, busy pubs and crowds of people. It's nice to be within walking distance of a beach, a nice cafe or a lake, but not absolutely essential. I'm very happy having Evie as my writer's retreat, or to spend hours reading. I do research and choose sites where we can do nice walks, wander to local cafes and even those that are close to cycle routes when I take my bike.

Here is the huge, important question.

Does Mr M love campervan life?

No!

And there is my dilemma. I absolutely love campervan life and would, given the chance, now live in Evie, but that would be Mr M's idea of hell. What's the answer then? Compromise. As with anything in a marriage, you have to look at both sides. Mr M knows and understands that it was my all-time dream to have a campervan, and he encouraged me to follow it when I was given the opportunity. There are things that Mr M enjoys, like relaxing in the sunshine or the shelter of the drive away awning, so long as he has his book or access to the internet. He loves chatting with other campers, and sometimes I think he's been kidnapped, as he can disappear for an hour or so when he gets distracted with some conversation or other.

So, our compromise is that during the cold winter months, if I go away, I go alone or with Florence. As the weather gets warmer and we go to sites that Mr M likes, such as Blair Castle Caravan Park or Skelwith Fold, he will quite happily come along.

I've voiced my concerns with Mr M that I am spending time apart from him when I go on solo trips, but he assures me that it's OK. He knows that adventures in Evie are important to me and actively encourages me to book trips. Maybe I should worry that he doesn't mind me going away without him, but I see it as having a wonderful, thoughtful husband who wants his wife to follow her dream.

Debra Murphy

Do I feel selfish?

Every single time I have an adventure without Mr M, I do, and I miss him all the time. I put an extra chair next to the table and his mug out for him when I'm making a cup of tea, but I'm never lonely. I cuddle a soft fleece at night if I'm missing him to feel as though he is next to me. At the same time, I love the luxury of a big double bed to myself.

Reflecting as I wrote this, I remembered a quote in the book, *Into the Wild*, by Jon Krakaurer, 'Happiness is not real unless shared'. Was that how I now felt?

When we chatted about the prospect of buying a campervan, Mr M thought he would like it. I thought he would, too. I don't believe he hates it all of the time. It's not his favourite thing to do. He's not a man for fine food and luxurious comforts, but he likes to have his own bathroom and sofa to relax on if he chooses.

If I had known in 2021, when I was deciding whether to spend my inheritance on Evie, that Mr M would not like it, would I have still bought the van? No, I don't believe I would. Owning a campervan was a lifelong dream, but having Mr M in my life tops any dream of mine. But don't tell him I've told you that.

I'm glad I bought a campervan. I've never regretted buying Evie because I've had some wonderful adventures, both with Mr M and alone. I had a special trip with Beatrix that turned out to be her last swim in Coniston before she had to cross the rainbow bridge. And, of course, I am now the coolest grandma ever with my trip away with Minnie in 2024. In July 2025, I already have four nights booked at Yellowcraig Campsite for another trip with Minnie, when we will definitely be putting up the drive away awning, as she was disappointed we didn't use it on our last trip. That will probably provide enough content for a whole new book: *Can Grandma and Minnie Put Up the Drive Away Awning in 20 Minutes?*

CAMPERVAN CAPERS

Of course, I've loved documenting my campervan journey and hope that you have enjoyed reading my book, for whatever reason you chose to buy it. Maybe I'll inspire you to buy a campervan yourself, or my calamities make you realise that it's not all rosy in campervan life, and you decide to spend your money on something else.

What's next for The Travelling Murphy's? Who knows. April 2025 brought another massive bill at MOT time as Evie needed some welding, but I'm assured that she's good to go for at least the next few years. As Mr M pointed out to me, the money I spent on the MOT is less than some people would spend on one holiday. I have lots of places I still want to visit, especially Camusdarach on the West Coast of Scotland, the far north of Scotland and Wales. And, of course, we need to take another trip to the Trossachs Holiday Park in Aberfoyle to see if the house of straw bales has been completed.

Will they be solo adventures?

Time will tell.

My final thought. If you dream of buying a campervan and get the opportunity, do it. Don't worry about what other people say. If you can afford it, buy the van. Just don't wear the same rose-tinted glasses I wore four years ago.

Debra Murphy

A Semi-Seasoned Campervan Woman's Useful Information

Buying your Campervan
There are many dealers and private sellers, but we chose to go to a dealer. As this is the only one I have any experience with, it's the only one I feel able to list. Unfortunately, you will not get the lovely Steve, the salesman, as he retired in 2025, but I'm sure there will be another suitably friendly and helpful salesman. Ask to speak to Graham in the Service Department and tell him Debra sent you.

Struans Leisure, Perth, Scotland
https://www.struans.com/

Be Part of A Gang
Joining one of the caravan clubs will give you discounts on stays at their sites, cheaper insurance and a whole range of information. I've listed the two main ones. The Caravan and Motorhome Club is the slightly more expensive of the two and doesn't allow tents to be pitched on its sites. The Camping and Caravanning Club is cheaper and always allows tents.

The Caravan and Motorhome Club
https://www.caravanclub.co.uk/

The Camping and Caravanning Club
https://www.campingandcaravanningclub.co.uk/

Drive Away Awning
Westfield Hydra 320 Travel Smart Air Drive Away Awning

In case anyone is wondering, the drive away awning we have is the Westfield Hydra 320 Travel Smart Air Drive Away Awning. There are probably millions to choose from, just make sure you buy one that fits your van.

CAMPERVAN CAPERS

Gas
There are two types of gas, Calor Gas and FloGas, and they cannot be interchanged without changing the connections.

Calor Gas
https://www.calor.co.uk/

Flogas
https://www.flogas.co.uk/

Werner 7 Tread Aluminium & Steel Platform Step Ladder
B&Q
Standing on these, I can now clean the top of Evie. It's a bit daunting reaching right over the roof, but at least I can see out of the skylight windows now when I'm lying on the bed.

Cleaning Your Campervan
MB14 Caravan & Motorhome Exterior & Interior Wash & Wax

I've recently discovered this fabulous cleaning product, which gets rid of all the dirt, grime and, importantly, that green mould stuff that grows in the grooves by the windows, doors, and mirrors. You can use it anywhere on the van, and it leaves the outside with a waxed look. It's expensive but well worth every penny. I bought mine at the Caravan and Motorhome Show in Glasgow last year. I believe you can also buy it online.

GO Outdoors
https://www.gooutdoors.co.uk/

Be warned: You enter this place at your peril, and it can seriously harm your bank balance. This store has everything you need, including stuff you didn't know you needed!

Debra Murphy

Campsites

I've been fortunate enough not to stay at a site that I wouldn't go back to, but I do have my favourites, such as Blair Castle and Skelwith Fold. I've listed all the sites mentioned in the book in the order they appeared. The information I've listed was current at the time of visiting.

This year, there is a one-off additional electric hook-up charge of £35 at Skelwith Fold. I don't feel this is extortionate, considering how power suppliers are increasing their costs. Although this is the first time I have noticed it, I'm pretty sure that this will become the norm on other campsites in the future.

Immervoulin, Strathyre, Scotland
https://Immervoulinpark.co.uk/
- Independent site
- Site can be prone to flooding due to its location near the river
- Walking distance from the lovely Broch Cafe
- Right beside Sustrans Cycle Route 7
- Fishing on site
- Dog-friendly
- Not open all year

Maragowan, Killin, Scotland
https://www.caravanclub.co.uk/
- Caravan and Motorhome Club Site
- Tents not permitted
- Walking distance from Killin Village, several cafes, hotels, the Co-op and The Falls of Dochart
- Right on the Sustrans Cycle Route 7
- Fishing onsite
- Dog-friendly
- Not open all year

CAMPERVAN CAPERS

The Trossachs Holiday Park, Aberfoyle, Scotland
https://trossachsholidays.co.uk/
- Independent Site
- Not within walking distance of any shops or cafes
- 5 minutes from Sustrans Cycle Route 7
- Dog-friendly
- Open all year

Skelwith Fold Caravan Park, Ambleside, Cumbria, England
https://skelwith.com/
- Independent site
- Now apply a one-off charge for electric hook-up
- Fabulous onsite shop and amazing library
- Walking distance from bus stops with regular buses to take you to Ambleside, Coniston and beyond
- Walking distance from Chesters by the River Cafe
- Plenty of gentle walks around the site
- Tents not permitted
- Dog-friendly
- Not open all year

Blair Castle Caravan Park, Blair Atholl, Perthshire, Scotland
https://atholl-estates.co.uk/stay-with-us/
- Independent Site
- Well-stocked shop onsite
- Tents permitted
- Booking fee includes free access to Blair Castle Gardens and a discount on a tour of inside the castle
- Walking distance from Blair Atholl with a handful of shops, cafes and hotels
- Wonderful woodland and riverside walks around the site
- Sustrans Cycle Route 7 runs right past the site
- Dog-friendly
- Not open all year

Coniston Park Coppice Caravan and Motorhome Club Campsite, Coniston, Cumbria, England
https://www.caravanclub.co.uk/
- Caravan and Motorhome Club Site
- Website suggests that tents might be permitted, but you have to phone to arrange
- Dog-friendly
- Walking distance from Coniston Water and Coniston Village
- Not open all year

Ayr Craigie Gardens Caravan and Motorhome Club Site
https://www.caravanclub.co.uk/
- Caravan and Motorhome Club Site
- Tents not permitted
- Walking distance from Ayr Town Centre and Ayr Beach
- Dog-friendly
- Not open all year

Tyndrum Holiday Park
https://highlandholidays.com/holiday-parks/tydrum/
- Independent site
- Tents permitted
- Five minutes from Tyndrum Village, the Green Welly Stop, Real Food Cafe and other restaurants and hotels
- Right on the West Highland Way
- Dog-friendly
- Open all year

Berwick Seaview Caravan and Motorhome Club Campsite
https://www.caravanclub.co.uk/
- Caravan and Motorhome Club Site
- Tents not permitted
- Walking distance from Berwick-Upon-Tweed
- Dog-friendly
- Not open all year

CAMPERVAN CAPERS

Yellowcraig Caravan Club Site
https://www.caravanclub.co.uk/
- Caravan and Motorhome Club Site
- Tents not permitted
- Five-minute walk to an amazing beach
- Dog-friendly
- Not open all year

Camusdarach Campsite, Arisaig, Scotland (I have not visited yet, but it is on my bucket list)
https://www.camusdarach.co.uk/
- Independent site
- All I can say is that it is in one of the most scenic parts of the Scottish Highlands between Arisaig and Mallaig on the Road to the Isles.
- Tents permitted
- Dog-friendly
- Not open all year

Oban Camping and Caravan Site
https://www.campingandcaravanningclub.co.uk/
- Camping and Caravan Club Site
- Tents permitted
- Caledonian Cycle Route 78 runs right past the site
- Dog-friendly
- Not open all year

**Dunbar Camping and Caravan Site
(I had an adventure there in April 2025)**
https://www.campingandcaravanningclub.co.uk/
- Camping and Caravan Club Site
- Tents permitted
- 15-minute walk to a fabulous beach
- Dog-friendly
- Not open all year

Debra Murphy

Acknowledgements

It has been said that it takes a village to raise a child. That might well be said about writing a book because the number of people who have helped me on the way to completing another project would certainly fill a village. I like to think of you all as my writing family.

To all my readers. Thank you. I still can't believe that people want to spend their hard-earned money on my written words.

Everyone at Struans in Perth who has looked after Evie for me, keeping her on the road, and allowing me to continue on my campervan journey, especially Steve, the salesman, and Graham, the fab service manager. You are keeping my dream alive.

Thanks to everyone in the Adria Twin Camper Van Owners Facebook group, who are always there to give advice or to cheer me on when things are not going as planned on my adventures.

Over the last five years, my friends and family have all listened, advised, laughed, moaned and cheered as I've produced chapter after chapter to be read out at any opportunity.

To everyone in the WTB Scotland gang, especially Rhona, Elaine and Paul, for being such a supportive group and allowing me to continue my love of chatting, baking and sharing cake with like-minded people, thank you.

To the people who have proofread my words to ensure that I have, commas in the the right place and that all my are words in the right order.

CAMPERVAN CAPERS

Ruth, Geraldine, Jim, and Jindra, thank you for your continued support and motivation. You are all fabulous.

To Rhona, thank you for the cakes. You always seem to know when I need a Caulder's moment.

Greg, for your on-going support for and pushing me to do more. You are a legend.

For the Rotary Club of Kilsyth, who have taken me into their group and boosted my ego when it was flagging.

For all the libraries that have supported me from the very beginning of my writing journey, thank you. As a child, libraries introduced me to the wonder of books, so it's now a privilege to have you host my talks and book launches.

Jessica, what can I say! You add magic to all my books. Without your illustrations, they would still be just words.

To Ben and Chloe, thank you for your love and support. It must be tough having me as your mum.

Finally, to my wonderful Jim. What can I say? Thank you is simply not enough. You are my biggest critic and my fiercest supporter. I truly love you.